ISBN 3-89417-090-5

Publishing House: Philippka-Sportverlag, P.O. Box 15 01 05, D-48061 Münster
© 2000 by Philippka-Sportverlag

Published as volume 2 of the series of textbooks "SUCCESS IN SOCCER"
Editor: German Soccer Association (DFB)

DFB-coordinator: Markus Weidner

Final Editing: Sean McAfee, Dietrich Späte

Editing of the series: Gero Bisanz, (DFB)

Production manager: Silke Büchter, Werner Böwing, Gudrun Quilling

Layout and Design: Thorsten Krybus

Translations: Patrick Hubenthal

Illustrations: Frauke Hehn

Cover photo: FIRO

Photos: Bongarts (pages 12, 14, 17, 19, 27, 45, 47, 51, 67, 75, 94, 217, 220, 222, 238, 256, 258, 259, 266 right, 267, 274, 275, 276, 281, 283); Hiegemann (pages 20, 21, 22, 23, 29, 33, 37, 38, 39, 41, 52, 108, 109, 118, 119, 156, 257, 266 in the middle and photo series pages 263 through 265 and pages 278/279); Daschner (pages 42, 58, 66, 100, 139); Maxwitat (pages 44); Minkus (pages 277); Müller (pages 107); Hyballa (pages 98). Other photos and photo series: FIRO

Printing: Aschendorff, Münster, Germany

SUCCESS IN SOCCER

Advanced Training

for Developing the Serious Player

(Ages 14-18 and Amateurs)

by Gero Bisanz and Norbert Vieth

Published by the German Soccer Association (DFB)
in conjunction with the DFB's training staff

CONTENTS

CHAPTER 6 Condition Training 217

CHAPTER 7 Goalkeeper Training 273

Accelerate the Globalization of the Game

**Joseph S. Blatter,
FIFA President**

Football is the world's game, played by people of all ages and backgrounds. However, just as no two football matches are alike, no two countries have the same needs.

Development is an area of FIFA's mandate that lies very close to my heart. My first position at FIFA was that of Director of Development Projects, under the guidance of João Havelange, with whom I shared the objective of accelerating the globalisation of the game, in this respect as in many others.

Over the last 25 years, I have seen the development programmes grow and expand, touching ever more countries and people around the world. The results of these initiatives have been reflected in the encouraging performances of representatives from the world's less developed nations at FIFA competitions. Differences in standards and football infrastructures are slowly but surely being reduced, and although the gap still exists between the traditional powers and the rest, this gap is narrowing.

It is therefore most gratifying to know that besides FIFA, national associations such as the DFB, also play a crucial part in the development of our game by making its vast store of soccer knowledge available to coaches throughout the world.

FIFA welcomes this initiative launched by one of its largest and most successful associations and wishes to thank the authors and the DFB for their efforts designed to benefit the sport of soccer.

Europe's Footballing Capital of the Future

Where there is a ball, there will be players chasing it: Soccer unites people, and, in European soccer, frontiers have been non-existent for a long time now. While many stars playing for top European clubs may be „foreigners", they are hugely popular with the local crowds, quite irrespective of their nationality.

Likewise, the coaching and development areas are growing ever closer together. Great strides have already been made towards the creation of a UEFA Coaching diploma system.

**Andy Roxburgh,
Technical Director
of UEFA**

Nevertheless, it is youth soccer and the promotion of young talent where a united European approach becomes increasingly important. After all, these young players are Europe's footballing capital of the future. UEFA's various youth competitions are an important stepping stone as they provide the stars of the future with an early opportunity to prove themselves on the international scene. By then, any top youth player worth his salt should be fully conversant with the essentials of the game. In the final analysis, it will always be the youth sections of the clubs which set the stage for attractive and successful soccer at top level. Any coach working there is teacher, psycho-logist and protector all rolled into one. On and off the pitch, these coaches greatly influence their pupils' development as human beings and foot-ballers alike. Therefore, the quality of European soccer tomorrow is very much a function of the quality of teaching and promoting talent today. UEFA expressly welcomes the efforts made by the German Soccer Association (DFB) to provide youth coaches at all levels with new and up-to-date technical literature. I am confident the DFB's initiative will provide other soccer nations with some valuable teaching materials for inclusion in their development programs.

Soccer Coaches Are Important to Society

**Egidius Braun,
President, DFB**

When the DFB was founded 100 years ago in Leipzig, it numbered just 86 teams. Today we have almost 27,000, with over six million members. Each weekend, more than 150,000 teams, at every age and skill level, compete for that deciding goal.

The spell of this incredibly simple sport remains unbroken. Since soccer is obviously such a popular sport, we should never underestimate the social and political power. Soccer "playfully" teaches children such virtues as helpfulness, responsibility and tolerance. It arms them against drugs, delinquency and other negative influences. Being a member of a team brings social contacts and a sense of inclusiveness that help to counteract modern society's tendencies toward isolation.

So every qualified coach and manager helps to guarantee that the players will enjoy the game, that the fascination of soccer will live on, and, ultimately, that the game will continue to fulfill its social function. The purpose of this book is to make it a little easier for our youth and amateur coaches to do their important job!

Amateur Soccer Is Our Foundation

There's no doubt that professional teams play an important part in the promotion of top talent. However, most of today's stars began their careers on amateur youth teams. There are many excellent players on adult amateur teams who are able to jump right into professional soccer without ever having belonged to one of the Bundesliga youth teams. On the other hand, for a talented 18-year-old who has just left a professional club's youth team, an ambitious amateur team can often provide the perfect opportunity to continue playing and eventually qualify for national – and international – level play.

Gero Bisanz, DFB

All of this makes one thing clear: Germany's 27,000 amateur teams are the true foundation of our talent promotion, and an enormous reservoir of promising players. The potential for attractive, successful soccer tomorrow is here today! It's up to us to cultivate all these talents with effective, up-to-date training methods, at every level of youth and amateur soccer.

That's why the goal of this book is to help coaches of 16- to 18-year-olds (as well as amateur coaches) make their training as successful as possible.

Good luck, and have fun!

Norbert Vieth,
Editor of "fußball-
training,"
Official Coaching
Magazine of the DFB

Gero Bisanz

Norbert Vieth

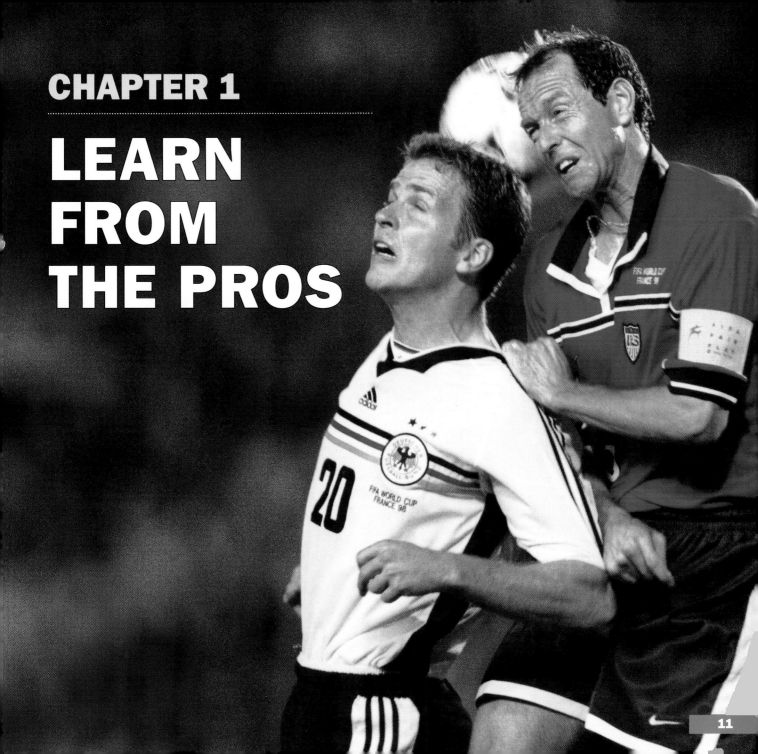

CHAPTER 1

LEARN FROM THE PROS

Soccer Trends

In soccer, a concept that works today may be obsolete tomorrow. That's why no soccer-playing nation can afford to ignore trends in international soccer or cling to "traditional" soccer concepts for too long, no matter how successful they may be.

Trends are new developments in national and international soccer: They're attractive, but more importantly, they work.

1. The game is faster

This means, first of all, that top-level players must be aple to run at top speed over a whole range of distances. It also means that the game in tight spaces is faster than ever, because defenders are getting better and better at "closing down" the space around the ball. In the future, the player with the ball will have less time to get oriented and decide how to handle a situation. Quick sprints to get open and show for passes, narrow escapes from tight spaces, fast dribbling and exciting 1 v. 1's: These are just a few of the features of this trend.

2. Technically and tactically, the game is more demanding

• Rigidly assigned positions and roles aren't likely to succeed in the future; today's game calls for tactical flexibility. Quick orientation, quick decisions, and quick adaptations to the situation at any given moment — that's what today's soccer is all about.

• Therefore, defense concepts of the future will be flexible arrangements. Direct man-marking will be rare. Instead, an active, "ball-oriented" defense, aimed at attacking the opposition quickly and effectively disrupting its attack, will become more and more important.

• Attackers will have to be technically skilled, creative and bold to get past these compact defense formations. They'll have to use a variety of tactics and play an attacking game at all positions.

• Players must develop the ability to respond correctly to a variety of different situations, even under extreme pressure. The "interchangeability" of all individual players will be more important than ever. Players will be required to take on a greater variety of roles and interact more with their teammates, so they'll have to be in good shape, both physically and mentally. Still, we'll never be able to do without individual stars.

3. Teams are more compact

Internationally successful teams are already becoming compact, well-organized units. Individual players' talents are effectively integrated, not "suppressed." Solo players and individualists find a place in the overall concept as "stars" (in the positive sense) who serve their team.

4. Attacking concepts are more variable and effective

• A compact defense is the foundation of effective soccer. However, the attack-oriented

Lothar Matthäus versus Luis Hernandez: The names may change, but there will always be international stars to attract the fans.

Illustration 1

Major Trends in Professional Soccer

1 • The basic attacking formation is effective and attractive

6 • Attack building is confident, technically sound and flexible

2 • Speed-oriented soccer: Fast-paced plays at all positions throughout the match

7 • Strength of will, team spirit and tactical discipline are more keys to success

3 • Every member of the team is able to adapt tactically to any situation

8 • The attack combines solo plays with quick, unpredictable combination plays

4 • Technique is perfect, even at high speed, in tight spaces, and under opposition pressure

9 • Valuable individualists are integrated into a unified team

5 • Ball-oriented, active defense creates compact defense formations

10 • Many goals are scored on corner kicks and free kicks

playing style is gradually becoming more and more essential to success at the international level. As more teams improve their defensive performance, it becomes more important for their opponents to improve their attacking game!

• Basically, the only way to beat a compact defense formation is a flexible, dynamic attacking game. Above all, the midfielders must become more mobile (as a group), in all directions. As the heart of the team, they have to be equally strong on attack and defense.

• Fast, accurate sequences of short-range passes are an effective attack tactic. Therefore, teams should make a point of practicing quick pass sequences under extreme time and opposition pressure until they're perfect. Players can build combination plays around these attack patterns without sacrificing creativity and the element of surprise.

• Individual attacking skills make up yet another basic element of the modern attacking game. Confident solo plays "shake up" the opposition's defense and create chances to score.

5. Good mental and social skills will always be important

Even when all the necessary basic skills are in place, optimum performance only becomes possible when players feel good about themselves as players and about the match.

A good mental and social climate is an indispensable part of every team's "arsenal." Strength of will, self-confidence, an ability to be self-critical, perseverance, determination, team spirit, tactical discipline, an ability to focus and a willingness to take risks: These are the qualities that characterize tomorrow's top players.

In the nineties, Brazil's Ronaldo (right) was the perfect example of the world-class attacker: a good dribbler, a fast sprinter, a skilled faker and a "goal hunter" who was constantly on the move. The top teams of the future will have to include at least one Ronaldo, if not two. . . .

Illustration 2

The Consequences For Today's Youth Soccer Training

Top-Level Soccer Demands:	Youth Training Must Deliver:
Technique	
• Perfect technique at every position • "Positional technique" based on basic techniques	• Creative ball handling • Systematic, age-appropriate technique training
Tactics	
• Tactical flexibility • "Active" defense • Creative attacks built around attack patterns	• A broad tactical education • An introduction to modern attack and defense concepts
Condition	
• Excellent condition for all players • Superior speed for top players	• Match-oriented, soccer-specific condition training • Talent promotion with a strong focus on speed
Psychology	
• Integration of team spirit and individuality • Mental qualities that lead to success	• Training for the "soccer personality" • Promotion of creativity and fun

What Do These Trends Mean For Youth and Amateur Soccer?

Trends in world soccer are important orientation points for every soccer-playing nation, but we should be selective about which trends we adopt. And copying the methods of whichever team happens to be on top at the moment (after the World Cup, for example) doesn't make any sense either. Different social conditions, mentalities, or talent promotion systems can condemn this kind of blind imitation to failure.

But most of all, soccer players have certain "typical" characteristics and advantages. The Germans will never match the technical brilliance of the Brazilians, or possess the same gift for movement, but they have other strengths instead, strengths that make an important difference when it comes to performance.

We must analyze trends in world soccer as carefully as possible. Every big international tournament is a source of new ideas for the national teams, an occasion for them to rethink their own concepts and make corrections as necessary. The same can be true for youth and amateur teams as well. However, we should always consider our own national needs and potentials before making any changes. For example, we might switch from a sweeper system to a flat four if it made our team's game more attractive and/or effective¯but not just to follow an international trend.

Remember: Consistency is one of the strengths of German soccer too!

What is the German Approach to the Game?

• An attack-oriented, dynamic playing style based on a well-organized, disciplined defense.
• An attractive midfield game, with lots of variation and quick, flexible shifts from attack to defense and back.
• Lots of options for attacking, based on an ability to shift from carefully controlled attack building to sudden surprise attacks/counterattacks.
• An offensive, "active" defense that quickly disrupts the opposition's attack and mounts a focused attack on the player with the ball.
• A 1 v. 1-oriented playing style: aggressive, but always fair, focusing on skill and the need to look past individual 1 v. 1's to the game as a whole.

And How Do We Develop Our Approach to Training?

This description of the "German approach" could also be a profile of any top German soccer player.

Every match played by the German national team and the Bundesliga clubs is an example for Germany's youth players, a display of soccer as it's played at the top level the level they hope to achieve someday too. But to do that, they and their coaches have to practice, practice, practice. And for that, they need a carefully balanced training plan. The objectives and contents of training should follow naturally from the conditions of match play at the professional level. But of course, the concepts have to be "filtered" for youth and amateur players and broken down into simple age-appropriate steps.

To achieve a realistic training concept, we have to consider some other conditions too:
• opportunities to schedule practice sessions
• frequency of practice (sessions per week)
• requirements specific to the ability level in question.

Last but not least, practice should always be based on principles that are practical and have proved effective in the past.

Illustration 3

The German Approach to Soccer

World Trends in Professional Soccer

The Strengths of German Soccer

The German Approach

- Attack-oriented, dynamic playing style based on a compact defense
- Attractive midfield game with lots of variation and quick, flexible shifts
- Attacks that shift from controlled attack-building to sudden charges
- Offensive, "active" defense in flexible formations
- Playing style that's 1 v. 1-oriented but always fair

Training Concepts

Match Concepts

The State of German Soccer

14- to 18-Year-Olds – The Situation Today

Without a doubt, soccer is Germany's number-one sport. Millions of fans identify with soccer. 80 percent of Germans surveyed after the 1990 World Cup in Italy described themselves as being "fundamentally" interested in soccer. And more recent statistics show that this percentage increased even more after the 1996 European championships. Season after season, Bundesliga fans break their old attendance records. Soccer mania has taken over Germany.

Active players are pouring into both men's and women's teams. In 1997, 9830 new teams joined the DFB¯an increase of 250,273 players over the year before. In 1999, the DFB was made up of 109,711 youth teams, ranging in age from 6 to 18. This is an incredible potential, but also a huge responsibility in terms of coaching: Providing qualified youth coaches for all these teams has become a top priority. It's especially important for clubs to provide good coaches for the 14- to 18-year-olds, because these ages are an exceptionally critical period (see Illustration 4).

The rate of increase for this particular age group is relatively low: In 1999, Germany had 19,142 teams between the ages of 14 and 18, or only 482 teams more than in 1998.

Naturally, these increases are nowhere near the waves of new players joining at the younger levels. Compared to the number of youth teams overall, the number of 14- to 18-year-olds is actually declining.

There are a number of possible reasons for this trend. Players may be:
- becoming more interested in other free-time activities,
- handling more responsibilities at school or work,
- switching to more casual sports,
- getting bored with their team's practices,
- becoming frustrated with inflexible team structures.

When a training program starts to copy the past just because "we've always done it that way," then it's time for a change. And we can start by answering the following questions:
- How can we make the game of soccer more contemporary and attractive, to keep up with the changing interests of our young players?
- How can we make a traditional sport youth-friendly?
- How can we compete with all the other sports and free-time activities and keep our players on the team?
- What do young players need from soccer? What can our league offer them?

What This Means For Youth Coaches

No matter how much things change, kids still come to soccer leagues for one major reason: to play serious soccer. In the future, we have to make this asset even more attractive and youth-friendly: The top priority is to make soccer exciting and fun. Young players want to learn the game and improve as soccer players, which means they expect certain things of their coaches. „Coaching from the gut" isn't good enough! Careful planning takes time, but there's no way around it.

At the same time, many young players are looking for something else as well. The older they get, the more they're interested in social contact, relaxation, entertainment, etc. So soccer teams have to be able to supplement their soccer offerings with other fun activities as well!

Illustration 4

Youth Soccer: Problems and Solutions

	Problems	Possible Solutions
1	• ·Practice is based too much on adult soccer – boring exercises instead of exciting games	• Make practice age-appropriate, systematic without sacrificing fun and creativity
2	• Other free-time activities distract kids and make soccer a "drop-in" sport	• Offer non-sports activities to fulfill social needs (social gatherings, trips, education)
3	• There aren't enough qualified coaches and managers; many coaches aren't licensed	• Work harder to attract and train adults, and to integrate interested youth
4	• Coaches and parents distort the game's values by focusing exclusively on success	• Redefine "success," putting individual improvements in performance ahead of victory

Women's Soccer: Better Than Ever

The idea that professional soccer is a "motor" driving positive trends in youth soccer is just as true for women as it is for men. Thanks to the success of the German women's team, the whole system of women's and girls' soccer has recently been revamped. Their first major victory, winning the European Championship in 1989 on their home turf in front of 22,000 cheering fans, sent a clear signal to the public, and it convinced thousands that women's soccer

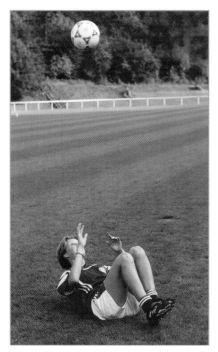

Strengthening exercises (with the ball, of course) should be a basic part of every training program for both girls and boys.

could be a high-quality, high-performance sport. And then the women's team really got rolling: They won the European Championship again in 1991 and 1995, were finalists in the 1995 World Cup and qualified for the first women's Olympic soccer tournament in Atlanta in 1996. In 1997, a re-formed, much younger DFB team won yet another European Championship with its own attractive brand of attacking soccer.

This winning streak was directly responsible for the boom in girls' soccer. In 1999, more than 700,000 girls and women belonged to soccer teams in Germany.

At the same time, Germany's women have instituted a number of "professional" structures that promise to raise performance levels even higher, ensuring Germany's position at the top for some time to come:

• In 1997/1998, the Northern and Southern Divisions were unified, creating a single Bundesliga with 12 teams. This consolidation has improved performance and the overall quality of the game, and increased media attention as well.

• Attempts to improve the talent promotion system and attract more girls at the youngest age levels have been going on for some time now. Various international tournaments have been organized for girls ages 16 to 20, and a national championship for 19-year-olds will soon be a reality.

In many cases, the rapid growth of women's soccer has served to bring women's and men's soccer closer together. Rules, age- and performance-based divisions, official competitions, coaching licenses and training programs: "Unisex" standards are now the norm in all of these areas. Basic principles and guidelines for practice and

match play are the same for both women and men.

Therefore, almost any statement we can make about amateur men's soccer will be equally valid for women.

For true success in amateur soccer, learn these basic rules by heart:

• Practice and match play have to be fun.
• Fun and performance go hand in hand.
• Players can only improve their performance in a positive team atmosphere.
• The coach should be both a partner and an example.

For women as for men, training and coaching can only be effective if they're adapted to fit the abilities, attitudes and motivations of the team in question.

Illustration 5

Women's Soccer: Past and Future Development

Women's and Girls' Teams in the DFB

1983	1984	1985	1986	1987	1988	1989	1990	1991	1992	1993	1994	1995	1996	1997	1998	1999
3284	3430	3443	3300	3137	3058	2997	2902	3109	3606	3868	4040	4415	4760	5512	6600	6891

Basic Principles

- Practice must motivate players to improve their own performance
- The joy of playing soccer is more important than anything else
- Comprehensive athletic training is the necessary foundation for an attractive game

Future Objectives

- Win new coaches for women's teams and train them as well as possible
- Improve the level of play by improving practice
- Make the game even more successful and attractive

The Many Faces of Amateur Soccer

Weekend after weekend, millions of amateur soccer players take the field to compete against each other. But the term "amateur" applies to all kinds of players, and we can distinguish different levels on the basis of their ability, their willingness to practice and the reasons why they play (including expectations that have nothing to do with sports).

The tournament system of the DFB and its state associations creates a solid structure that groups all these different teams into classes, from the Oberliga down to the county leagues. Certain characteristics (motivation, ability, practice intensity, etc.) clearly distinguish one level from the next.

Amateur soccer comes in many varieties. When it comes to organizing and coaching an amateur soccer team, there's no single formula that's guaranteed to work for everyone. Still, there are certain general guidelines that will help any amateur team men, women, boys or girls find success.

Illustration 6a

The "Hierarchy" of Amateur Soccer

Upper Level

- Performance is the top priority
- Daily practice sessions are the norm
- Players strive to bring every aspect of their game up to the same high standard

Mid-Level

- The goal of practice is to improve performance
- A positive practice atmosphere is important
- The coach is the liaison between players and the league

Lower Level

- Fun and social contact are priorities
- Like-minded players meet to practice and compete
- The coach is more like a friend and a teammate

Higher Level = Greater Demands

Oberliga

| Practice Intensity |

| Technical Standard |

| Tactical Standard |

| Conditional Standard |

| Performance-Orientation |

| Recognition of Players |

| Recognition of Coaches |

| Competitive Thinking |

| Team Strength |

County League

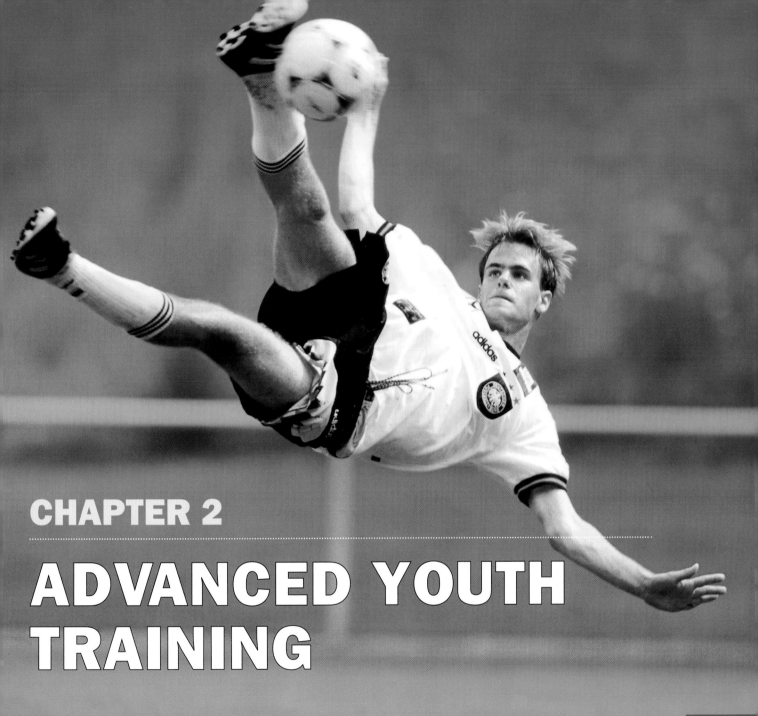

CHAPTER 2

ADVANCED YOUTH TRAINING

The DFB Training Concept

From Beginner to Pro

Everyone knows that in soccer, it's a long way to the top. With a systematic and focused training program, we can help our boys and girls make it all the way.

Step 1: Setting Training Objectives

The ultimate purpose of youth training is to teach and promote attractive, effective, forward-thinking soccer. This goal has far-reaching effects on training; it influences technique, tactics, condition and psychology.

For youth training, the challenge is to break down "the big picture" of soccer into a coherent set of training objectives, and to work out a long-term training program that introduces these objectives systematically, each one building on the one before. These training "stages" are relatively age-independent at first.

Skipping any stage of the process inevitably leads to deficiencies, and "filling in the gaps" later on can be extremely difficult.

If we want our youth to develop steadily and completely as soccer players, we have to give them time, consistency and patience.

Step 2: Adapting Objectives to Age Levels

From infancy to adulthood, the typical path of mental and physical development can be divided into distinct phases.

Observation of these phases has led to step-by-step models of development, which can be valuable aids to youth coaches and managers. However, each individual player also has unique characteristics that should never be ignored.

The age levels and characteristics assigned to each phase should always be regarded as rough estimates. The transitions from one phase to the next are fluid. Yet, despite their limitations, developmental models are essential to any systematic training program. Soccer training can only be effective if each stage of the program is adapted to the characteristics of the corresponding age level. At every age, general developmental characteristics should help to determine the objectives, methods, content and intensity of the training program.

Good 1 v. 1 skills are essential! 1 v. 1 exercises should be a regular part of practice, at every age level.

Illustration 1

The DFB Youth Training Structure

Age	6 – 8	8 – 10	10 – 12	12 – 14	14 – 16	16 – 18
class	F	E	D	C	B	A
Main Objectives	• Have fun playing soccer • Learn basic athletic movements		• Improve soccer skills • Practice technique and tactics		• Practice playing soccer • Perfect technique and tactics	
Training Stage	Basic Training		Intermediate Training		Advanced Training	

Stage-by-Stage Training

We recommend a youth training structure divided into three stages:

- basic training
- intermediate training
- advanced training

Each stage should include only those training objectives that are appropriate to that level of development, so that players can make the most of their mental and physical assets at every point along the way.

These stages also correspond to the DFB's standard age classes (see Illustration 1).

Children's Training

Children's training covers ages 6 through 14; in the DFB age class structure, this corresponds to Classes F, E, C, and D. It is divided into two sections: The first one, basic training, includes 6- to 10-year-olds (Classes F and E). The second, intermediate training, includes 10- to 12-year-olds (Class D) and 12- to 14-year-olds (Class C).

Youth Training

Youth training refers to 14- to 16-year-old boys and girls (Class B) as well as 16- to 18-year-old boys (Class A). This stage is also known as advanced training. Around the world, children's and youth training are known collectively as "youth training."

Familiar Faces and Latecomers

Ideally, youth training starts at age 6 and extends to age 16, for girls, and 18, for boys. Throughout this entire period, the primary objective is to teach every aspect of soccer step by step. The best way to achieve steady, continuous progress is for children to start practicing regularly between ages 6 and 8. That way, age, development level and training objectives correspond perfectly at every step .

When young players don't start practicing until later, they miss out on basic training. However, most boys have had other athletic experiences, so they can catch up with the rest of the team relatively quickly. Not so for the girls, unfortunately: Many of them have never had any other experience with sports, and so they have to do both basic and intermediate training at the same time.

Coaches have to be especially understanding of these "latecomers" who have missed the first stage of training. The very first step should be a careful evaluation of their abilities and potentials, so that the training process can be tailored to address any deficiencies.

Stage 3: Advanced Training

Soccer Training

The third and final stage of youth training is advanced training; it includes boys ages 14 through 18 and girls ages 13 through 16.

At this age level, most boys and girls are performing at a relatively high level, and willing to show it on the field. These factors make it an extremely good time to achieve focused, steady improvments in performance.

As always, though, the objectives and contents of each practice session must be precisely adapted to players' current abilities and potentials. "Advanced training" continues to build on the training objectives of the

earlier stages: Having fun playing soccer is still as important as ever, but learning by playing is gradually expanding its role to become focused training.

The specific objectives of advanced training are:

- Solidify the techniques learned in the past, and to adapt technical-tactical sequences to heightened physical abilities (such as greater strength and improved coordination).
- IImprove techniques and tactics specific to each positional group.
- IImprove team tactics at the 11 v. 11 level.
- Continue developing soccer-specific

condition.

- Expand players' knowledge of relevant soccer theory.
- Promote self-awareness and responsibility.

Technique Training

At the DFB exhibition tournaments, youth players lay it on the line, and even the best turn out to have technique problems here and there. Their basic technique may be solid, as long as they have plenty of room to move and time to get the ball under control and/or pass it. But when space is restricted and the pressure is on, their technique problems are revealed.

Furthermore, many talented young players still haven't developed the skills required to deal effectively with difficult situations, or to play with real control. **Technical deficiencies limit tactical ability.** And advanced training is an ideal time to work on acquiring, improving and solidifying technique: At this age level, the biggest changes of puberty are over, so players' observational skills are well-developed and their coordination is very good (the second "golden age of learning"). It's another excellent opportunity to bring technical skill up to a high level in a relatively short period of time and to get results fast. Addressing technical deficiencies at a later date is extremely difficult and time-consuming if this chance is missed!

Remember: Time spent on technique training is never wasted!

Still, technique training programs must

Fortunately, "latecomers" have a good chance to make up for lost time: Ages 14 through 18 are considered the second "golden age of learning."

Illustration 2

14- to 18-Year-Olds: An Overview (1)

Developmental Characteristics	Objectives	Contents
• The second phase of puberty is marked by significant improvements in abilities related to learning and performance: – The body increases in width to balance earlier increases in height (result: better coordination); – Strength increases; – The organs adapt to the body's increased mobility. • Significant advances are possible with systematic training at this stage. • However, there are still important differences between boys and girls: "dynamic mobility" and strength develop to a greater extent in males than in females.	• Solidify, refine and perfect basic techniques and tactics; and adapt them to the higher demands of match play • Focus on specific aspects of individual, group and team tactics: – positional roles within the team, – changing rhythms, – dividing up the field, – ball-oriented defense, – confident attack building and game on the wings, – counterattack, – shifting the area of play • Solidify and improve condition with motivational, soccer-specific exercises: – speed, – basic endurance, – soccer-specific endurance, – strength (all aspects), – mobility • Promote self-confidence, self-awareness and responsibility	• Systematically planned but varied exercises for groups of various sizes, focusing on specific technical-tactical points • Supplementary exercises for the same technical-tactical points: – with specific corrections, – with a steady increase in time and opposition pressure • Individual practice sessions (to address specific weak points) • Practice games with larger teams, to develop a concept of team tactics • Endurance runs between sessions or regeneration runs after sessions • Exercises to improve soccer-specific condition • Sprinting and jumping exercises, races for the ball • Regular exercises to improve strength and mobility

Illustration 3

14- to 18-Year-Olds: An Overview (2)

Practice

At this age, boys and girls. . .

- grow muscle at an accelerated rate, balancing their physical proportions.

- display improved coordination and increased "dynamic mobility" as a result of these changes.

- show marked improvements in strength and speed.

Consequences

- "Match technique training," i.e. solidifying basic techniques under time and opposition pressure, is the main focus of practice.

- Condition should be improved by playing; specific conditional factors may be isolated but should always be improved in a soccer-specific manner.

- Basic team tactics and positional roles should be a third area of focus.

Competition

At this age, boys and girls. . .

- are growing out of the typical "ego-centered" thought patterns of puberty and starting to focus more on teammates and objective problems.

- are able to assume specialized positions and roles within the team, due to better comprehension of complex sequences of events and a more realistic self-assessment

Consequences

- The coach must observe each player's strengths and characteristics, and then determine position assignments, playing style and playing systems accordingly.

- For youth players, an attack-oriented attitude and a playing system with three forwards are ideal.

- Encourage initiative, creativity, and above all, fun!

Management

At this age, boys and girls. . .

- have matured into independent individuals, with their own needs, opinions and characteristics.

- strive for even more independence and expect to be recognized as equal partners.

- act much more self-confident.

Consequences

- Young people need lots of room for personal development.

- Positions of responsibility in and around the team can be good starting points: leading a practice group, helping to organize sessions, setting up a non-athletic activity, etc.

- Young adults need to be convinced! Every instruction or piece of advice must be justified. A good reason carries more weight than authority.

follow certain rules if they are to produce optimal results.

Rule 1: Games and Exercises Must Work Together

Small-sided games form the foundation of technique training. However, technical-tactical games should always be supplemented with exercises that simulate actual moves and plays. That's because the only effective way to improve a move is to practice it again and again, without opposition pressure. Also, it's a lot easier for the coach to give advice and make corrections during exercises than during matches.

For these reasons, the most effective form of technique training is a carefully planned combination of exercises and small-sided games, all focusing on the same technical concept.

Whether it's a free kick, a corner kick or a cross, the inside instep kick calls for precision.

Rule 2: Make the Exercises Demanding

Technique exercises should always be just barely manageable. This can be accomplished by varying the difficulty of the exercises to match the team's ability level.

The most important objective is to speed up technical sequences systematically but without losing quality. In the end, players should be able to execute every technique at the high speeds required for match play. Remember: If players want to be prepared for match conditions, then they have to practice their technique under those conditions.

Tactics Training

Solid technique is the first prerequisite for effective tactics, because technique can either enhance or limit a player's tactical repertoire. So when players practice to make their technique more dynamic and flexible, they're also improving all the individual and group tactics they learned at the intermediate level.

The next step, though, is to go beyond individual and group tactics to team tactics, as practiced in match play (11 v. 11). For 14- to 18-year-olds, team tactics breaks down into two main areas: First, they have to become familiar with the various duties of the different positions within the team; and second, they have to learn team tactical concepts.

Condition Training

No matter what age level you're training, it's important to make condition training **"game-based"**. In other words, use specialized variations on the game of soccer to improve condition. Every individual aspect of condition (power, speed, endurance, mobility) must be presented in a "package" that's motivational and closely related to the game. Of course, there's nothing wrong with using condition-specific exercises every once in a while, as long as the main focus is always on the ball.

More information on conditioning can be found in Chapter 6.

Illustration 4

Working With 14- to 18-Year-Olds

1 Always make sure the atmosphere in and around the team is positive and anxiety-free.

2 Establish conditions for trust: Give each player individual attention on a regular basis.

3 Be patient and understanding of non-athletic problems (school, parents, friends).

4 Ask your players about their way of life.

5 Encourage players to be independent and create plenty of opportunities for responsibility.

6 Set a good example as an athlete and a human being.

The Match: 11 v. 11

The Match as a Part of Training

Matches play a valuable role in soccer training at any age‑provided they're adapted to the interests and abilities of the players being trained!

Team and field size aren't the only things to adjust, either. Concepts, systems, positional roles and requirements must be age-appropriate as well.

Game systems and tactics should never be too hard or too easy!

The DFB Approach for Youth

Starting with players as young as age 10, youth coaches should begin teaching an attack-based approach to match play (11 v. 11) and building the types of players that top-level soccer requires. Position assignments should be considered especially carefully.

• Attack patterns led by three forwards (two outside forwards and one center forward) and supported by the midfield have the clear advantage. In the future, the game on the wings will become even more critical, because defenders are going to keep closing up the space directly in front of the goal. However, every attacker – even the forwards – must be able to switch to defense in an instant and start disrupting the opposition's attack.

• As far as the rest of the team is concerned, coaches may assign positions and roles in a number of different ways, depending on their own approach to the game, their players' individual strengths, and the opposition's playing system.

However, it's extremely important to assign defense positions intelligently. There are various possibilities:

1. If you choose to use a sweeper, the sweeper should never be too far behind the main defensive line. Instead, the sweeper should be out in front, actively helping fellow defenders and creating 2 v. 1 situations wherever possible. Keeping the sweeper in the midst of the action can also be helpful on the attack, because he can immediately help build the attack in the midfield. And the sweeper has more room in the midfield, regardless of whether the opposition is using two forwards or three.

When the opposition has two forwards, then it's enough to have two defenders in addition to the sweeper. On the other hand, if the opposition has three, then the sweeper should stay close to the inside defender, so that the two outside defenders can engage attackers trying to break through on the outside.

2. When the sweeper consistently plays alongside the other defenders, it can be considered a "flat defense." A flat defense can involve three or four defenders; the four-person version is known as the "flat four." In this scenario, the sweeper ultimately becomes a bona fide inside defender, engaging attackers trying to break through in the middle. The other inside defender

Creative forwards have never been as valuable as they are today!

actively attempts to win the ball, or else covers the sweeper's back.

Youth coaches should always remember that game systems should never be too hard or too easy for the players. Find the playing style that's perfect for your team and all its potential.

Illustration 5

Playing Systems for Youth Soccer

1 Flexible sweeper and three defenders

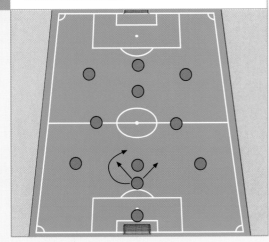

2 Flexible sweeper and two defenders

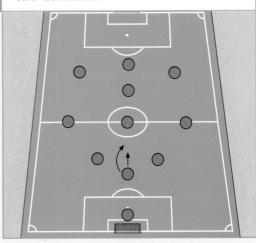

3 Two defenders and a "front sweeper" in the midfield

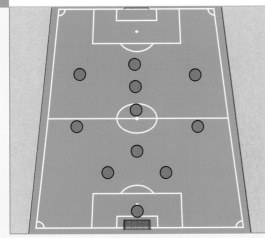

4 Two permanent inside defenders and two outside defenders (flat four)

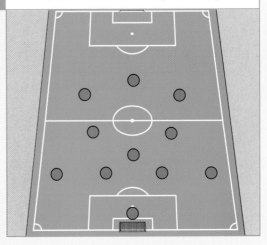

CHAPTER 3

ADVANCED
AMATEUR
TRAINING

The Complex World of Amateur Soccer

A Coach's Work

The primary objectives of upper-level amateur soccer are improvements in performance and success on the field. Since the success of the team ultimately depends on each individual player's ability to perform, the coach's job, first and foremost, is to improve individual performance.

Next, the individual players should ideally complement each other as completely as possible. The purpose of the team-building process is to allow players to realize their full potential for working together.

Putting these factors together, we can begin to define the profile of the „ideal" coach: someone who encourages individual players and helps them grow, who motivates, who monitors individual performance and makes corrections, who initiates and guides the team-building process. The coach is responsible for practice sessions, matches (coaching), education and team psychology. Ultimately, though, coaches have to look beyond the soccer field if they want to succeed, because performance and success depend on a complex array of other influences. In fact, the team and the coach are surrounded by them: the structure of the league, interference from sponsors, contact with spectators and fans, cooperation with the media. The effects of these factors on a team's performance are not to be underestimated.

In other words, while athletic expertise is indispensable for successful coaching, it's not enough by itself. Today, the amateur coach must be more versatile than ever to meet all these demands. All too often, the coach has to be a manager too. To be truly successful, coaches have to be just as active, creative and competent off the field as they are on it.

There is no one "recipe" for successful coaching. It's up to each coach to analyze his own team's situation and develop his own solutions accordingly.

Coaching is just one of the many jobs of an amateur coach. The pros have huge staffs of managers and administrators to deal with the work of running a soccer team but at the amateur level, the coach has to do it all.

Illustration 1

Factors Influencing Amateur Soccer

Work/Employer	Match	The Public (Media/Spectators)
Family	Coach / Player	Sponsors
The League	Practice	The Association

The Practice Session

Soccer Should Be Fun...

So the "outside" of successful amateur soccer is a comfortable, supportive environment. On the "inside," though, the most important motivator for most players is, and always has been, fun. It's fun to chase the soccer ball, and it's fun to outplay the opposition and win with the help of your teammates. The competition, the joy of movement, the opportunity to rise to a challenge these are the attractions of the soccer experience.

We can't state it clearly enough: The amateur coach's duty, above all else, is to fulfill these expectations for his players. If players don't enjoy practicing, then they won't practice. Many of them spend their days coping with the demands and occasional stresses of their jobs, and they don't want the soccer field to be another "workplace." They want to forget about their jobs, have fun and just play soccer!

... But Don't Forget Performance!

On the other hand, practice has to be more than entertainment, especially at the upper amateur levels. After all, performance is also an important motivator for both players and coaches. They want to help their team win matches, and they want to improve their own individual performance at the same time. As they learn to handle the ball with more skill, they expand and perfect their technical-tactical repertoire; this improves the team's performance and makes the game more fun for everyone. So practice has to be performance-oriented. We coaches have to figure out the best way to combine both requirements (performance and fun) in one training program.

The basic approach at all levels of amateur soccer is to develop a wide variety of exercises and to use them systematically. Individual practice sessions will be structured differently, depending on training objectives; detailed guidelines are found in Chapters 5 and 6.

Improving performance can be hard work, but don't forget to have fun doing it!

Illustration 2

Practice-Related Duties

THE COACH

MATCH PLAY	PRACTICE	MANAGEMENT
(Organization and Leadership)	(Organization and Leadership)	(Individual and Team)

PLANNING	EXECUTION	EVALUATION
• Formulating objectives for the team • Long-, middle- and short-term practice planning (concepts and methods) • Accounting for logistical factors (time, team size, weather, etc.)	• Keeping things running smoothly, being flexible • Ensuring that exercises are fun and interesting • Setting an example that keeps players motivated	• Leading post-practice discussions with the team (praise and criticism) • Writing post-practice reports • Incorporating new information into practice planning

Individual and Team Supervision

The Amateur Coach as Team Manager

An attractive training program and a well-organized team environment are important for good performance but there's still more. Teams are prevented from playing their best when individual players are bothered by personal problems, or when some elements of the team don't get along with others.

This brings us to the next set of duties facing the amateur coach: managing and advising his players. In this role, the coach has to be a psychologist and a teacher.

As manager and advisor, the coach must balance two interrelated objectives:
• Help each player develop important psychological qualities on a long-term basis: self-awareness, the capacity for self-motivation, strength of will and a willingness to get involved. These are the characteristics that define the "soccer personality."
• Encourage healthy relations among team members: mutual help and respect, based on a balanced distribution of roles and responsibilities and a natural team hierarchy. Contacts between players can damage, stabilize or even improve performance, so coaches have to be conflict resolution experts.

Management duties are never done, and they're different for every team. For each new situation, the coach has to find a new and appropriate way to use his influence, depending on his own personality, the personalities of the players involved and the structure of the team.

When it comes to influencing players, though, the most important factor of all is definitely the coach's own personality. That's why charisma, persuasiveness and trustworthiness are such desirable qualities. The best way for a coach to motivate and influence players is to be excited about soccer and show it!

Every amateur coach's dream: Thanks to a legion of helping hands, the DFB head coach is free to concentrate on coaching!

Illustration 3

Management-Related Duties

```
                        ┌─────────────────┐
                        │     TRAINER     │
                        └─────────────────┘
        ┌───────────────────────┼───────────────────────┐
        ▼                       ▼                       ▼
┌────────────────┐    ┌──────────────────┐    ┌────────────────┐
│   MATCH PLAY   │    │    MANAGEMENT    │    │    PRACTICE    │
│ (Organization  │    │   (Individual    │    │ (Organization  │
│ and Leadership)│    │    and Team)     │    │ and Leadership)│
└────────────────┘    └──────────────────┘    └────────────────┘
```

INDIVIDUAL PLAYER	TEAM
• Providing motivation to perform • Promoting mental stability • Providing individual and social training • Advising about personal problems (family, job, finances, etc.) • Helping with injuries and illnesses	• Resolving external conflicts • Resolving internal conflicts • Shaping team structure and hierarchy • Encouraging positive group dynamics • Integrating new players

The Match

Match Play at the Amateur Level

Winning matches is the ultimate objective, and it's the point of all the coach's and players' efforts. Week after week, match performance is the result of all those practice sessions. Of course, a single match is not a reliable index of the quality of a team's training; it's well-known that the final score in a game of soccer is the product of many factors, not all of them predictable. However, if we observe a team's standing and, more importantly, its performance over a longer period of time,

When the match is over, it's time for the coach to do long-range planning.

we can indeed draw conclusions about the quality of its training program.

In the end, the performance-oriented approach is indispensable because it's the foundation for success. Lasting improvements in individual and team performance can only be achieved with a systematic approach to playing and practicing.

There are a number of effective methods for improving individual performance and team success.

Before the Season Starts

• Selecting the starting lineup and assigning positions sets the course for the whole season and should be considered carefully, after a comprehensive evaluation of the previous season. Each member of the lineup must complement the others in terms of position, personality and approach to the game.

• The match itself must be perfectly organized. That's why it's important to build a good "team behind the team" (managers, physical therapists) well ahead of time.

During the Season

In addition to the long-term duties, the work directly related to the match is also very important: preparation before the match, coaching during it, and careful evaluation afterwards. These duties also include:

• Developing tactics based on analyses of your team and the opposition

• Conducting tactical orientations with the team (individual and group discussions, team meetings)

• Providing tactical advice and reorientation during the match itself, based on up-to-the-minute observations

• Making effective use of the half-time break (making tactical corrections, reassigning roles, changing the lineup, treating injuries, etc.)

• Thoroughly evaluating and discussing the match afterwards.

Illustration 4

Match-Related Duties

THE COACH

| **MANAGEMENT**
(Individual
and Team) | **MATCH PLAY**
(Organization
and Leadership) | **PRACTICE**
(Organization
and Leadership) |

LONG-TERM

- Evaluating the previous season
- Talent scouting
- Setting objectives for the season
- Observing matches (evaluating opponents)
- Handling logistical problems for home and away games

SHORT-TERM

- Preparing the team and individual players for new tactics
- Providing mental orientation
- Selecting the starting lineup
- Leading the team during the match (replacing players, using the half-time break)
- Evaluating the match

CHAPTER 4

PRACTICE AND MATCH PLAY: THE BASICS

Tactics and Tactics Training

What Are Tactics?

The rules and basic idea of soccer give the game a simple, clear structure:
Defenders try to win the ball and keep their opponents from scoring; attackers try to score.

Achieving these objectives is a matter of careful consideration and planning, resulting in a plan of action known as tactics. Tactics include all the plans and plays a team uses to score and prevent goals. Tactical action is expected of individual players (individual tactics), positional groups (group tactics) and the team as a whole (team tactics).

Individual Tactics

The term "individual tactics" covers all the attacking and defensive moves an individual player must master in order to deal with typical game situations successfully; it's the foundation for group and team tactics. To use individual tactics, players must have a good command of technique and be in excellent condition. They must also be able to comprehend game situations quickly and apply appropriate tactical knowledge. They must be able to draw on all of their physical, mental and technical potential and use it as the situation requires.

General individual tactics includes all of the technical-tactical basics of the game, i.e. individual techniques and how to use them regardless of position in any situation.

However, specialized individual tactics, are also an important part of training. These are individual actions that are specific to particular positions or roles. For example, when players are defending, they have to use different tactics than they would if they were forwards.

Concepts

TACTICS

• Tactics put technique and condition into action, in a way that's carefully planned and success-oriented.

Individual Tactics

• Individual tactics are purposeful actions an individual player can take to deal with various game situations.

Group Tactics

• Group tactics are the ways in which the different parts of the team (positional groups) work together.

Team Tactics

• Team tactics are an interdependent set of attacking and defensive concepts that involve all members of the team.

Match Tactics

• Match tactics are tactics required especially for a specific match.

Group Tactics

Soccer is a team game, which means that success is only possible if individual players are organized, clearly focused and working together for a common purpose group tactics.

As with individual tactics, we can distinguish between general and specialized group tactics.

"General group tactics" refers to standardized variations of combination play in groups, which all players must practice and perfect. "Specialized group tactics," on the other hand, describes prearranged actions involving one or more positional groups, as determined by team tactics and playing system. For example, the sweeper should have certain arrangements with the man-markers, the midfielders should plan routes in advance, etc.

Illustration 1

Basic Soccer Tactics

Soccer Tactics

Attack

Individual Tactics	Group Tactics
general individual tactics	general tactics starting at the 2 v. 2 level

Defense

Individual Tactics	Group Tactics
specialized tactics (position- and role-specific)	specialized tactics involving more than one positional group

Team Tactics

- fast (counter)attack
- solid attack building
- set plays
- combined defense
- ball- and zone-oriented defense

Attack/defense

Match Tactics

- strengths and weaknesses of the opposition
- strengths and weaknesses of individual opponents
- outside influences
- developments during the game

Team Tactics

Team tactics cover all the ways in which the entire team works together.

Of course, all team tactical concepts must be based on the abilities of individual players, because team tactics are impossible without a broad repertoire of individual and group tactics. All decisions regarding team tactics affect every individual player, because team tactics determine the ways in which they work together within their positional groups, and even the tactics they use on solo plays.

Attackers have two basic alternatives in terms of team tactics: either fast counter-attack or slower, safer attack-building. There are also other possibilities that bridge the gap between these two extremes.

Modern defense is characterized by its opponent-marking methods and its ball-oriented approach, which can lead to pressing in more intense situations.

Match Tactics

Ultimately, the key to success is perfecting a team tactical concept and the underlying individual and group tactics.

However, both coaches and players have to be flexible and adapt the basic tactical concept to current conditions, changing it from one match to the next if necessary. For example, scouting may reveal that the opposition has particular strengths or weaknesses, either as a team or on an individual basis, and adjustments will be necessary. On the other hand, outside influences such as field size, weather, spectators and referees can also influence team tactics.

Of course, unexpected events in the course of a single match can also lead to short-term adjustments. Some possibilities are: the score, important players being absent or expelled from the game, weaknesses on either team, changes in the opposition's tactics and/or personnel, etc.

Still, the fundamental goal should be to maintain the basic tactical concept at all times, even in critical situations and in spite of any disruptive influences. After all, any team that can define the game in favor of its own strengths will have the tactical advantage and this should be the ultimate goal of all tactics training!

Tactics Training

Tactics training has two basic objectives:

First Objective

A long-term tactics training program should teach players a wide range of individual and group tactical possibilities, so that they have versatile, effective solutions for even the most challenging game situations.

Second Objective

Players must also be prepared to assume the specialized roles and positions prescribed by the team-tactical concept, especially at the upper levels.

In actual practice sessions, the two objectives may overlap, and concepts, methods and demands on players will variably considerably from one level to the next.

Lower-Level Tactics Training

At lower age and ability levels, tactics training is designed to teach all elements of individual and group tactics in a systematic sequence over the course of years:
• dribbling, passing, ball control, shooting (with follow-up play and, ultimately, with opposition pressure)
• shifting quickly from defense to attack and back
• basic forms of combination play: showing for passes, getting open, wall passes, take-overs, etc.
• defensive behavior in basic situations, starting with 1 v.1s.

When these basic individual and group tactics have been taught, then the next step is to teach team tactics, always remembering to tailor the concepts to the players' abilities.

Illustration 2

Tactics Training: Guidelines

1 Offer exercises that simulate match conditions and intensities!

4 Plan a series of exercises focusing on the same concept, each more complex and difficult than the one before it!

2 Whenever possible, offer open-ended exercises that encourage players to take the initiative!

5 Involve the player in the learning process with demonstrations, corrections, questions and discussions!

3 Exercises should be difficult enough to make players work, but not impossible!

6 Teach players as wide a range of tactics as possible!

Upper-Level Tactics Training

At the upper age and ability levels, tactics training focuses more on developing an overall tactical concept, designed specifically for the team in question. A coordinated, smoothly functioning team is the ideal.

To develop unique team tactics, we must answer the following questions:

• What kind of players are we working with? Which positions would be a good "fit" for new players?

• Can all of our players work with a single tactical concept, or do we need to take different abilities and attitudes into account?

• What type of defense (e.g. ball-oriented defense) should we use?

• What type of attack (e.g. counterattack, wing attack) should we use?

Protecting the ball in 1 v. 1 play is one of the basic tactics of soccer.

• Which set play sequences should we practice most?

It's also extremely important to give upper-level players adequate preparation for the next match. The week before the match, devote some practice time to developing tactics specifically for use against the next opponent, using specially designed exercises and practice games.

Objectives For All Levels

There are certain objectives that technical-tactical training should always fulfill, regardless of age level:

• Developing expertise in basic and positional techniques

• Laying a foundation for an attractive, attack-oriented playing style

• Promoting involvement, creativity, a willingness to improvise and take risks, and an intuitive feel for the game

• Developing the optimal defense concept at both group and team levels.

But how can we achieve these demanding goals in the long term?

Tactics Training: Basic Principles

Teaching the Basics

The more confident players are in their ball handling, the more flexible their game will be, which improves their chances of handling even difficult situations successfully. Therefore, tactics training relies heavily on improving and/or solidifying technical skills in typical situations.

Players must be able to execute all techniques with precision, even at high speeds and under opposition pressure.

The principles of basic tactics training are:

• Take plenty of time to teach each technical-tactical concept.

• Combine exercises and practice games that focus on the same concept.

• All exercises must have match character.

• Corrections should always refer to specific game situations.

• Be sure to involve players in the learning process.

• Provide challenges appropriate to players' abilities.

Teaching Specialized Tactics

In addition to the basic individual and group tactics, upper-level players must fulfill a more complex set of tactical requirements. They must also perfect the specialized elements of team tactics, step by step.

Here too, there are certain basic principles:

• Players and coaches must work together to develop team tactics. If everyone identifies with the concept, motivation improves dramatically. That's why the players should help develop each tactical guideline.

• No tactics can produce team harmony; it only comes about as a result of patient, painstaking work.

It's up to the coach to initiate and encourage the learning process, starting with exercises designed to focus on specific tactical concepts.

Then, during the exercises, the following steps should take place:

1. The coach analyzes the game situation and notes problems.

2. The coach interrupts play, describes the situation and asks for alternative solutions that might work better. Actively involving the players in solving a concrete problem is a much better way of teaching tactics than a purely verbal explanation from the coach.

3. The players then resume play and try out the alternative they've developed.

• "Helping players help themselves" is the motto of this type of tactics training. After all, the ultimate objective is a high degree of tactical flexibility and initiative. Instead of just memorizing tactical patterns, players should learn to take responsibility for themselves and their teammates, and always focus on finding solutions to the real, often unforeseeable problems that arise on the soccer field.

Tactics are becoming the most demanding part of performance-oriented soccer today. That's why it's so important to expand our training methods and improve the overall quality of tactics training. For both players and coaches, tactics training is an ongoing challenge!

Tactics and Systems

Tactics and playing systems are closely related and influence each other extensively. This is because tactical concepts and approaches cannot work effectively unless roles and positions are organized into a logical structure.

This type of positional structure is called a "playing system" or "basic formation." In soccer, we usually break formations down into three positional groups, which are a natural extension of the basic structure and idea of the game: defenders, midfielders and attackers (forwards).

Each of these positional groups is assigned its own area and roles. The names commonly given to playing systems, such as 4–4–2 or 3–5–2, only tell us how many of a team's players are assigned to each positional group. In other words, these names can only convey a limited amount of information, since they only describe a team's starting formation. They tell us nothing about a team's styles of attack and defense, nothing about the way individuals and groups actually play.

To get a more informative picture of playing systems and the way they determine how players play, we must first understand and visualize where they play. This allows us to visualize each player's typical "sphere of influence." This is what makes the term "playing system" more comprehensive and informative.

Modern Playing Systems

Today we distinguish between two basic approaches to the game; the main difference between them is the role of the sweeper.

In the first case, the sweeper is a major figure, while the second dispenses with the sweeper altogether. However, both types allow teams to use both 3–5–2 (or 3–4–3) and 4–4–2 (4–5–1, 4–3–3) formations.

When playing with a sweeper, the most important question is the sweeper's role: whether this player plays behind, with or in front of the defenders. A sweeper who reacts appropriately and flexibly to game situations gives his team a major advantage!

4 – 4 – 2

The 4 – 4 – 2 system is nothing new (it's always been a favorite in England), but it became significantly more popular during the early 1990's. At the 1990 World Cup in Italy, most teams were still playing with a sweeper, but in the U.S. in 1994, almost half of the teams were using some type of flat defense.

The 4 – 4 – 2 System

General Characteristics

- The 4 – 4 – 2 system does not necessarily call for a specific type of defense, but it's generally combined with a zone defense.
- The four defenders and four midfielders can effectively cover the entire width of the field, which makes it relatively easy for them to realize a basic principle of zone defense: moving with the ball as a unit.

Defenders	Midfield	Attackers
• The four defenders form a line. Therefore there is no definite sweeper, even if one player generally stays back a bit to cover his teammates. • The "flat four" moves toward the ball as a complete unit in order to restrict the space available to attackers. • Whenever possible, two defenders should put pressure on a single attacker, making it nearly impossible for him to dribble or complete a through pass.	• The midfield is divided lengthwise into four zones, with each midfielder responsible for one zone. The result is a formation with two "outside" and two "inside" midfielders. • When their team loses the ball, all four midfielders should move toward the ball to restrict space around it. • With only two forwards in front, midfielders may sometimes move up to fill spaces in front of the opposition's goal.	• A system with only two forwards requires more tactical flexibility. • Since a forward's primary function is to score, the two forwards should make scoring their ultimate objective on every play. • They can also be effective assisting teammates supporting from behind. • If the forwards lose the ball, they instantly become the first line of defense: They slow down and interfere with the opposition's attack.

3 – 5 – 2

Germany won the World Cup in Italy in 1990 with this basic formation, and most Bundesliga teams are using it today, because of all the tactical possibilities it offers. The basic midfield formation and the tactical orientation of the sweeper are particularly versatile!

The 3 – 5 – 2 System

1 Goalkeeper
5 Sweeper
Defender 3
4 Defender
Center Midfielder
2 Outside Right Midfielder
10
6 Outside Left Midfielder
7 Right Front Midfielder
8 Left Front Midfielder
9 Right Forward
11 Left Forward

General Characteristics

- The classic 4 – 3 – 3 system has gradually evolved, expanding the role of each position.
- The most significant change: Outside defenders play a major role in the attack. As a result, most coaches started filling these positions with similar types of players (strong on both attack and defense) and doing without a true winger.
- With slight shifts in the positional groups, the 4 – 3 – 3 system evolved into the 3 – 5 – 2.

Defenders	Midfield	Attackers
• The sweeper can play behind or in front of the defenders, depending on the player's abilities, game situation and overall tactical concept. During attack building and pressing situations, the sweeper can move past the defenders and into the midfield. • The defenders may be assigned directly to the opposition's forwards. It's best when each defender stays on one side and covers whichever defender is attacking there.	• Each team should organize midfield roles and positions. • One common system involves a pair of midfielders on each side. The fifth midfielder takes the center position and plays defense, switching to the attack as the situation requires. • In another version, four midfielders form a line across the field. The position of the fifth (attacking) midfielder is filled by an attack-minded "playmaker."	• The two forwards must initiate powerful, flexible attacks against the opposition's defense, and score goals. • They should play not just in the center, but also on the wings, crossing frequently as they close in on goal. • If they lose the ball, they should switch to defense immediately. Their job is to delay and/or interfere with the opposition's attack building, ideally allowing their team to win back the ball.

Illustration 3

Tactical Concepts: An Overview

Individual Tactics

Attack

- Include lots of variations in your dribbling
- Use a broad repertoire of fakes to outplay opponents
- Use variations in dribbling to get out of tight situations
- Show for passes at the right moment
- Make your passes accurate, versatile and appropriate to the situation
- Be prepared to control any pass on the ground or in the air, even under pressure
- Use a variety of shooting techniques

Defense

- Attack players who already have the ball; use positional play, pressure and fakes to force the opponent outside and win the ball
- Block attackers (nearby or far away) who are waiting or showing for passes

Group Tactics

Attack

- Set up combination plays actively and intelligently
- Create passing options for teammates by getting open and showing at the right time (the foundation of good combination play)
- Make combination play easier by spreading out in all directions
- Watch teammates and coordinate your showing runs with them
- Know combination plays (wall pass, overlapping, wall pass fake) by heart, and use them
- Know the attacking combinations in the middle and on the wings

Defense

- Know how to defend against a greater, equal or lesser number of opponents

Team Tactics

Attack

- Know how to build attacks from the rear:
  1. Covering the field
  2. Passing safely
  3. Switching the area of play
  4. Taking advantage of opportunities to score
- Know how to counterattack quickly:
  1. Starting from a defensive formation
  2. Switching quickly to the attack after winning the ball
  3. High-speed dribbling, diagonal and through passes
  4. Scoring quickly
- Know standard variations for free kicks and corner kicks (both direct and indirect)

Defense

- Defend effectively with a coordinated team effort
- Present a united front in the midfield (midfield press)
- Use offensive pressing (attacking the opposition deep in their own half) as the situation requires

SIS TEACHING MEDIA

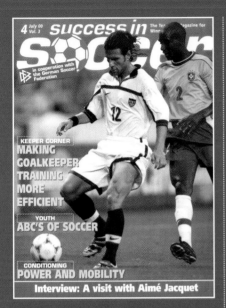

SIS MAGAZINE

is dedicated exclusively to modern training methods. With information on techniques and tactics providing critical training support for soccer players at all levels – from youth league all the way up to the National Team. All articles with lots of diagrams and photos.

6 issues per year.

SIS BOOK SERIES

Vol. 1: "Basic Training" gives easy to understand basic information for training and educational support for boys and girls (ages 6 to 14) as well as a variety of different training methods. 132 pages.

Vol. 2: "Advanced Training" gives information for pratice and match play for young players (ages 14 to 18) and adults. It covers these areas: Tactics and tactic training, condition and condition training, goalkeeper training and practice planning. 288 pages.

SIS VIDEO SERIES

Part 1 and 2: "Fun and Games", I and II, show how young players (ages 6 to 10) can be motivated and trained for success on the field. 65 min. each.

Part 3 and 4: "Advanced Technique Training", I and II, provide an overview of coaching and competition for young players (Ages 11 to 14). 85 min. each.

For price information please contact SUCCESS IN SOCCER:

North+South America: SIS, Manni Klar, phone 1-888-828-4263 (U.S. only), 1-505-889-3680, fax 505-855-7725, email: us-order@successinsoccer.com

UK: The Coaching Store, phone 07041-514000, fax 07041-519999, email: sales@coachingstore.co.uk, order online at: www.coachingstore.co.uk

AUSTRALIA: SOCCER AUSTRALIA, phone 02 9267 0799, fax 02 9267 2559, email: aus-order@successinsoccer.com

Other Countries or Continents: Philippka-Sportverlag (GER), phone +49-251-230050, fax +49-251-23005-99, email: int-order@successinsoccer.com

Condition and Condition Training

What is Condition and How Can We Improve It?

Strictly speaking, condition refers to a player's physical attributes. It is subdivided into basic categories of endurance, power, speed and mobility.

What are the guidelines of up-to-date, practical condition training?

● One of the most important principles of modern soccer applies directly to condition training: Practice and match play have a huge influence on each other. Training objectives must come directly from match play, because their purpose is to improve

> ### Note
>
> **Condition is...**
>
> ● not the same thing in soccer as it is in other sports. For example:
> 1. A soccer player's speed is different from a sprinter's
> 2. A soccer player's endurance is different from a cross-country runner's
>
> ● ...shaped by demands that are unique to soccer
>
> ● ...most easily improved by soccer-specific games and exercises

performance for match play. Training can't prepare players to do their best in match play unless it follows this rule.

However, a basic characteristic of soccer (as opposed to other sports) is its complexity. Every game situation is shaped by inter-actions between technique, tactics and condition. While the tactical concept gives players general orientation, they must be able to apply their technical skills and conditional attributes appropriately in each situation. How could a team execute a tactical plan like "controlled attack building," for example, unless they were able to use basic techniques like passing and receiving? What's the point of tactical instructions like "man-marking" if the opposition has superior speed and endurance?

These intimate connections among the various components that make up perform-ance must always be considered and included in condition training. Balanced, efficient combinations of individual techni-cal, tactical and conditional elements should occupy most of a team's practice time. That's the best way to improve perfor-mance!

● This basic approach to modern soccer training has important consequences for the contents of practice. Every exercise must be related directly to the demands of match play. It's useless to practice some-thing that never occurs in actual match play. In short: The best soccer training has match character. This is just as true for technical-tactical training as it is for condition

1 v. 1 situations are extremely tiring! Therefore, in the ideal 1 v. 1 practice session, playing times are short and breaks are long.

training. All aspects of condition must be trained in a soccer-specific way, especially in youth soccer. That includes endurance training, speed/takeoff power training and coordination training.

Illustration 4

Condition in Soccer

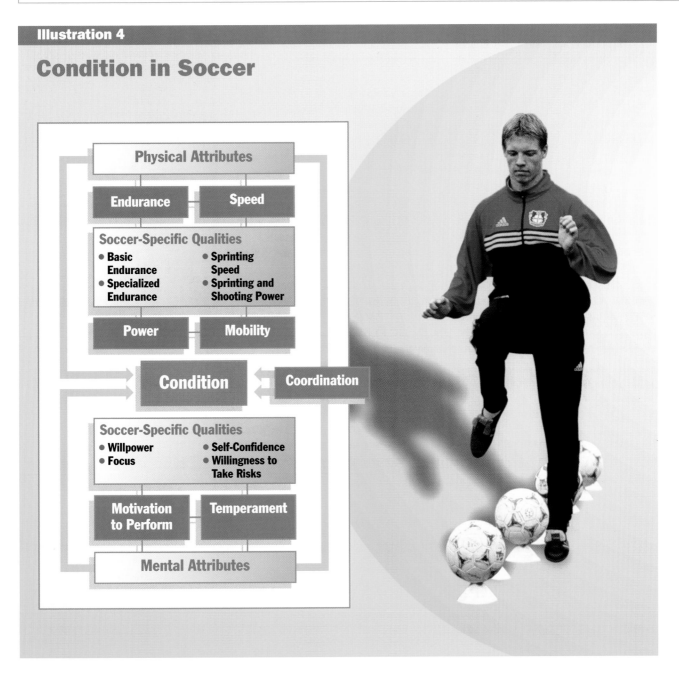

• The best way to establish a relationship between practice and match play is with game-based exercises. This refers to all soccer games on goals that simulate match conditions, from simple (1 v. 1) to complex (10 v. 10).

The coach's job is to set training objectives and find exercises that correspond to them. Changing certain aspects of these exercises can make them simpler or more complex, or it can highlight a particular conditional attribute for special training.

When planning exercises to improve soccer-specific endurance, make sure that the level of exertion is not too high or too low.

As a rule of thumb, the larger the practice group, the longer the playing time can be. With smaller groups, on the other hand, the level of exertion tends to be more intense, so playing times must be shorter, and breaks between exercises must also be longer!

Note

Condition training must be...

• ... designed to prepare players for the real demands of the game

• ... thoroughly play-oriented, with a strong focus on practice games

• ... balanced: Levels of exertion during practice must be the same as in match play

• ... fun: A play-oriented structure promotes fun and creativity at the same time

To summarize, here's an overview of the most important guidelines for modern, soccer-specific condition training:

• The best condition training is match-based and systematic. That way, players develop their condition in a soccer-specific direction.

• Practice sessions should consist primarily of exercises with different objectives, team sizes, field sizes and playing times. This efficiently combines condition training with technical-tactical training, but still allows coaches to focus on specific concepts.

• For maximum motivation, always include the ball.

• A play-oriented structure promotes fun and creativity at the same time.

• Improve soccer-specific endurance with a comprehensive, highly active warm-up program (technique exercises); active regeneration between exercises and games; and a relatively long cool-down run.

• Comprehensive condition training also includes exercises for mobility, speed and takeoff power, usually built into the warm-up period. But here, too, methods and intensities should always be match-oriented!

Ideally, soccer training should have "match character." That's why we focus on practice games from 1 v. 1 to 10 v. 10.

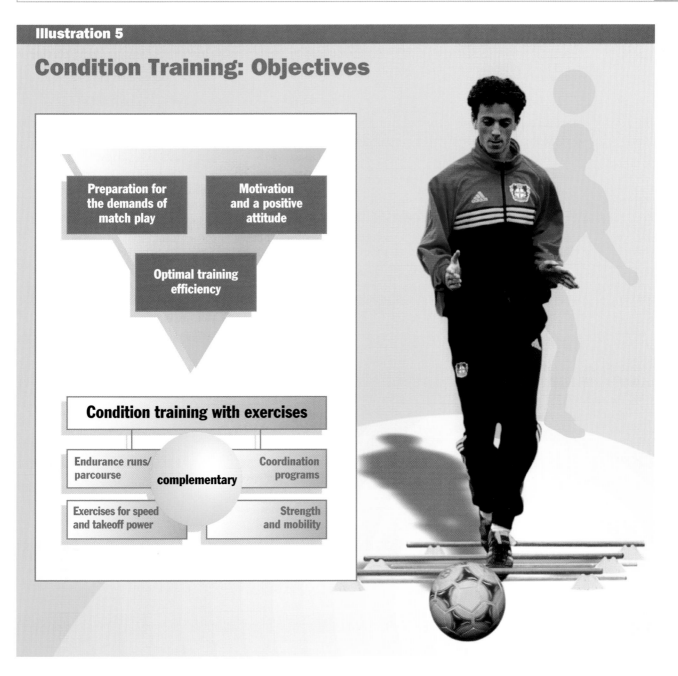

Illustration 5

Condition Training: Objectives

Preparation for the demands of match play

Motivation and a positive attitude

Optimal training efficiency

Condition training with exercises

Endurance runs/parcourse

complementary

Coordination programs

Exercises for speed and takeoff power

Strength and mobility

Practice Planning

The Value of Practice Planning

No team can achieve lasting improvements without careful, long-term practice planning. If coaches want to bring out the best in their players, they have to spend time planning. This is because long-term improvements in performance are only made possible by a series of well-conceived practice sessions, each one building on the one before it. Occasional departures from the plan are no problem, as long as a common theme is in place, giving the coach an overview of what's been accomplished so far, and what is still to come.

Exertion should be carefully monitored and controlled.

Developing a Practice Plan

Step 1: Analyze the Situation

• It's impossible to formulate realistic objectives without thoroughly analyzing all the factors influencing a team's performance: personalities, attitudes, environment of the team and individual players, practice conditions, league structure ...

Step 2: Define Objectives

• After careful analysis, it's possible to define objectives for different time frames (short-, middle- and long-term). Some objectives may be more clearly defined than others.

• However, the coach should always work together with players to set these objectives. This way, the team will identify with the objectives; otherwise, conflicts are sure to arise, preventing optimal performance.

Step 3: Make a Plan

• Now it's possible to start on the actual planning, using your association's calendar as a general outline and scheduling objectives to coincide with fixed dates (the start of the season, matches, breaks and vacations).

• The individual practice sessions will ultimately be filled with specific games and exercises. This is the time to seek out appropriate exercises, adjusting their range and intensity to fit your own training program.

Step 4: Conduct Practice Sessions

• The practice session reveals the quality of the planning. Flexible, short-term changes may be made during the session itself, if necessary.

Step 5: Ongoing Evaluation

• A continuing evaluation of the training process is a valuable tool for improving the way you plan and conduct practice sessions. Problems may occur in execution, planning, or even the formulation of objectives; regardless, take note of all of them and correct them.

• The match is the ultimate indicator of whether practice planning has achieved its objectives. However, the score alone is not the only criterion. The action itself is important, as is the performance of individual players, groups and the team as a whole!

Illustration 6

Practice Planning Step by Step

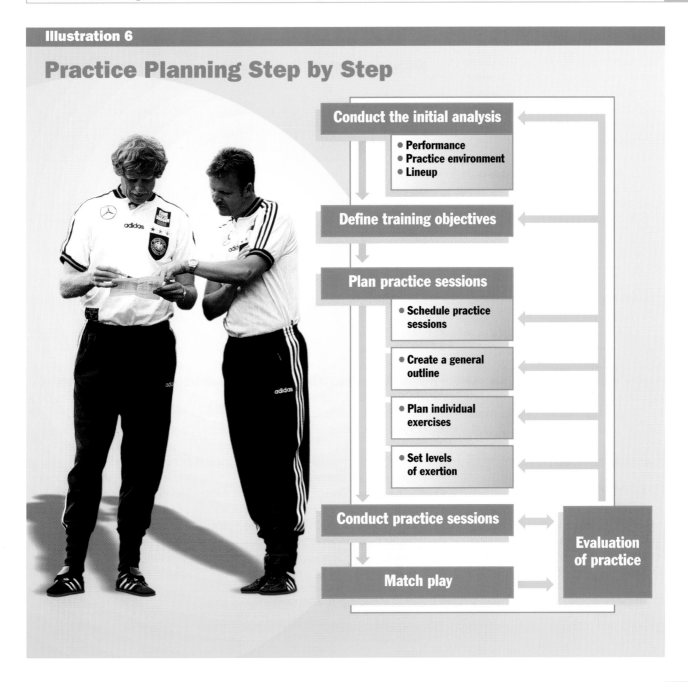

Conduct the initial analysis
- Performance
- Practice environment
- Lineup

Define training objectives

Plan practice sessions
- Schedule practice sessions
- Create a general outline
- Plan individual exercises
- Set levels of exertion

Conduct practice sessions

Match play

Evaluation of practice

Planning a Season

The soccer season is ordinarily divided into six segments that begin and end at important fixed dates (beginning of season, match dates, end of season). The point of training is both to achieve optimum individual and team performance, and to stabilize a team's form over the course of an entire season. In order to accomplish this, each segment of the season has its own unique priorities.

Illustration 7

Planning a Season

Pre-Season		Fall Season		
July	August	September	October	Novem

Pre-Season

Objectives
- Developing basic condition (with a focus on soccer-specific endurance)
- Solidifying basic technique
- Practicing the elements of individual tactics for attack and defense
- Refining group and team tactics (developing a playing system)
- Integrating new players
- „Breaking in" the team

Suggestions
- Always include the ball!
- Practice should be systematically developed, concept-based and game-oriented!
- Make sure that levels of exertion are appropriate and well-balanced!

Fall Season

Objectives
- Continued improvement of basics
- Refining team tactics and system
- Specialized training
- Individual training to address weaknesses, cultivate strengths
- Position-specific training
- Solidifying basic condition

Suggestions
- Integrate what you learned from the last match into this week's practices!
- Plan your training program in the long term, but be flexible in your response to the team's current condition (adjust exertion levels accordingly)!
- For lasting improvements, devote plenty of time to each technical-tactical concept

Winter Break

Objectives
- Recovering from the fall season (vacation over the holidays!)
- Physical examinations, healing injuries
- Active regeneration (running, stretching)

Suggestions
- Players must have sufficient time for "active regeneration" after the stresses of the fall season.
- Indoor tournaments must not be allowed to interfere with this process. Schedule no more than a few at the end of the break, just before the spring pre-season.
- Motivate players to do condition training on their own during the break!

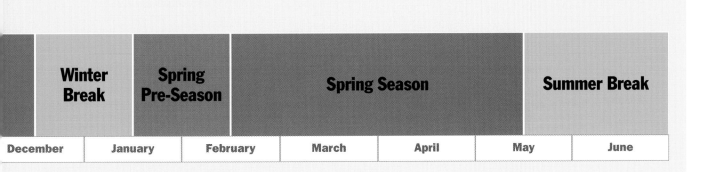

| December | January | February | March | April | May | June |

Winter Break — Spring Pre-Season — Spring Season — Summer Break

Spring Pre-Season

Objectives
• Reestablish basic condition
• Overcome tactical and other problems from the fall season
• Adapt the team to winter ground conditions)
• Prepare mentally for the start of the spring season

Suggestions
• The strain of playing in winter conditions makes it especially important not to over-exert players. Get them in shape, but don't overwork them.
• The practice plan for the spring pre-season is a guideline, nothing more. When unforeseen events arise (overexertion, sudden weather changes), be prepared to respond flexibly and improvise.

Spring Season

Objectives
• Maintain form through the end of the season
• Learn from each match and preparing accordingly for the next
• Refine the team's playing system
• Promote individual players
• Fun and motivation throughout the season

Suggestions
• Plan to focus on individual technical-tactical concepts over longer periods of time (3-5 weeks) to achieve lasting improvements and overcome weaknesses.
• Structure practice to be attractive and game-oriented, to keep motivation and performance at a high level. Observe the team and be sensitive to its needs.

Summer Break

Objectives
• Recover from the spring season
• Heal injuries
• Get excited about the upcoming fall season
• Plan and organize the training program for the upcoming year

Suggestions
• Vacation should be an opportunity for players to forget about soccer for a while. However, after a break, they should start playing other sports to stay in shape.
• The coach should review the past season and decide how to improve performance next year.
• After analysis, which positions need to be strengthened? Does the playing system need to be changed?

Planning a Week

It's a good idea to create weekly plans (from match to match) as well. The first step is to define the focus for each day.

Be sure to consider the following:
● Frequency of practice: How many sessions in a week?
● Match intensity: Are there two matches coming up this week? How intense was the last match?
● Observations of current performance: Which areas need immediate attention? Which areas need work now in order to be ready for the championship games later?

Always plan exercises and exertion levels at the same time and in conjunction with one another. Never think of practice sessions as isolated units, because optimal improve-ments are only possible when sessions are part of an overall structure, each reinforcing the others.

Different types of exercises (e.g. power, en-durance or technique training) require differ-ent amounts of recovery time. By planning the schedule of sessions and regeneration periods for a week, the coach can actually have a positive influence on players' conditi-on. The more often a team practices, the more important this is.

With a good mix of objectives, exercises and methods, you can avoid overexerting players and provide an optimal balance of exertion and rest in most of your practice sessions.
● The overview on page 67 offers general guidelines for structuring concepts and exertion levels, based on the number of practice sessions per week. Of course, the specifics of your training plan depend on the specific situation of your team!

Two Sessions Per Week

● Exercises should be at least as intense as match play. This applies to all elements being practiced.
● Tuesday should be devoted to small-group exercises for soccer-specific condition training, while Thursday's practice should focus more on group and team tactics!

Three Sessions Per Week

● Plan a soccer-specific condition training session for Tuesday.
● Focus on intensive technique training on Thursday and group and team tactics on Friday!

Four Sessions Per Week

● The last practice before the match should include some special speed training, team tactics and sometimes set play practice.

What's the next session going to be about? What will we be working on? Answering these questions and explaining your training plan to players ahead of time can save valuable practice time.

Illustration 8

Weekly Practice Planning

Two Sessions/Week	
Mo	
Tue	● Exercises focusing on condition
Thu	● Exercises focusing on tactics
Fri	

Three Sessions/Week	
Mo	
Tue	● Soccer-specific condition training
Thu	● Intensive technique training
Fri	● Group and team tactics training

Four Sessions/Week	
Mo	● Regeneration training (e.g. technique exercises)
Tue	● Soccer-specific condition training
Thu	● Group and team tactics training
Fri	● Match tactics training ● Set plays

Basic Principles

- Most exercises should be complex and play-oriented.
- Integrate technique exercises into the warm-up period.
- Primary objective: To provide enjoyment and fun!

Basic Principles

- Again, exercises should be complex and play-oriented.
- Fill out the week with game-oriented condition exercises focusing on isolated aspects of condition.

Basic Principles

- Combine ball-handling exercises with a regeneration program.
- Don't overwork players: Balance exertion and rest.
- Take time to prepare players for their opponents

Planning a Session

The last stage of planning is the individual practice session.

Starting from the general plan, we now define objectives and contents for a single practice session and plan the session accordingly.

The coach's job is to find appropriate games and exercises, organize the session efficiently and set the desired levels of exertion. By planning an individual session, you create a reasonably accurate preliminary picture of the 60–120 minute period in which you'll be working with the team.

Each practice session is divided into three sections, all of which should help players achieve the main training objectives.

Warm-Up

• Plan warm-up just as carefully as any other section.

• Provide interesting warm-up exercises with the ball (an opportunity for technique training)

• Warm-up should also prepare players for the concepts to be covered in the main session whenever possible.

• Warm-up exercises should get steadily more intense

Main Session

• Only focus on a few concepts during the main session, and stick with them until you see definite results. The right balance of exertion and rest is also important here.

• Schedule exercises that require players to be well-rested and in ideal condition (e.g. technique training, speed and coordination exercises) for the beginning of the main session.

• Don't "overload" practice, i.e. don't pack too many concepts into one session. It's better to spend a longer period of time on one concept until you see true improvements.

• Plan the overall flow of training carefully. It makes things much easier when logistics (group size and composition, field size) remain the same from one exercise to the next. This eliminates "downtime" and makes the session more efficient. But remember, it's impossible to foresee every logistical problem. Coaches have to be able to improvise too!

Cool-Down

• Use the cool-down period to work on the technical-tactical concepts practiced in the main session one more time.

• Cool-down runs are not the only way to end the session. You can also offer interesting exercises (especially shooting exercises) to raise spirits and build self-confidence.

Even the German national team takes advantage of warm-up to do intensive technique training.

Illustration 9

Planning a Practice Session

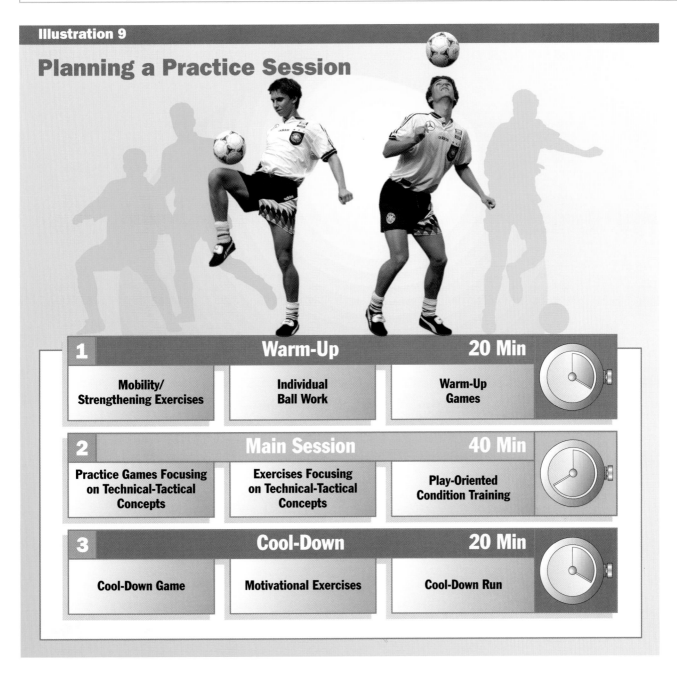

1	Warm-Up		20 Min
Mobility/ Strengthening Exercises	Individual Ball Work	Warm-Up Games	

2	Main Session		40 Min
Practice Games Focusing on Technical-Tactical Concepts	Exercises Focusing on Technical-Tactical Concepts	Play-Oriented Condition Training	

3	Cool-Down		20 Min
Cool-Down Game	Motivational Exercises	Cool-Down Run	

CHAPTER 5

TECHNIQUE AND TACTICS

Practice Planning: Basic Information

Something for Everyone!

In the next three chapters, we'll present a comprehensive, carefully structured collection of exercises and practice games designed to improve technical and tactical skills. But first, a few general comments:
The theoretical information presented in Chapters 1 through 4 was designed for as wide a range of coaches as possible, including both youth and amateur levels. The practical information that follows is no different.

For instance, we have a team of 14- to 16-year-olds playing in the Kreisliga and practicing twice a week: Their coach needs age-appropriate, attractive methods for teaching them the basics of technique, tactics and condition. Then on the other hand, we have an ambitious Oberliga team that practices and competes under almost professional conditions: Their coach wants to know every critical detail of how to refine the team's overall tactical concept and perfect the individual attributes that make up conditioning.

One thing is clear: The demands, contents and concepts of soccer training vary widely with age and ability level.

Finding the Right Exercises

Nevertheless, the following practical section offers valuable information to all coaches who want to improve their day-to-day training.
• Most of the exercises include supplementary information that makes it easy to integrate them into a training plan, regardless of the details of a specific team's situation (such as ability level). We recommend (and have tested) simple variations that can

Special ball-oriented exercises can be an effective way to work on specific aspects of conditioning, such as sprinting speed.

make the majority of exercises and games easier or harder. All a coach has to do is find the appropriate variation.
• For logistical reasons, some exercises are intended for specific target groups. For example, most of the simple technique exercises that teach and solidify basic skills are ideal for younger or lower-level players. Many of the condition exercises, on the other hand, are tailored to upper-level players. These condition exercises are the only ones that require standard levels of exertion to improve endurance, speed, power or mobility.
• To help coaches see at a glance which exercises correspond to which level (whenever it was not immediately clear), we have assigned them to our three training levels. The chart on the next page shows which teams belong to which level, as a general rule.
• However, keep in mind that this chart is no more than an aid to orientation. Ultimately, only the coach can decide whether a specific exercise fits a team's current playing level, practice conditions, level of exertion, etc.

Practice: Levels of Difficulty

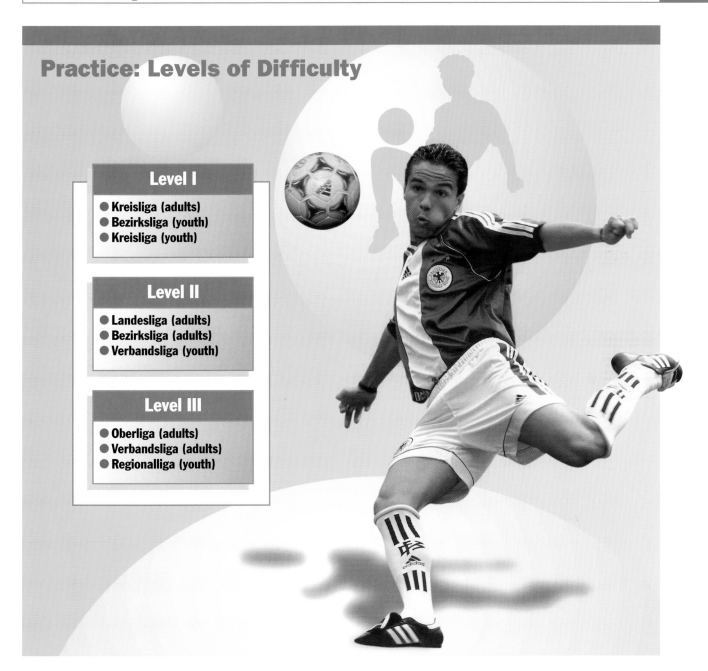

Level I
- Kreisliga (adults)
- Bezirksliga (youth)
- Kreisliga (youth)

Level II
- Landesliga (adults)
- Bezirksliga (adults)
- Verbandsliga (youth)

Level III
- Oberliga (adults)
- Verbandsliga (adults)
- Regionalliga (youth)

Basic Technical Skills

The Importance of Technique Training

Complex exercises should be the primary ingredient of modern soccer training. However, it's also important to return to technique often, isolating individual skills and improving them. After all, basic techniques are a soccer player's "tools."

Just like a painter or a violin virtuoso continually perfecting his stroke, the soccer player must practice the basic techniques again and again in order to optimize them. Only by repeating the basic patterns thousands of times in simple exercises, honing and "automating" the techniques, do players develop the ability to use these techniques effectively, even under pressure. In fact, the ease and creativity of the world-class player are the result of countless repetitions of the basic patterns over many years of "special technique sessions."

The more practice time a team has, the more time it'll have to work on difficult techniques like the bicycle kick. If, like most lower-level teams, they don't have that much time, players still have a chance to make some improvements on their own.

Step-by-Step Guidelines

Achieving technical perfection depends on two complementary processes. These processes must be taken into account in long-range practice planning, and they must be a part of each individual practice session as well:

1. Refining and automating basic technical patterns with simple exercises.
2. Using a variety of techniques, as determined by tactics, in practice games from 1 v. 1 to 11 v. 11.

In the overview on pages 78 and 79, we illustrate the most important basic technical skills in detail.

Trends in Technique

Certain trends are obvious in today's top-level soccer, trends that have a direct influence on the way we structure and conduct technique training at all age and ability levels. Success in today's game depends entirely on the technical perfection of all players. They must be able to execute all the basic techniques at top speed, in tight spaces and under pressure.

We can also identify some important new demands in terms of individual technical elements:

• Focus on Fakes

In the past, fakes and tricks belonged exclusively to forwards and midfield attackers. Today, fakes are part of almost every play, at every position. This is true for ball control, but especially for dribbling. The purpose of faking is to deceive opponents as to a play-

Illustration 1

Systematic Technique Training Should Include...

- A proper demonstration of the skill in question

- Frequent repetitions of the basic moves, executing them as accurately as possible

- Corrections and specific suggestions from the coach

- The various ways to use each technical element in simple game situations

- Motivated players who are fully focused and ready to learn

Technique: Foundations

Technique Training for 6- to 10-Year-Olds

- **Objectives**

1. Learn the major technical skills (in crude form): dribbling, passing, shooting.

2. More importantly: Have fun playing soccer

- **Contents**

1. Games and exercises to promote coordinated ball handling (exercises with rolling, bouncing and flying balls, as well as small group games).

2. Motivational, age-appropriate exercises to teach basic techniques.

3. Free soccer games with small teams, on goals (2 v. 2, 3 v. 3, 4 v. 4).

Technique Training for 10- to 14-Year-Olds

- **Objectives**

1. To systematically learn and solidify technical skills (dribbling, passing, shooting, ball control, heading).

2. To develop versatility in using these techniques in different situations (e.g. under opposition pressure).

- **Contents**

1. Motivational solo exercises to improve coordinated ball handling.

2. Attractive, age-appropriate exercises to solidify basic techniques.

3. Small group games focusing on specific technical-tactical concepts.

er's true intentions. This gives attackers, for example, enough space to set up the next play. Since fakes have become so important, they deserve special attention in technique training.

- Players never really "finish" learning fakes. Even the very best players can still improve: for example, by making their movements more dynamic, or simply by expanding their repertoire. When it comes to fakes, practice really does make perfect!

- Players are always in need of suggestions and demonstrations for new tricks. These may come from coaches, teammates, opponents or professional soccer players.

- When teaching fakes, it's especially important to work systematically, i.e. from easy to hard.

• Flexible, Coordinated Dribbling

The days of dribbling the ball in one direction with a few swift kicks using the same foot are long over. These days, opponents attack from all sides in rapid succession. Under these circumstances, the attacker's only hope of keeping posession (not to mention breaking through the defense) is to use all the different surfaces of both feet in quick alternation. Using both feet and flexibility are essential for dribbling. Fast "footwork" is also important.

Players must be able to change their position in an instant with quick, small steps. Creativity and surprise are the main characteristics of this type of play. However, we can still define some basic patterns of flexible dribbling; as with fakes, the only way to perfect these patterns is to repeat them again and again.

Exercises for Technique Training

- In addition to small group games (the basis of technique training), practice must also include match-character technique exercises.

- These exercises allow players to practice individual techniques over and over, without interruptions.

- It's easy to make immediate, specific corrections on the individual movements.

- The level of difficulty can be systematically increased and adapted to the team's current ability level. Opposition pressure, speed and space can also be varied. Technique exercises should always be just barely within the range of players' abilities.

- Interesting technique exercises are perfect for warm-up.

- If the objective of technique training is to expand and ultimately perfect players' technical abilities, then it's important to praise good plays and provide objective criticism on problems.

Illustration 2

The Building Blocks of Technique Training

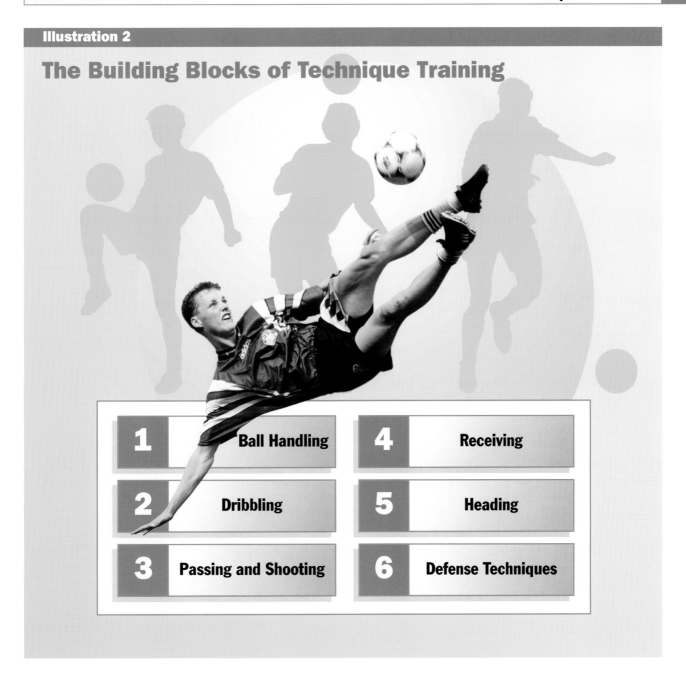

1	Ball Handling		**4**	Receiving
2	Dribbling		**5**	Heading
3	Passing and Shooting		**6**	Defense Techniques

Basic Techniques: An Overview

Technique in Today's Soccer

In soccer, "technique" includes all legal and effective movements that may be required to achieve a specific objective (scoring/preventing goals). People who claim that past players were technically better than today's are living in the past. The fact is, today's players face a much harder challenge, because they have to apply their technical skills to much more complicated problems. Over the years, the technical standard in soccer has been constantly rising to keep up with a faster pace of play, more dynamic 1 v. 1's and more refined techniques.

Dribbling

Dribbling to Maintain Possession
- Shield the ball with your body
- Look up from the ball
- Dribble into open space

High-Speed Dribbling
- Cover open spaces with long-range, carefully controlled dribbling
- As before, look up from the ball

Dribbling and Faking
- Keep the ball close to the foot for fakes and changes of direction
- Use different dribbling techniques and fakes

Inside-Foot Kick

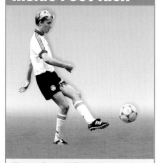

Passing With the Inside of the Foot
- When passing with the inside of the foot, keep the ankle of the kicking foot stiff and point the toes out and up

Heading

Heading From a Standing Start
- Hit the ball with the forehead whenever possible!
- Use the entire upper body for power

Heading From a Jumping Start
- The direction of the jump should be more upward than forward
- Take off from one leg whenever possible!

Basic Techniques: An Overview

For the reasons outlined above, the basis of attractive, successful soccer is mastery of basic techniques, even under the most demanding conditions. Players must practice their technique exercises frequently to master all the techniques they'll need in today's soccer, and keep practicing them until they're perfect. For every technique there is clearly defined ideal form. These ideal techniques are valuable orientation points for training, but in practice, each player develops a personal form based on his or her unique personal characteristics. The purpose of training is to develop and maintain these personal forms.

Instep Kick Techniques

Full Instep Kick
- Place the plant leg next to the ball and keep the ankle of the kicking leg stiff, toes pointing down
- Lean forward slightly

Inside Instep Kick
- Approach diagonallyl to the kick direction
- Plant leg next to the ball
- Kick the ball with the inside of the instep.

Outside Instep Kick
- Plant leg beside or slightly behind the ball
- Point the kicking foot inward and strike the ball with the outside of the instep

Receiving

Receiving With the Inside/Outside (On the Ground)
- At the first contact, give way slightly with the receiving foot and raise it a little

Receiving With the Inside/Outside (In the Air)
- The calf of the receiving leg should form a "roof" over the ball as it lands

Receiving With the Thigh or Chest
- Let your chest sink slightly at the moment of contact
- It's also possible to receive while jumping

Fakes: An Overview

Effective Faking

Players who know how to "fake out" their opponents aren't just entertaining the spectators; they're also creating advantages for their team.
Mehmet Scholl is the perfect example of this type of player, and on the following pages, he demonstrates a series of effective fakes.
It's important to perfect a variety of fakes at all age and ability levels, because they're essential to success in soccer.
Players can't really use fakes effectively until they're able to execute them automatically. Fakes have proved to be a valuable way to get out of tight spaces, and should be a part of every player's technical repertoire.

Body Fake With Lunge Step

  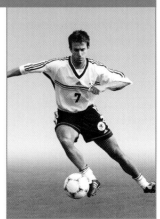

● Start the fake a short distance away from the opponent...

● ...take a wide lunge step to the outside behind the ball...

● ...then go the other way with the outside of the opposite foot.

Shooting Fake

● Fake a shot with a clear "wind-up" motion...

● ...then stop the shot at the last instant...

● ...and change direction with the outside of the foot.

Fakes: An Overview

As always, creative outside forwards, with their wide repertoire of fakes, are indispensable for mounting effective wing attacks and getting past tight defense formations. And central attackers should also be able to use a variety of fakes to put the opposition under pressure in the middle.

Rivelino Trick

- While dribbling at moderate speed, start the fake...

- ...with a quick "step-over" over the rolling ball...

- ...then go the other way with the outside of the same foot.

Rivelino Trick With Hop-Over

- Start the fake with a "step-over" from the outside to the inside...

- ...set the foot down just long enough to start the other way....

- ...and chip the ball over the opponent's leg.

Fakes: An Overview

Step-Over

- Dribble toward an opponent who's blocking your path...

- ...and just before you reach the opponent...

- ...lunge step to the outside over the ball...

- ...and go the other way with the outside of the other foot.

Double Body Fake With Lunge Step

- Dribble diagonally toward the opponent to engage him...

- ...then a wide lunge step to the outside (in front of the ball)...

- ...followed by a second lunge step in front of the ball...

- ...then start moving away in the direction of the first lunge step.

Fakes: An Overview

Ronaldo Trick

- Start by pulling the ball to the left with the sole of the right foot...

- ...then plant the right foot in front of the ball...

- ...step over it with the left...

- ...and start sprinting explosively in the opposite direction.

Scholl Fake

- Dribble toward the defense, then change direction...

- ...fake a convincing pass...

- ...break off the pass at the last moment...

- ...and go the other way with the inside of the passing foot.

Ball Handling

Ball Handling in Practice and Play

Skillful, creative ball handling is a sign of high-level technique. Ambitious players who want to achieve this level must practice regularly with the ball on their own and try out every possible move. In addition to fakes and tricks, juggling exercises are also perfect for individual ball handling practice. Individual sessions are also a great way to combine technique and coordination training and improve body control.
As coach, it's up to you to remind players how important individual ball handling training really is.

Focus On:

Juggling

Technique/Coordination

Tricks and Fakes

Juggling
- While juggling the ball, move along a preset course from start to finish as quickly as possible. Set up competitions between two players.
- First juggle only with the thigh, then only with the head. You can vary the number of times you juggle the ball with a given body part.
- Now juggle only with the thigh, varying the height as often as possible.
- Juggle with lots of quick touches. Switch legs in a steady rhythm (e.g. after every five touches).
- Juggle only with the head. Who can manage the most touches in a row?

Technique and Coordination
- Pass the ball back and forth between your feet while:
– moving forward
– moving backward
– turning around
- Start out dribbling. At the coach's signal, kick the ball a bit farther ahead and stop it with:
– the head
– the buttocks
– the forearm
– the knee.

- With a partner, pass one ball back and forth with the feet and another with the hands; or pass both balls with the feet.
- While juggling, bounce the ball up over your head, sit down quickly and catch it. As you stand up again, throw the ball up high enough so that you can continue juggling.
- While dribbling, kick the ball a few meters ahead, then go after it while performing the following movements:
– knee lifts/fast knee lifts
– heel kicks/skipping
– sideways steps
– simulated header
– one- or two-legged jumps
– squatting jumps
– 360-degree turns
– quick lunges to the left or right

Tricks and Fakes
- See pages 80 to 83 and 89 for fakes

Basic Pattern	Juggling
Complex Juggling Proper juggling should include as many different parts of the body as possible: head, chest, thigh, instep, shoulder, heel, inside of foot, etc.	

Variation 1	
Quick Instep Touch Juggle the ball with the instep only, using lots of quick touches. Try to keep the ball as low as possible. Who can be the first to reach 30 (40, 50) touches in a row?	

Variation 2	
Vary the Height Once again, juggle the ball with the instep only, with lots of quick touches. At intervals, bounce the ball as high as your head once, twice or three times in a row, then continue juggling as before.	

Variation 3

Juggling

Instep Kick to Chest Level
Juggle with the instep only. Now the ball must bounce up to chest level or higher every time. Who can manage the most touches in a row?

Variation 4

Low, Higher, Head Level
Juggle the ball with your foot. At intervals, bounce it over your head, then juggle it a few times with your head.

Variation 5

Vary the Height
Juggle with the instep only, constantly varying the height (from low juggling with lots of quick touches to juggling above head level).

Variation 6	Juggling
Instep – Thigh – Head Juggle in the following order: instep – thigh – head, repeat.	

Variation 7	
Instep – Thigh – Chest Juggle in the following order: instep – high – chest, repeat.	

Variation 8	
Unlimited Creativity Juggle the ball with various body parts and as much variation as possible. There should be no limits on your creativity!	

Exercise 1

Exercises for Technique and Coordination

Trapping With the Knee
Start out dribbling. At intervals, stop the ball briefly with the knee, then start dribbling again immediately. Advanced: Pull the ball behind the plant leg with the sole of the foot, then sprint away in the opposite direction.

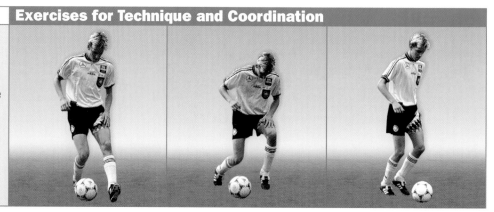

Exercise 2

Stopping the Ball by Sitting on It
Start out dribbling, changing direction frequently. At intervals, stop dribbling by sitting on the ball for a moment, then get up again immediately and keep dribbling.

Exercise 3

Juggling With 360-Degree Turns
For advanced players: While juggling with the instep, bounce the ball high up over your head, turn completely around one time and continue juggling without a break.

Exercise 1

Stopping and Starting

Dribble straight ahead with the outside of the foot, then point your toes and set your foot down on the ball for a moment. Immediately start moving the ball to the side with the outside of the same foot.

Tricks and Fakes

Exercise 2

Lunge Step Over the Ball

While dribbling at an easy pace, take a lunge step (from the outside to the inside) over the ball, plant your foot briefly and start moving the ball in the other direction with the inside of the other foot.

Exercise 3

Step-Over

While dribbling forward, step over (away from) the ball to the outside, shift your weight onto that leg and start dribbling in the opposite direction with the outside of the other foot.

Dribbling

Dribbling in Practice and Play

Dribbling is an indispensable basic technique. Opponents normally attack from all sides, making the space available for dribbling incredibly tight, so players' dribbling techniques must be as versatile and flexible as possible. The coach's job is to prepare them accordingly with an up-to-date technique training program.

Dribbling with the inside of the foot

...with the outside

...with the instep

Basic Exercises

Players perform the following dribbling exercises in a marked field (each player has a ball):

• Change direction as often as possible.
• Dribble:
– with the right foot only
– with the left foot only
– with the outside of the foot only.
• Dribble with lots of quick touches.
• Dribble at high speed, changing direction often but always keeping the ball under control.
• Turn halfway around and continue dribbling with the inside or outside of the foot.
• Change speed as often as possible.
• Periodically integrate a "favorite fake" into your dribbling.
• Turn all the way around (alternate between turning to the left and to the right).
• As above, but after each turn, keep dribbling a few meters further at high speed.
• Zigzag dribbling: Move to the right, then to the left in rapid succession – alternating the dribbling foot at first, then using the right/left foot consistently.

• Alternate easy dribbling with sprints.
• Switch feet in a steady rhythm, e.g. 3 times with the right foot, then 3 times with the left.
• Alternate using the outside and the inside of the same foot, switching on each touch.
• You have four different "gears" for dribbling, and you "shift" at the coach's signal.
• Stop the ball, then start dribbling diagonally for a few meters.
• As above, but turn and dribble in the opposite direction.
• Kick the ball ahead, catch up to it and dribble it close to your foot for a few meters.
• As above, but perform a fake or half-turn after catching up with the ball.

Basic Sequence	Dribbling Through Goals	Variations
Dribble through a number of 2-meter-wide goals, one after the other: • Change direction/speed frequently • Dribble around both "goalposts" using the inside/outside of the foot **Level I**		• Dribble around both "goalposts" in a figure eight • Change direction at each goal line • Turn all the way around with the ball (dribbling with the inside/outside of the foot) at each goal line • Sprint quickly across the goal line (with the ball)

Basic Sequence	Dribbling Through Double Goals	Variations
Dribble through a number of 3-foot-wide "double goals," one after the other: • Slalom dribbling through the goals • Figure-eight dribbling through the goals **Level I**		• Approach from the front: Dribble through the first goal at an easy pace, change direction quickly and dribble through the next one at high speed • Approach from the side: Dribble around the cones with lots of quick touches • Approach from the side: Stop the ball briefly at each cone

Basic Sequence	Dribbling in a "Cone Jungle"	Variations
Dribble to each cone, one after the other, and perform the following moves as you go around them: • Fake left, then dribble past on the right • Fake right, then dribble past on the left **Level I**		• Double fake: Fake left, fake right, dribble past on the left • Execute a shooting fake, then switch directions just before each cone • Pull the ball back behind the plant foot, then dribble away to the side (just before each cone) • "Step-over" (scissors trick) at each cone

Passing and Shooting

Passing and Shooting in Practice and Play

First-class combination play is just one of the marks of a top team, and one requirement of good combination play is accurate passing, even at high speeds and under opposition pressure. But combination play is not an end in itself in soccer; sooner or later, all combinations should lead to a shot. So it's also a question of mastering the right shooting technique for every situation (depending on position with respect to the goal, amount of pressure, goalkeeper's behavior etc). The next exercises deal with both techniques.

Practical Training Tips

Inside-Foot Kick

Inside Instep Kick

Full Instep Kick

Shooting Exercise 1

One goal with goalkeeper; each player has a ball:
- Dribble straight toward the goal and shoot.
- Dribble diagonally (try different angles) toward the goal and shoot.
- Dribble away from the goal, turn and shoot.
- Dribble through a slalom course (different angles) and shoot.
- Fake before shooting.
- Dribble a short distance, then kick the ball ahead, catch up with it and shoot from the top of the box.
- While juggling the ball, move into the penalty area and volley.

Shooting Exercise 2

A passer (Player A) stands about 20 meters in front of a goal with goalkeeper, and the other players (B) stand further back in the backfield (each of them has a ball). B passes to A, who passes back. B runs to receive the ball from A, dribbles and shoots. Then B becomes the passer, and A joins Group B.
Variations:
- B shoots directly.
- A square passes into B's run-ning path, and B shoots directly.
- A kicks a variety of passes to B (on the ground, in the air (low), square, to the left or right, etc.). B may control the ball briefly or shoot directly.
- A moves to various positions around the penalty area: B shoots from various angles.

Basic Passing Exercise

Players move around a marked field in pairs, with one ball for each pair:
- Free combination play
- Players are limited to two touches before passing back.
- A dribbles, changing direction often, and plays a wall pass with B (players switch roles).
- Free combination play, all passes in the air.

Basic Sequence	**Passing Through Cone Goals**	**Variations**
In pairs, players pass the ball back and forth through various small goals (two meters wide): Which pair is the first to pass through 10 goals?		• Which pair can execute the most passes in three minutes? • Two to four defenders (wearing jerseys or otherwise marked) interfere with the pairs by blocking their passes through the goals (without staying on the same goal all the time!)
Level I		

Basic Sequence	**Passing Through Double Goals**	**Variations**
Pairs of players move from one double goal to the next, passing back and forth as follows: • Wall pass across both goal lines (A) • Direct pass and back pass over each of the two goal lines (B)		• Which pair can play wall passes through all the double goals first? • A slalom-dribbles through one double goal, then passes in the air to B. B receives the ball and dribbles through another goal, etc.
Level I		

Basic Sequence	**Passing and Shooting**	**Variations**
Two players pass the ball back and forth as they move toward a goal with goal-keeper, then shoot from a marked line: • Both players are limited to two touches in a row (direct passes preferred) • They should also switch positions while passing (crossing paths)		• The coach dictates specific combination plays, e.g. wall pass – through pass
Level I		

Receiving

Receiving in Practice and Play

What makes a good combination play? On one hand, passes must be solid and precise, but on the other hand, players must also be able to receive and control the ball with confidence. If a team wants to dominate the game, they have to maintain possession of the ball, and to do that, they need players who can receive every pass – on the ground, in the air, hard or soft – even in the tightest of spaces and under opposition pressure.

The inside of the foot

… .the outside of the foot

… a body fake

Practical Training Tips

Basic Exercise 1

Two players, with one ball between them, move freely about a marked field (15 x 15 meters), staying about 10 meters apart at all times. A passes to B, who receives, dribbles and passes back, etc.

Variations:
- Only passes on the ground
- Only low passes in the air
- Execute a body fake before receiving and controlling each pass
- Change speed and direction frequently
- B shows for the pass with a quick sprint before receiving
- As above, except A's pass is perpendicular to B's running path

Basic Exercise 2

Two players stand in a 10 x 10-meter field. Two others ("passers") have one ball each and stand about five meters outside the field on different sides. They both pass simultaneously to the two players in the field. They receive and control the pass while moving, then pass to the other passer. Switch roles after two minutes.

Variations:
- Passers pass from the side, so field players must receive and control perpendicular passes
- Passes in the air
- 1 v. 1 in the field, with only one ball: The attacker must get open, receive the pass, and pass to the other passer

Basic Exercise 3

An attacker stands in front of a goal with goalkeeper and receives a number of passes from several other players in rapid succession, from various directions. The attacker controls each ball and shoots.

Variations:
- Only passes on the ground, or in the air
- Vary the height and/or force of passes

Basic Sequence

Receiving Passes on the Ground

Variations

A group of players stands in the back-field: The first player passes on the ground to an attacker in the penalty area, who dribbles a short distance toward the goal and shoots.

The attacker always receives:
- with the inside of the foot.
- with the outside of the foot.
- while executing a body fake.
- behind the plant leg.

Level I

Basic Sequence

Receiving Passes in the Air

Variations

Like Exercise 1, except the passes are in the air.

The attacker always receives:
- with the inside of the foot.
- with the outside of the foot.
- with the chest.
- with the thigh.
- while executing a body fake.
- behind the plant leg.

Level I

Basic Sequence

Combination Play

Variations

Pairs of players move from goal to goal; each pair has a ball. A passes through one goal to B, who receives and controls the ball, dribbles to another goal and passes through it to A.

The attacker always receives:

- with the inside of the foot.
- with the outside of the foot.
- while executing a body fake.
- behind the plant leg.

Level I

Heading

Heading in Practice and Play

In recent years, heading has become more important for both defenders and attackers.
By the end of the 90's, the percentage of goals scored on headers (after crosses and especially after corner and free kicks) was higher than ever before.
It's not exactly easy to learn heading technique, though – which makes regular heading training all the more important.

Two-Legged Jump

One-Legged Jump

Turning Header

Practical Training Tips

Basic Exercise 1
Players practice in pairs:
- A throws, B heads the ball back. Switch roles after 10 headers.
- B takes off with both legs from a standing position.
- B takes off from one leg after a short run.
- A throws first to the left, then to the right. B runs to meet the ball, turns from the waist and heads the ball back to A.
- After throwing, A runs first to the left, then to the right. B turns from the waist in order to head the ball back to A.
- A throws in different directions (sometimes directly to B, sometimes to the side). B heads the ball back.
- A drop-kicks the ball, and B heads it back.

Basic Exercise 2
Group A (throwers) stands next to a goal with goalkeeper, while Group B (attackers) stands further back in the backfield.
The first player from Group B receives a ball and heads it at the goal.
Afterwards, both players switch groups.
Variations:

- Attackers must take off from behind a line about seven meters in front of the goal.
- Competition: Which player can score the most goals in 10 minutes?
- The throwers drop-kick the ball.

Basic Exercise 3
Groups and positions as above: The first player in Group A crosses in front of the goal, and the first player from Group B heads the ball on goal. Both players switch groups after each play.
Variations:
- Crossers dribble a short distance before crossing.
- Alternating right and left crosses.

Basic Sequence	Heading Triangle	Variations
Three players form a triangle, about five meters on each side. A throws to B, B heads to C, C catches and throws to A, etc. Level I		• Players drop-kick the ball (instep kick) instead of throwing it. • All players head the ball. • Players head from a standing position or with a short running start. • Players vary the way they throw (sometimes directly to the receiver, sometimes to the side).

Basic Sequence	Heading in Two Directions	Variations
Three players stand in a straight line. The two outside players have one ball each and take turns throwing to the inside player, who heads each ball back. Players switch positions and roles periodically. Level I	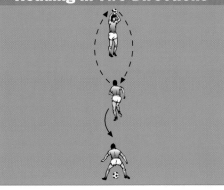	• Outside players drop-kick the ball (instep kick) to the inside player. • The inside player heads from a standing position or with a short running start. • Outside players vary the way they throw (sometimes directly to the receiver, sometimes to the side).

Basic Sequence	Heading on Goal	Variations
B and C take turns throwing to D, who heads each ball at the goal. After ten plays, D becomes the new goalkeeper, B becomes the attacker, and A joins the throwers. Level I	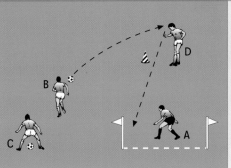	• Players head from a standing position. • Players take off with one leg for the header with a short running start. • The attacker gets one point for each successful shot. After ten minutes, which player has scored the most points?

Defense Techniques

Defense Techniques in Practice and Play

Ideally, good defense should include good positional play, interception of passes, and stopping the attack in 1 v. 1 situations. However, in many situations, the best solution is a slide tackle. Players who have mastered the slide tackle and use it properly foul less often! Important: The slide tackle is not just a "disruption;" it should always be used to win the ball. Ideally, a defender will be able to start a new attack after tackling. That's why it's also important to practice the block tackle, a variation specifically designed for winning the ball.

Practical Training Tips

Inside Slide Tackling
- Kick the ball to the side with the inside of the foot that's further away from the ball.
- Alternative: the outside of the foot that's closer to the ball.

Block Tackling
- Block the ball with the inside of the foot.
- Get close to the ball before tackling.
- Turn your upper body toward the ball.

Basic Exercise 1
Players move in pairs among random small goals. Each pair has a ball. A passes through an open goal from about five meters away. B runs around the goal and attempts to secure the ball with a block tackle, then pass it back through the goal to A. Switch roles after five tackles.
- Which pair can execute the most block tackles in two (or three) minutes?
- Which pair can be the first to execute 10 correct block tackles?

Basic Exercise 2
A stands between two cones 12 meters apart. B and C each have a ball and stand outside these cones, each about 10 meters away. They take turns passing toward "their" cones, timing their passes so that A has just enough time to meet each pass and secure it with a block tackle. After four tackles, two of the players switch roles.
Variations:
- A must pass back after each tackle.
- A kicks each ball directly back with a slide tackle (inside or outside)

Basic Exercise 3
Players stand in pairs on the endline next to a goal with goalkeeper. Each pair has a ball. The first pair moves into the field together; A dribbles until B wins the ball with a block tackle, dribbles toward the goal at top speed and shoots.
Variation: After losing the ball, A goes after B and plays 1 v. 1 to stop B from scoring.

Basic Exercise 4
As above, except several players (attackers) are waiting about 30 meters in front of the goal. B tackles as above, but kicks the ball into the path of the first attacker, who receives the pass and shoots.

Basic Sequence	**Tackling Through Goals 1**	**Variations**
A passes into the space between two small goals, runs after it and uses a slide tackle to kick it through one of the goals to B, who then joins Group A. A takes over B's position, etc. **Level I**		• A tackles only with the inside/outside of the foot. • Make the goals smaller/larger. • A has to kick the ball further ahead and run faster to catch up with it.

Basic Sequence	**Tackling Through Goals 2**	**Variations**
The first pair moves into the space between the two small goals; A's dribbling is intentionally "open." At the right moment, B tackles so that the ball goes through one of the goals. Then A and B take over for the players behind the goals. **Level I**	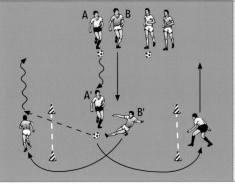	• A tackles only with the inside/outside of the foot. • Make the goals smaller/larger. • Vary the dribbling speed. • Vary the "openness" of the dribbling.

Basic Sequence	**Tackling Through Goals 3**	**Variations**
A gives the ball a gentle kick into a square marked by cones, then immediately moves behind one of the sidelines of the square. Player B runs after the ball at top speed, meanwhile watching to see where A goes, and uses a tackle to kick the ball to A as accurately as possible. **Level I**		• Vary the force of the initial kick.

Tactics Training: The Basics

How to Use This Section

The catalog of exercises in this chapter is based on the system of theoretical principles for tactics training outlined on pages 48 through 56.

To summarize once again, the two basic objectives of tactics training are:

1. To teach basic individual and group tactics within the framework of a long-term, well-organized training process.

National team players have to practice their 1 v. 1 play too...

2. To develop team tactics that build on this elementary tactical repertoire. The higher the players' ability level, the more refined their team tactics can be.

In practice, these two objectives tend to overlap, and as a result the concepts and demands involved in tactics training vary from one level to the next.

Tactics training also varies considerably from team to team. That's why it's impossible to create a uniform training plan or a fixed sequence of exercises that follows a strict progression from one concept to the next. Coaches have to develop plans appropriate to their own specific situations.

However, our catalog of exercises is a source of valuable information for coaches of all ages and ability levels.

Using the Catalog of Exercises

Specialized team and match tactics are always built on a foundation of solid individual and group tactics. Before a team can perfect its overall concept of the game, it has to raise its individual and group tactics to a high level. Therefore, we've included a broad spectrum of exercises that focus on individual and group tactics.

In the interest of making the catalog systematic and easily accessible, we've divided all of the exercises into attack and defense, according to their overall objectives.

In terms of structure and suggested corrections, each exercise focuses specifically on either attack or defense, but all of them are complex enough that they allow a team to practice both aspects simultaneously.

The exercises on group attack tactics are subdivided into two basic situations: "Combination Play to Maintain Possession" and "Combination Play to Score." Once again, these exercises accentuate group attack tactics, but at the same time they benefit the team in other ways as well.

The team tactics exercises are also clearly organized. The attack-oriented exercises are divided into "Solid Attack-Building" and "Attacking with Speed."

The defense-oriented exercises all teach ball- and zone-oriented defense as a fundamental principle of modern defense.

This creates three basic alternatives for defense tactics at the team level: attack pressing, midfield pressing or a compact ine in front of the goal.

These differ in terms of which part of the field the team generally occupies and where they attack the player with the ball.

Illustration 3

How the Exercises Are Organized

Basic Exercises	TACTICS	Supplementary Exercises

Contents/Concepts

- 1 v. 1 on two goals with goal-keepers
- 1 v. 1 on one goal with goalkeeper
- 1 v. 1 + neutral players on goals

INDIVIDUAL TACTICS

1 v. 1 Attack

1 v. 1 Defense

Contents/Concepts

- 1 v. 1 + extra player (focus on maintaining possession)
- 1 v. 1 after a pass on one goal with goalkeeper
- 1 v. 1: header after a cross

Contents/Concepts

- Space-oriented exercises (focus on maintaining possession)
- Passing games (focus on controlled combination play)
- Games (4 v. 4, 5 v. 5 etc.) on two goals, focusing on shooting
- Games on two goals, focusing on moving with the ball

GROUP TACTICS

Combination Play to Maintain Possession

Combination Play to Score

Ball- and Zone-Oriented Defense

Contents/Concepts

- Group tactics exercises involving combination play followed by shooting
- Efficient, well-organized shooting exercises
- Exercises in which attackers out-number defenders, or vice versa
- Small group games on goal lines

Contents/Concepts

- Games on goals involving two or three zones
- Games on goals with additional wing zones and goals
- Large-group games on goal lines
- Games on goals with various pressing zones

TEAM TACTICS

Solid Attack Building

The Counterattack

Line Defense, Midfield and Attack Pressing

Contents/Concepts

- Combination/ shooting exercises on the wings
- Fast counterattacks on various goal zones
- Group tactics: line defense
- Group tactics: midfield pressing

Organization of the Exercises

The following sections all follow a consistent pattern: For each concept, we present both basic and supplementary exercises.

Basic Exercises

The basic exercises include lots of additional information that make it much easier for you to use them in your own training program, regardless of your team's practice conditions or ability level.

• With simple adjustments to the basic sequence, you can make any of these exercises easier or harder. It's just a matter of finding the right variation to make the exercise match your team's abilities.

• Many a practice session has failed because it was poorly organized, even though it contained all the right exercises. It's impossible to foresee every organizational problem ahead of time. That's why the ability to improvise is so important! On the other hand, many typical problems are predictable. Our organizational tips help you get around these pitfalls and ensure that your sessions go smoothly.

• For best results, each exercise should be accompanied by corrections and demonstrations. Our suggested corrections highlight the main concept for each exercise and make it easier to give the necessary criticism.

Supplementary Exercises

The basic exercises are followed by supplementary exercises for each concept. Here, too, some additional information can help make things run more smoothly.

Unlike the basic exercises, the supplementary exercises are not designed to be easily adapted to different ability levels, so it's up to you to pick out the ones that are most appropriate for your own team.

Other Information

Throughout the catalog of exercises, we've provided suggestions to help make your tactics training program more efficient, instructive and attractive. By taking a systematic approach to each individual tactical concept, you can create simple situations for practice.

These basic situations should become progressively more and more complex. The overviews on pages 103 and 104 illustrate how you can use these situations to work on and ultimately perfect each tactical concept.

Using fakes to fool an opponent – a mainstay of individual tactics practice

Illustration 4

Individual and Group Tactics for Attackers: Concepts

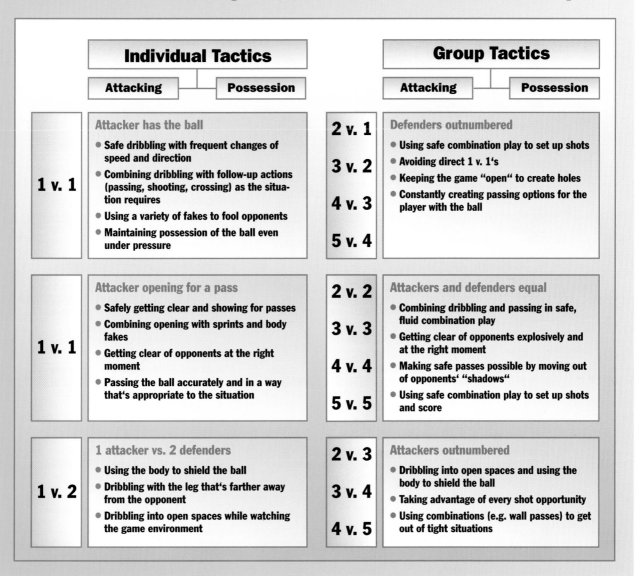

Individual Tactics

Attacking — Possession

1 v. 1

Attacker has the ball
- Safe dribbling with frequent changes of speed and direction
- Combining dribbling with follow-up actions (passing, shooting, crossing) as the situation requires
- Using a variety of fakes to fool opponents
- Maintaining possession of the ball even under pressure

1 v. 1

Attacker opening for a pass
- Safely getting clear and showing for passes
- Combining opening with sprints and body fakes
- Getting clear of opponents at the right moment
- Passing the ball accurately and in a way that's appropriate to the situation

1 v. 2

1 attacker vs. 2 defenders
- Using the body to shield the ball
- Dribbling with the leg that's farther away from the opponent
- Dribbling into open spaces while watching the game environment

Group Tactics

Attacking — Possession

2 v. 1

3 v. 2

4 v. 3

5 v. 4

Defenders outnumbered
- Using safe combination play to set up shots
- Avoiding direct 1 v. 1's
- Keeping the game "open" to create holes
- Constantly creating passing options for the player with the ball

2 v. 2

3 v. 3

4 v. 4

5 v. 5

Attackers and defenders equal
- Combining dribbling and passing in safe, fluid combination play
- Getting clear of opponents explosively and at the right moment
- Making safe passes possible by moving out of opponents' "shadows"
- Using safe combination play to set up shots and score

2 v. 3

3 v. 4

4 v. 5

Attackers outnumbered
- Dribbling into open spaces and using the body to shield the ball
- Taking advantage of every shot opportunity
- Using combinations (e.g. wall passes) to get out of tight situations

Illustration 5

Individual and Group Tactics for Defenders: Concepts

Individual Tactics

1 v. 1 — Attacker has the ball
- Stopping opponents at the right moment and forcing them back
- Positioning the body to allow breakthroughs only to the outside
- Watching for the right moment to attack the ball while forcing the attacker backwards
- Attacking the ball while moving in the same direction as the attacker

1 v. 1 — Attacker opening for a pass
- Staying in position to reach passes before opponents can reach them
- Constantly staying on the "inside line" between opponents and the goal
- Keeping opponents and ball in view at all times, paying attention to attacking plays
- Moving directly toward the ball whenever a pass can be intercepted

1 v. 2 — 1 attacker vs. 2 defenders
- Slowing down the opposition's attack by forcing them back
- Using positional play to isolate one opponent
- Waiting for a chance to attack the ball

Group Tactics

2 v. 1, **3 v. 2**, **4 v. 3**, **5 v. 4** — Attackers outnumbered
- Sending two defenders at once to attack the player with the ball
- Attacking decisively, focusing all efforts on winning the ball quickly
- Using 1 v. 1 play to pressure the player with the ball and prevent passes
- Using positional play to "drive" attackers into teammates' zones

2 v. 2, **3 v. 3**, **4 v. 4**, **5 v. 5** — Attackers and defenders equal
- Stopping, deflecting and/or attacking the player with the ball
- Limiting the opposition's space by moving with the ball
- Working closely together to keep each other covered
- Discussing new situations and responding as a group

2 v. 3, **3 v. 4**, **4 v. 5** — Defenders outnumbered
- Stopping the player with the ball and attacking, depending on the situation
- Forcing the attack outside, isolating individual opponents
- Moving to the ball, forming a defensive line

Illustration 6

Team Tactics: Concepts

	Attack		**Defense**
Solid Attack Building	• Creating openings for passes all over the field • Building solid combination plays involving square, diagonal, deep and back passes • Shifting the area of play from one side of the field to the other • Using combinations to create and take advantage of goal openings	**Line Defense/ Midfield Pressing**	• Pulling all players far back to form a compact and strong defense • Creating a solid unit in the midfield • Winning the ball in the midfield with decisive attacks (pressing) • Using attack pressing occasionally, as the situation requires
Speed Attack	• Limiting the opposition's space with a strong defense • Quick shifts: Starting a fast, determined attack after winning the ball • Moving forward with as many players as possible (depending on the situation) after winning the ball • Using high-speed dribbling and diagonal and deep passes as well as shooting	**Deep Pressing**	• Mounting determined attacks to win the ball before it even crosses the centerline • Using attack pressing appropriately (on long back passes, after your own corner kicks and throw-ins, etc.) • Periodically "pressing" forward (at the start of the game, when the opposition is ahead or uncertain) • Moving as a unit toward the ball

Set Plays	• Mastering a few standard variations for:
	  – direct free kicks
	  – indirect free kicks
	  – corner kicks
		Set Plays	• Mastering the basics of wall formation on direct and indirect free kicks from various distances
			• Developing an effective, organized defense against the opposition's free kicks

How to Use These Exercises

• When choosing exercises, always make sure you can run them smoothly under your practice conditions (see inset, right).

• Plan to spend relatively long periods of time on individual tactical concepts, using different games and exercises. Stay focused and make the exercises systematically harder. Each exercise requires a certain amount of lead time. Don't give up if some things don't work right away. If necessary, make the exercises easier, for example, by enlarging the field or the goal, by allowing unlimited touches, by adding some neutral players, etc.

• The playing times given are general guidelines only. When it comes to exertion levels, it's especially important to observe players carefully and make breaks longer or shorter as necessary.

• When introducing new exercises, remember the following rules:

1. Explain the most important points (field size, special rules, scoring, tactical concepts, etc.) briefly and precisely.
2. All members of a group should be at more or less the same level of ability.
3. If necessary, let players run through the basic motions once, then interrupt to clear up any confusion or further questions.

• The side- and endlines must be clearly visible. If you can't use preexisting lines, then use cones or other markers. Always practice position-specific tactics in the same spaces players would encounter in a real match.

• Turn breaks into active rest periods whenever possible, for example with easy technique exercises, stretching and limbering exercises, easy runs, etc.

• While players are performing the exercise, pay attention to the following points and make changes to the rules if necessary:

1. Are the practice groups approximately equal in strength?
2. Is the field too big/too small?
3. Are the goals too big/too small?
4. Are the playing times and rest periods appropriate? Players must be able to execute all the plays at top speed and with full concentration.
5. Above all (after allowing for a certain amount of lead time): Are the players really practicing the concept in question?

Practice Planning

Practice Field

What type of practice field is available? Are there other teams on the grounds at the same time? Will you have to make arrangements with them?

What are the ground conditions? Do they rule out certain exercises? Can the field be divided so that all players can practice without disturbing each other?

Equipment

What type of equipment is available? Are there enough balls for each player to use one, if necessary? If not, how can you organize practice so that each player gets the maximum amount of contact with the ball? What can you use as markers? Can you have your equipment and markers ready so that it doesn't take too long to switch from one exercise to the next?

Group Size

How many players do you have? How many do you expect at practice? How many groups and fields will you have to have for effective learning in small groups? What can you do if your groups prove to be too different in terms of numbers or ability?

Illustration 7

Training for Success!

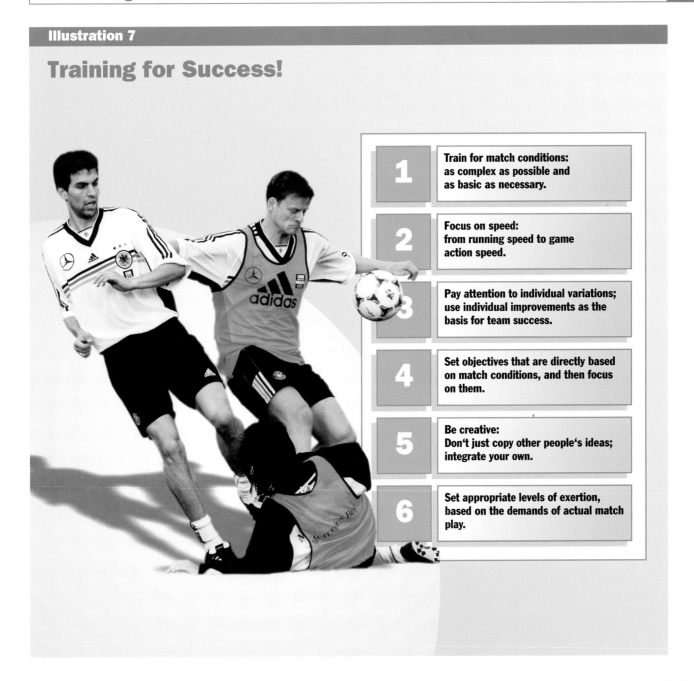

1. Train for match conditions: as complex as possible and as basic as necessary.

2. Focus on speed: from running speed to game action speed.

3. Pay attention to individual variations; use individual improvements as the basis for team success.

4. Set objectives that are directly based on match conditions, and then focus on them.

5. Be creative: Don't just copy other people's ideas; integrate your own.

6. Set appropriate levels of exertion, based on the demands of actual match play.

Individual Tactics: 1 v. 1 Attack

The Basics of Individual Attack Tactics

For attackers, individual tactics include all the tactical skills an individual player needs in order to win 1 v. 1's, meet the requirements of group and team tactics, and handle typical game situations. The foundation for all of this is a good command of technique, so that players can react flexibly and appropriately to any situation.

In the course of a game, players are constantly encountering 1 v. 1 situations that can mean the difference between keeping and losing the ball. 1 v. 1's make follow-up plays possible and can ultimately decide the outcome of the match.

That's why one of the best-known sayings in soccer is, "the team that wins the 1 v. 1's wins the game." And it's also the reason why technical-tactical 1 v. 1 skill is indispensable for a successful attacking game at any level of play.

Effectively improving individual tactics improves the entire team's game. After all, solid combination play and demanding attack concepts depend on the abilities of individual players. That's why 1 v. 1 training should be a regular, carefully planned part of every training program.

The spectrum of situations players may encounter is wide, but for attackers, there are two basic tactical situations:

• In **Situation 1**, the attacker already has the ball and dribbles toward the opponent in hopes of maintaining possession, outplaying the opponent and finishing with a follow-up action (more dribbling, a pass, a cross or a shot).

• In **Situation 2**, the attacker does not yet have the ball and must get clear of the opponent, show for a pass from a teammate and receive it safely. At the same time, the attacker must also try to get into the best position possible to control the ball or start dribbling.

In today's soccer, it's important for attackers to be able to handle both basic situations.

On one hand, the spread of ball-oriented defense concepts has made the space available to attackers ever smaller. Creative, determined solo plays are the best way to get past tight defense formations, but attackers can only pull these plays off if they have perfect technique, an aggressive playing style, an intuitive feel for the game and a broad repertoire of fakes. Such players are in particularly high demand for outside forward positions, especially if they have strong dribbling skills.

On the other hand, solo attacks are extremely difficult when defenders outnumber attackers. Maintaining control of the ball is important for solid attack building, and especially for keeping the ball at the front of the attack. Each individual player must be able to protect the ball against opponents, even under intense pressure.

All of this means that regular 1 v. 1 training is essential for attackers at every level of play.

The 1 v. 1 Situation: Attack

Basic Sequence

- The attacker dribbles toward the goal at full speed.
- As soon as an opponent blocks his path, he slows down and keeps the ball closer to the foot.
- He fakes, then kicks the ball past the opponent into an open space and goes after it.

1

2

3

Illustration 8

Training Objectives

General

Attacker Without Ball

- Be confident about showing for passes from teammates.
- Use sprints and fakes to get clear of opponents and to win time and space so you can receive passes without interference.
- Pick the right moment to get clear (open passing lane and eye contact).

Attacker With Ball

- After receiving a pass, turn as far as possible toward the opposition and their goal; otherwise, shield the ball securely.
- Maintain possession even when two opponents are attacking you: Keep the ball as close to your feet as possible and change directions frequently while dribbling.
- On solo plays, use fakes and explosive sprints to get past opponents.
- After getting past an opponent, follow up with a pass or shot; don't give opponents another chance to attack you.

Special

For Defenders

- Use your dribbling skills to get out of pressing situations in front of your own goal, then follow up with a safe pass.
- When your team wins the ball, switch immediately to the attack and use your 1 v. 1 skills to outplay opponents.

For Midfielders

- Use a variety of dribbling moves to protect the ball against attacks by opponents and build your team's attack.
- Use determined, high-speed dribbling to get past opponents and set up a shot or cross, depending on the situation.

For Forwards

- Use your dribbling skills to shield the ball from opponents and pass it to teammates as they move up.
- Use fakes to outdribble opponents in tight spaces, then place a well-aimed shot.

Setup/Sequence

Four players line up behind each endline of a 30 x 20-meter field.

The first two play 1 v. 1 on two goals with goalkeepers.

Playing time: 30 seconds, then the second pair plays, etc.

For the first round, each player in Group A has a ball; then for the second round, each player in Group B has one.

After each pair has played six times, which group has scored more goals?

Alternating 1 v. 1's on Two Goals

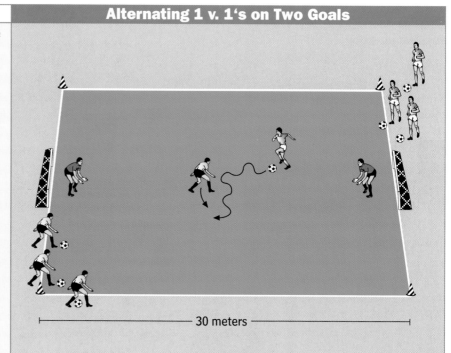

|—————— 30 meters ——————|

Focus On:
- Changing speed in 1 v. 1 play
- Using a variety of fakes
- Scoring opportunities

Tips for Coaches
- Have extra players waiting.
- Retrieve stray balls quickly.
- Pairs should switch positions every 30 seconds.

Tips for Players
- Try to draw the defender to the outside so you can fake and then shoot.
- Use shot, pass and body fakes.
- Shoot as soon as you break through.

Variations

Level I	Level II	Level III
• Players who are waiting for their turns act as "passers" who stand around the outside of the field and help the attacker. • As above, but the passers are limited to two touches in a row (one to receive, one to pass). • Passers only help attackers from their own team.	• Like Level 1, but a direct shot after a pass from a passer counts double. • Two pairs play 1 v. 1 simultaneously. • The coach has all the balls and starts each round by passing on the ground from outside the field, so that each attacker has to start by receiving a pass.	• Three pairs play 1 v. 1 simultaneously. • The coach has all the balls and kicks a low pass in the air to each attacker, who receives it, then starts playing 1 v. 1.

Setup/Sequence

Four pairs play simultaneous 1 v. 1's on a field between two goals with goal-keepers (25 meters apart).
There are also two neutral passers on the field.
Each attacker tries to maintain possession until an opportunity arises to play a combination with one of the neutral players. Attackers may shoot only after a combination. If they score, they keep the ball; if not, their opponents get it.

Four 1 v. 1's on Two Goals With Two Neutral Players

— 25 meters —

Variations

Focus On:
- Shielding the ball
- Being aware of your surroundings
- Using open space

Tips for Coaches
- The neutral players should switch roles with the others after a while.

Tips for Players
- Protect the ball by shielding your opponent with your body.
- Changing speeds after passing.

Level I	Level II	Level III
• Team competition: Which group can score more goals? • Individual competition: Which player can score the most goals in two minutes?	• Neutral players must pass back on one touch to attackers. • After scoring, the shooter must dribble across the centerline before passing to a neutral player and starting a new attack.	• A one-time shot after a pass from a passer counts double. • Attackers must shoot on the first or second touch after receiving the ball from a neutral player.

Setup/Sequence

In a field twice the size of the penalty area, two teams of two play on two goals with goalkeepers (each team has one attacker and one defender).

Players must stay in their own halves. Defenders who win the ball pass to their attackers in the other half, who then play 1 v. 1 to score.

All other players watch the game while waiting for their turns. Two new pairs take the field every 60 seconds.

1 v. 1 + 1 v. 1

Focus On:

- Getting clear of an opponent
- Showing for passes
- Receiving and controlling passes under pressure

Tips for Coaches

- Assign no more than eight pairs to a field.
- Have extra balls ready.

Tips for Players

- Use a body fake to get clear of opponents.
- Get open for a pass with a quick sprint.
- Make eye contact with the player who has the ball.

Variations

Level I	Level II	Level III
• Players who are waiting for their turns act as "passers" who stand around the outside of the field and help the attacker. • As above, but the passers are limited to two touches (one to receive, one to pass). • Passers only help attackers from their own team.	• After scoring, attackers keep the ball and start a new attack on the other goal. • As above, but with 2 v. 2 in one half and 1 v. 1 in the other.	• Like Level 2, but with 3 v. 3 in one half and 1 v. 1 in the other. • As above, but with 1 v. 1 in one half and 1 v. 2 in the other.

Setup/Sequence

A passer stands five meters outside the penalty area, with a number of balls. Inside the penalty area, three pairs play separate 1 v. 1's (three attackers and three defenders).

One attacker shows for a pass and plays 1 v. 1 against the defender to score.

Any defender who wins the ball passes back to the passer.

After the 1 v. 1, the next pair plays, etc. Players switch roles after about five minutes.

Three 1 v. 1's in the Penalty Area

Focus On:

- Getting clear of an opponent
- Dribbling followed by a shot
- Faking out opponents

Tips for Coaches

- Opponents should be equally matched.
- Integrate with station training.
- Shooting exercises are good activities for breaks.

Tips for Players

- Work on receiving each pass safely and securely.
- Start faking out your opponent as soon as you receive the ball.

Variations

Level I	Level II	Level III
• After the initial pass, all three attackers can work together to score. • When attackers can't find an opportunity to break through, they can pass back to the passer, who then passes to the next attacker.	• Same as above, but with four pairs instead of three. • One passer stands at each corner of the penalty area with a number of balls. They take turns passing to the attackers in the penalty area, who play 1 v. 1 (or 3 v. 3) to score.	• A one-touch shot after a pass from a passer counts double. • The passers are stationed on the sidelines farther back in the backfield (about 30 meters from the goal). They pass in the air (high and low) to the attackers in the penalty area, who play 1 v. 1 or 3 v. 3 to score.

Exercise 1	4 v. 4 + Four Passers	Variations
Three groups of four: Groups A and B play 4 v. 4 on two goals with goalkeepers inside a 25 x 35-meter field. The players in Group C are passers who stand on the sidelines and endline of one half. They take turns passing to players in Group A, who try to score on Goal 1. If B wins the ball, they can counterattack on Goal 2. A and B switch roles after several rounds.	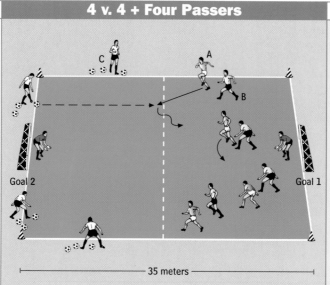	• Defenders are assigned to specific attackers, and attackers are not allowed to work together to set up shots. Instead, each attacker must receive a pass and play 1 v. 1 to score. • Low passes in the air. • Passers stand on the sidelines and throw the ball in to the attackers. • Attackers are not allowed to show for passes in the half where the passers are standing.

Exercise 2	1 v. 1 on Parallel Goals With Goalkeepers	Variations
Set up two goals side by side on an endline, about 15 meters apart. Mark a counter-line about 10 meters outside the penalty area. Players form pairs. The first attacker tries to get past the defender and score on one of the goals. Defenders who win the ball can counterattack by dribbling across the counter-line. Afterwards, the next pair plays.		• Team competition: Attackers form one team, defenders form another. All goals count toward team totals. • Defenders stand on the end-line between the goals and start each play by passing in the air to the attackers. • Before each 1 v. 1, the coach indicates a goal to the attacker. The defender doesn't know which goal the attacker has to shoot at.

Exercise 3

Players form two teams of three. One player plays 1 v. 1 in a 15 x 15-meter field against a player from the other team. The remaining players stand outside the field, one on each side.

The attacker in the field plays combinations with teammates and tries to keep the ball away from the defender for 30 seconds (or one minute). Field players and passers switch roles after each round.

1 v. 1 With Passers

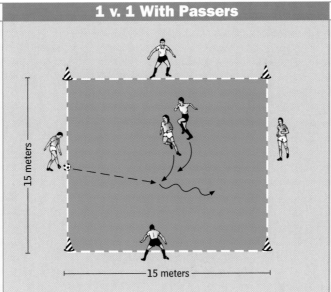

Variations

• Attackers can play combinations with all four passers in turn.
• Passers are limited to two touches in a row.
• Passers are limited to one touch.
• If an attacker passes to a passer from his own team twice, he switches positions with that player.
• Field players try to complete three combinations with their teammates.

Exercise 4

On each endline of a 15 x 25-meter field, set up three small goals about five meters apart. Divide players into two groups.

Three players from each group take the field to play three simultaneous 1 v. 1's.

Attackers may shoot at any of the opposition's three goals. The remaining players stand behind the goals to retrieve balls. Every 30 seconds, three new pairs take the field.

Three 1 v. 1's on Three Small Goals

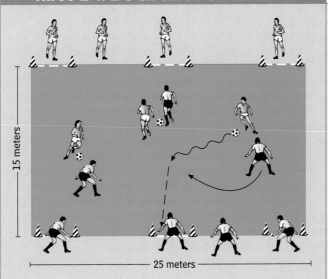

Variations

• Attackers must dribble through one of the opposition's goals to score. (The goals can be made somewhat wider.)
• Individual or team competition: Which player/team can score the most goals?
• Place only two goals on each endline.

Exercise 5	**1 v. 1 on Two Goal Lines Each**	**Variations**
Two players play 1 v. 1 on four three-meter-wide goals in a 15 x 15-meter field. Each player defends two adjacent goals. The player with the ball tries to get past the defender and dribble through a goal, scoring one point if successful. Playing time: 30 seconds to one minute	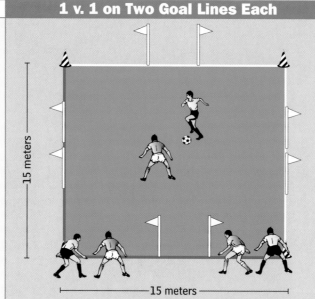	• As above, but with two pairs in the field at the same time. • Adjust goal width to players' ability level. • Instead of goals, attackers must dribble across one of the opponent's endlines.

Exercise 6	**1 v. 1 After a Pass on Goal With 'keeper**	**Variations**
Players form pairs (one attacker, one defender). The first stands in front of a goal with goalkeeper, 20 meters away. The remaining pairs stand on the endline next to the goal. A passer stands in the backfield with a number of balls. The first attacker tries to get clear of the defender to receive a pass. As soon as the attacker shoots, the next pair takes the field. Players switch roles every three rounds.	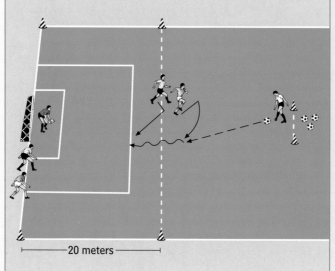	• Attacker and defender start from the endline; the attacker tries to get clear and the defender tries to win the ball. • The attacker must receive a low pass in the air. • Defenders who win the ball can counterattack on a small goal in the backfield. • After the attacker receives the ball, the passer can join in, creating a 2 v. 1 situation.

Exercise 7

Two groups of equal size stand about 25 meters away from a goal with goalkeeper. Players take turns playing 1 v. 1, one player from Group A (attackers) against a player from Group B. After three or four rounds, Group B switches to the attack.

1 v. 1: Solo Attack

Variations

- Opponents start out standing next to each other. Both movetoward the goal at the same time, and the attacker tries to score.
- The attacker starts out standing a short distance behind the defender, who stands with legs apart. The attacker kicks the ball between the defender's legs to start the 1 v. 1.
- Defenders who win the ball can counterattack on either of two small goals.

Exercise 8

Set up two goals with goal-keepers about 30 meters apart. Two attackers and one defender stand in front of each goal. On the right sideline of each half stands a "wing player," who starts each play with a cross. The attackers play 2 v. 1 to score, preferably on a header. Players switch roles every 10 rounds.

Heading on Goal After a Cross

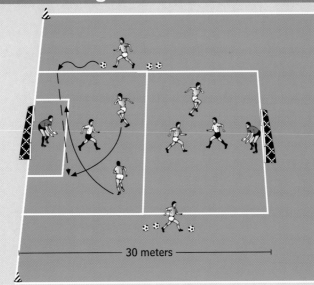

30 meters

Variations

- As above, but 1 v. 1 in front of each goal (new pairs every five or six rounds).
- Two "wing players" stand on each side and take turns.
- Use only one ball: If defenders (or the goalkeeper) win the ball, they pass to the right to the wing player, who crosses to the attackers in front of the other goal. If the attackers score, the goalkeeper throws the ball to the wing player in the other half.

Individual Tactics: 1 v. 1 Defense

The Basics of Individual Defense Tactics

For defenders, individual tactics include all the tactical skills an **individual** player needs to handle typical defense situations and meet the requirements of defense tactics at the group and team levels.

1 v. 1 play is often considered the basic unit of the game – with good reason, because even the best defense strategies depend entirely on the tactical skills of individual players. Like individual tactics for attackers, the game situations defenders typically encounter can be reduced to two basic situations:

• In **Situation 1**, the attacker already has the ball. Depending on the situation (position on the field and with respect to opponents, as well as available space), the attacker may stop and shield the ball, try a solo run or pass to a teammate. The defender responds accordingly, using "active defense" (e.g. attacks on the ball, both real and faked) to take the initiative and force the attacker to take certain actions.

• In **Situation 2**, the closest attacker does not yet have the ball but is trying to get open and take an active part in the attack. Depending on the situation, the defender can either attack as the attacker is receiving a pass, or try to keep the attacker from getting involved at all, by blocking or intercepting passes.

1 v. 1 Training Tips

Since 1 v. 1 skills are so important, players should practice the basic 1 v. 1 situations regularly, as part of a focused, concept-based training program. It's helpful to remember a few basic principles:

• **All** players must practice the basic repertoire of individual tactics (both attack and defense) constantly to keep their skills fresh. Defenders should put special emphasis on concentration and the ability to gauge situations and respond appropriately, while self-confidence and flexibility are especially important for attackers. Continuous training is the only way to achieve the necessary competence. The training program should devote a block of time to each individual element of 1 v. 1 play, using attractive games and exercises as well as specific corrections from the coach.

• After the basic skills of 1 v. 1 defense have been developed to a relatively high degree, players can begin position-specific training as well: Individually or in small groups, players practice the skills that will prepare them for the demands of their respective positional groups.

• Naturally, 1 v. 1 exercises should focus equally on both attack and defense skills. Many exercises make it easy to combine the two, but it's always most effective to focus on one tactical concept per session.

The 1 v. 1 Situation: Defense

Strategy Against a Dribbling Opponent

- The defender moves sideways and back, offering the attacker a breakthrough on the "safe" side (the outside).
- As soon as the attacker kicks the ball ahead, the defender attacks, moving almost parallel to the attacker and knocking the ball away with a slide tackle.

Illustration 9

Training Objectives

General

- **Try to stop dribbling opponents as quickly and as far away from your goal as possible.**
- **Always move along the "inside line" between the opponent and your goal.**
- **Always watch the ball and your opponent.**
- **Stay light on your feet and bend slightly at the waist so that you can move easily in any direction.**
- **Use defensive fakes while moving sideways and back.**
- **Put pressure on opponents; don't give them any time to set up effective follow-up plays.**
- **Direct your positional and running plays so that your opponent is forced outside.**
- **When opponents are waiting to receive passes, block the ball and intercept it if possible.**
- **Otherwise, attack them as soon as they receive the ball.**

Special

For Defenders

- **Watch how your opponents dribble (note strengths and weaknesses). Keep your distance from fast dribblers, and don't attack strong dribblers too soon.**
- **Be flexible: Move behind, behind and to the side or directly beside your opponent, depending on the situation.**

For Midfielders and Forwards

- **Use positional play to disrupt the flow of the opposition's game.**
- **Slow down their attack; move backwards, staying between opponents and your own goal.**
- **Don't let the attacker with the ball run past you!**
- **For attack pressing, move quickly and decisively to disrupt the opposition's attack.**
- **For a flat defense, on the other hand, go deep into the backfield, close down the playing area and put the brakes on the opposition's attack.**

Setup/Sequence

Two teams stand behind the endlines of a field: attackers on one side, defenders on the other.

One by one, the attackers dribble toward the opposite goal and shoot, while the defenders try to stop them. Any defender who wins the ball can attempt (just once) to counterattack on the opposite goal, while the former attacker defends. Afterwards, a new attacker and defender start the next round immediately.

1 v. 1 on Two Goals

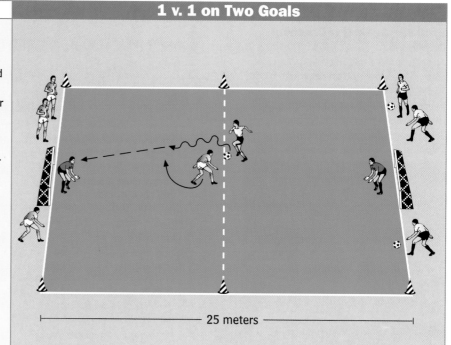

— 25 meters —

Variations

Focus On:
- Positional play
- Forcing attackers outside

Tips for Coaches
- No down time between rounds.
- Retrieve stray balls quickly.

Tips for Players
- Always stay goalside of your opponent.
- Offer an opening to the side, but block the direct line to the goal.
- Force the attacker to the outside.
- Attack the ball.

Level I	Level II	Level III
• Instead of just one counterattack attempt, defenders can keep trying until they finish. • An extra neutral player in the field helps the attackers: 2 v. 1 to score.	• The defenders have all the balls and start each 1 v. 1 with a pass to the attackers. Players return to their original positions after each round. • After a score, the same pair plays 1 v. 1 again with a new ball supplied by the coach.	• Each attacker must play against two defenders (1 v. 2) to score. · As above, but the second defender starts from the same endline as the attacker (but from the other side of the goal), so that the attacker can avoid the 1 v. 2 situation for a few minutes by moving quickly.

Setup/Sequence

Three (or four) pairs of players play 1 v. 1 simultaneously on two goals with goal-keepers, in a 40 x 35-meter field (about twice the size of the penalty area).
One player in each pair attacks on the right-hand goal, the other on the left-hand goal.

Three (or four) new pairs take the field every 60 seconds.

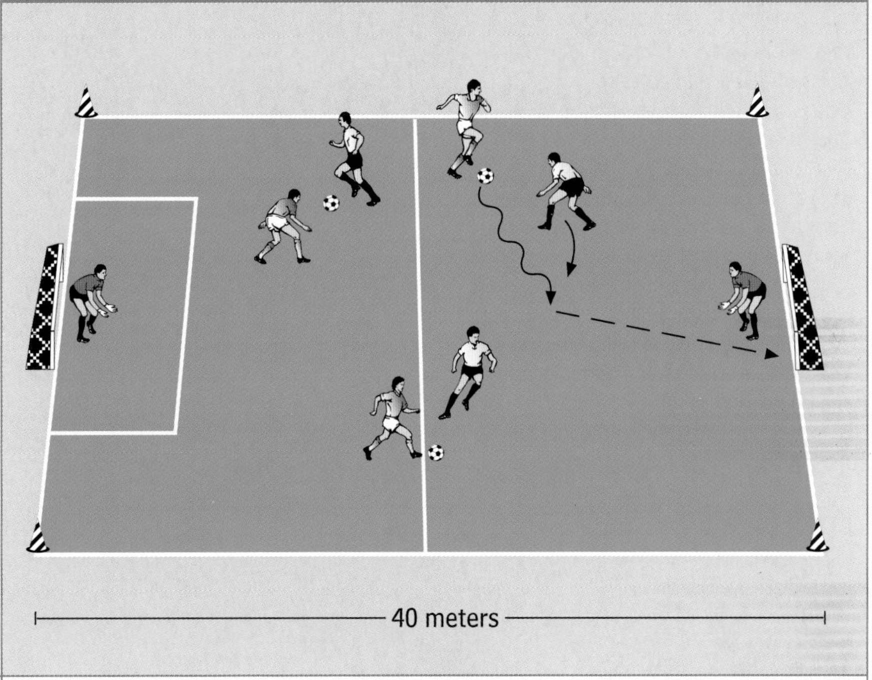

Three Simultaneous 1 v. 1's on Two Goals

— 40 meters —

Variations

Focus On:
- Positional play
- Blocking shots
- Counterattacking and scoring

Tips for Coaches
- If things are too confusing, reduce the number of pairs on the field.
- Have extra balls ready.

Tips for Players
- Don't fall for fakes!
- Don't let the attacker shoot.
- Stay light on your feet.
- Be aware of the action around the ball.

Level I	Level II	Level III
• All three pairs attack on a two-meter wide goal without goalkeeper. Attackers can score on either side of the goal but may not run through it. The game continues after a score. • As above, but on a five-meter wide goal with a goalkeeper. • Players attack on two end-line goals.	• Set up three small goals on each endline of a 40 x 20-meter field. Three pairs play 1 v. 1, as above. Attackers can score on any of the opposition's three goals. • As above, but attackers must dribble through the goal to score.	• After scoring, the attacker gets an extra ball from the endline and starts a new attack. • At the coach's signal, attackers must give up the ball to their opponents (quick attack/defense shift).

Setup/Sequence

Two teams of two play on a 20 x 25-meter field with two three-meter-wide goals (marked with poles).

One player from A attacks on the opposite goal against two defenders from B.

A second attacker waits by A's goal.

If the first attacker needs to, he can pass back to his teammate, who then starts his own solo attack (1 v. 2) on B's goal.

Any defender who wins the ball becomes the new attacker and plays 1 v. 2 against the two players from A, while his teammate takes the support position next to their goal, etc.

Maximum playing time: three minutes per round.

1 + 1 v. 2 on Two Goals

Focus On:
- Active defense: Pressure on the player with the ball
- Intercepting passes

Tips for Coaches
- Run through the exercise once with a demonstration group.

Tips for Players
- Put pressure on the attacker as soon as he's closer to you than he is to his teammate.
- When your teammate attacks the player with the ball, move in immediately to provide support and create a 2 v. 1 situation.

Variations

Level I	Level II	Level III
• As above, but with two standard goals with goalkeepers. The second attacker waits on the endline. • The second attacker may take the field behind his teammate and receive passes but may not shoot.	• Each team defends two small goals placed side by side (five meters apart). This makes defending more difficult because it expands the possibilities for attackers to include changes of direction and fakes.	• Each team defends three small goals placed side by side. • The second attacker can join the attack after a back pass; defenders must adjust instantly to a 2 v. 2 situation.

Setup/Sequence

Two 20 x 30-meter field halves are separated by a five-meter wide "forbidden zone." Players play a separate 4 v. 4 in each half. The four defenders in one half and the four attackers in the other form a team of eight. Attackers play combinations and attempt to dribble across the opposition's endline. If the defenders win the ball, they have to pass it to their teammates in the other half, who play combinations and attempt to dribble across their opponents' endline.

4 v. 4 + 4 v. 4

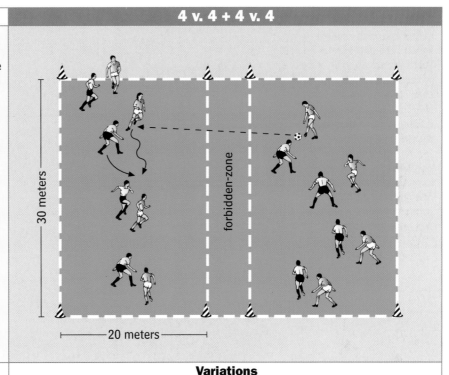

30 meters

forbidden-zone

20 meters

Focus On:
- Anticipating game situations
- Proper positional play
- Intercepting passes

Tips for Coaches
- Make sure you can tell the teams apart!

Tips for Players
- Don't block your path to the ball.
- Always keep your opponent and the ball in view.
- Move directly past your opponent to the ball as soon as you see a chance to intercept it.

Variations

Level I	Level II	Level III
• 3 v. 3 + 3 v. 3. • Same sequence, but each team defends two small goals on the endline.	• Same sequence, but with three small goals on each endline. • Make the "forbidden zone" seven meters wide.	• Same sequence, but with two goals with goalkeepers on each endline. • 5 v. 5 + 5 v. 5. • Make the "forbidden zone" 10 meters wide.

Exercise 1	Defender Facing Attacker 1	Variations
Set up two goals with goal-keepers about 30 meters apart. Two equally matched teams wait beside their goals. Each player in Group A has a ball. The first player from A dribbles a few meters and passes to Player B, then sprints after it to defend. B now plays 1 v. 1 to score. A can counterattack on B's goal after winning the ball. After each shot, the next player from A passes, etc.	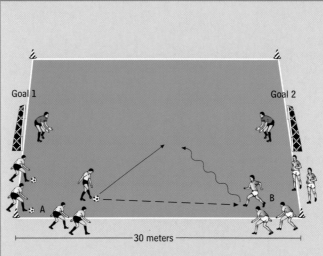	• A passes in the air to B, who controls it before the 1 v. 1. • Individual competition: After 10 rounds, which player has scored the most goals? • Team competition: Which group can score more goals in 10 rounds?

Exercise 2	Defender Facing Attacker 2	Variations
Set up three small goals about 30 meters away from a goal with goalkeeper. Two (or three) pairs of players stand at each small goal, waiting to play 1 v. 1. The first pair's attacker starts for the big goal and attempts to shoot, the other player acts as defender. Any defender who wins the ball can counterattack on his small goal. After a shot, the round is over; both players move down one goal and switch roles.	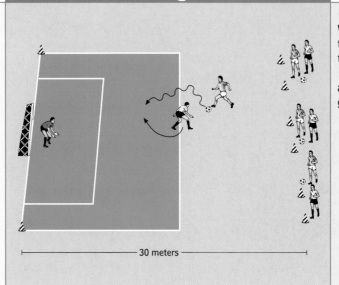	• Widen the countergoals: When defenders win the ball, they have to **dribble** across the goal line. • Defenders may counter-attack on any of the small goals.

Exercise 3

Set up two goals with goal-keepers about 30 meters apart. Several pairs of players (one attacker and one defender) stand next to each goal. The first pair's attacker passes into the center of the field and starts after the ball. The defender follows and attempts to keep the attacker from scoring on Goal 1. Defenders who win the ball counter on Goal 2.

The next round starts from the opposite goal.

Attacker Facing Away From Goal

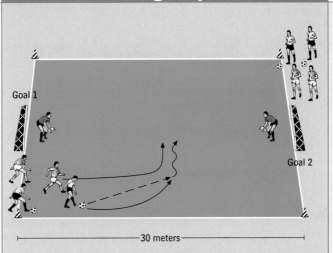

Variations

• Two pairs play simultaneously, one on each goal, but there is no counterattack: The round ends when the defender wins the ball.
• The attacker **dribbles** into the field, followed by the defender, and attacks on the goal from which they started.

Exercise 4

Same setup as Exercise 3. Six to eight players stand next to each goal. The coach stands on the sideline and passes into the center of the field.

After the pass, one player from each group runs for the ball. The player who wins it attempts to score. If defenders win the ball, they counterattack on the other goal, and their opponents become the new defenders.

1 v. 1 After a Pass

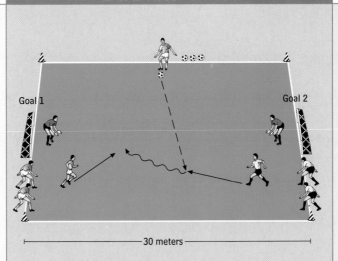

Variations

• Two players from each side take the field after the coach's pass and play 2 v. 2.
• The coach passes in the air.
• The coach kicks some passes on the ground, others in the air.

Exercise 5	1 v. 1 After a Pass 1	Variations

Set up two goals with goal-keepers about 25 meters apart; several pairs of players stand next to each goal.
The first pair stands in front of Goal 1. The attacker shows for a pass from the goalkeeper at Goal 2, receives it and plays 1 v. 1 to score on Goal 1.
Any defender who wins the ball can counterattack on Goal 2.
The next round starts with a pass from Goal 1.

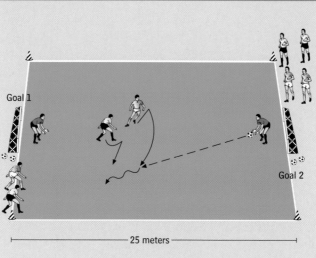

Goal 1

Goal 2

25 meters

- The goalkeepers throw the ball in (low).
- The goalkeepers kick passes on the ground.
- The goalkeepers kick low passes in the air.
- Goalkeeper competition: Which goalkeeper allows fewer goals?

Exercise 6	1 v. 1 After a Pass 2	Variations

Set up three small goals about 30 meters from a standard goal with goalkeeper. One pair of players stands at each small goal; three more are in the middle of the field.
One player at each small goal has a ball. The attacker at the first small goal passes to one of the attackers in the field, who plays 1 v. 1 to score. Any defender who wins the ball can counterthe small goal.
Then the next player passes to an attacker.

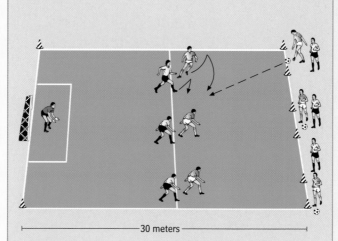

30 meters

- Attackers and defenders switch roles with their partners every three rounds.
- The attackers at the goals pass in the air (low).
- Make the countergoals wider; defenders must dribble across the goal lines to score.

Exercise 7

Two or three defenders stand behind the endline on either side of a goal with goalkeeper. Each has a ball. Two or three attackers stand at each corner of the penalty area.

A defender on the left passes diagonally to an attacker, who tries to shoot. A defender from the right moves up to stop the shot. Afterwards, the exercise continues with a pass from the right, etc.

1 v. 1 in the Penalty Zone on One Goal

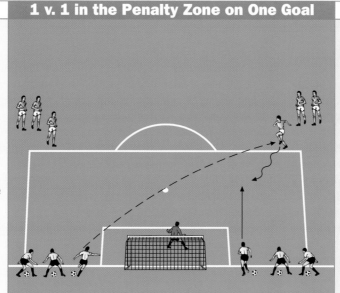

Variations

- Attackers must receive low passes in the air.
- After the pass, two defenders and two attackers (one of each from each side) take the field to play 2 v. 2 inside the penalty area.

Exercise 8

Inside the penalty area are two defenders and three attackers. A crosser stands on the sideline.

The attackers get clear and show for crosses, then attempt to score with a header. Defenders try to head or kick the ball away from the goal and to a teammate. After each cross, the players play until the situation has been clearly resolved.

The crosser switches sides every eight to 10 rounds.

2 v. 3 in the Penalty Zone After a Cross

Variations

- Attackers can also head or kick the ball to a teammate waiting outside the penalty zone, who then shoots (preferably directly).
- As above, but 3 v. 3 (4 v. 4) inside the penalty zone.
- As above, but with two attackers waiting outside the penalty area.

Group Tactics: Combination Play to Maintain Possession

Maintaining Possession

Maintaining possession, or staying in control of the ball in any situation, is a skill that's been developed (practically) to perfection by the world's top teams. First they master building a solid attack from the back, no matter how hard the opposition is pressing. This type of constructive opening play plays an exceptionally important role in today's game. Then, in the midfield and beyond, the focus shifts to maintaining possession. This phase is generally characterized by quick, flexible combination play, with lots of short passes and occasional long ones. Combinations involving lots of players are standard.

Not even the best team can afford to do without solo plays, which are integrated into combination play.

In recent years the speed of combinations in tight spaces has increased enormously. At the same time, active, ball-oriented defense has increased pressure on the player with the ball. Attackers have significantly less time to orient themselves and get on top of the situation than they used to. That's why safe, quick combination play is so valuable. When the pressure is on, perfect combination play is the only way for attackers to keep the ball.

Combination Play: The Basics
• "Creative ball handling" and well-developed ball coordination
• Versatile, accurate passing, even at top speed and under extreme pressure
• Safe, flexible receiving at top speed and under intensive opposition pressure
• Getting clear and showing for passes with well-timed sprints, body fakes and changes of direction

Standard Combinations
You can improve cooperation and enhance your team's effectiveness with a variety of combination patterns.

These quick, versatile attacking combinations are also a good way to get past tight defense formations.

Basic Sequence	Wall Pass	Characteristics
• Attacker B dribbles straight toward defender A. • Before the pass, B makes eye contact with "wall player" C, who is off to one side and open. B then passes to C from about two meters away. • At almost the same time, B sprints toward the goal in order to get past A as quickly as possible. • C passes back with one touch and accurately into the path of B, who then finishes the attack with a shot.		• The wall pass is an effective combination for two players. • With two precise passes, attackers can get past defenders. • The speed of the play and its potential for variation (e.g. the "wall pass fake," or a solo play by the "wall player") add an element of surprise. • Typical wall pass situations: 1. In the center of the attack, to set up a shot. 2. On the wing, to set up a cross.

The most effective combinations are the wall pass, the takeover and overlapping. Well-known additions to this basic repertoire include the wall pass fake and the pass to a third player.

Practicing Combination Play

For confident combination play, players must master the necessary basic techniques: dribbling, passing, receiving, ball control etc. The first objective of practice is to solidify these techniques, using match-oriented exercises that systematically increase in precision, speed and opposition pressure. This is followed by a variety of small group games designed to teach fluid combination play.

Finally these skills must be incorporated into the tactics of the team as a whole. This involves some other concepts:

1. Combination plays in positional groups
2. Changing the tempo and the area of play
3. Confident attack building and the game on the wings.

Objectives

General

- Incorporating dribbling and passing into fluid combinations
- Using short or long passes as the situation requires
- Confident combination play within positional groups
- Using group attack tactics

Basic Sequence	Takeover	Characteristics
• First, attacker B dribbles toward defender A, who blocks the path. • Just before reaching A, B changes direction and dribbles diagonally or laterally toward attacker C, while shielding the ball from A with his body. • Teammate C comes to meet B and takes possession on the side away from A. • Then C has to sprint away, keeping the ball close, to get out of the tight situation. • C finishes the attack with a shot.		• The takeover is an effective group attack tactic. • Attackers can use this combination to escape tight situations. • Typical takeover situations: 1. In the center of the attack, to set up a shot. 2. On the wing, to set up a cross.

Setup/Sequence

Two teams of six play in a field half or other marked area.

Using combination play, the attackers try to maintain possession as long as possible. If they lose it, the teams switch roles.

Attackers score one point for every 10 passes in a row.

Playing time: five minutes per round

6 v. 6 Game

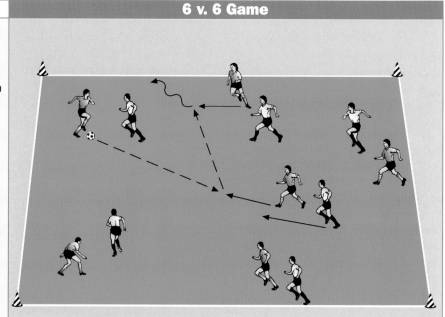

Variations

Focus On:

- Passing safely.
- Getting clear and opening to create opportunities for passes

Tips for Coaches

- The field should be rectangular (to simulate a standard field).
- When the ball goes out players dribble or pass from the point it left the field.

Tips for Players

- After you pass, get open again.
- Don't get "stuck" on one side.
- After a few short passes, try a long "opening" pass.

Level I

- Two neutral players (the coach can be one of them) help whichever team has the ball, to make combination play easier.
- Add goal lines: The teams attack on the sidelines. Attackers use combination play to **dribble** across the opposition's goal line (for one point).

Level II

- Teams don't switch roles until the attackers lose the ball three times. Attackers must pass directly until the first time they lose the ball; then they're limited to two touches. After they lose the ball a second time, touches are unlimited.
- All players limited to three touches.

Level III

- Each long pass to a teammate = one point.
- Each wall pass or takeover = one point.
- All players are limited to two touches (or one).
- Assign each player to a specific opponent.
- Set up six small goals (three meters wide) in the field. Each pass through a goal = one point.

Setup/Sequence

Three teams of four players each play in a marked field:

Teams A and B play 4 v. 4 on two goals with goalkeepers.

The players from C (passers) distribute themselves evenly along the two sidelines.

A's objective is to score as many goals as possible, on either goal. B, on the other hand, tries to maintain possession as long as possible and prevent A from scoring, in cooperation with the passers. Teams switch roles after five minutes.

Ball Keepers vs. Goal Hunters

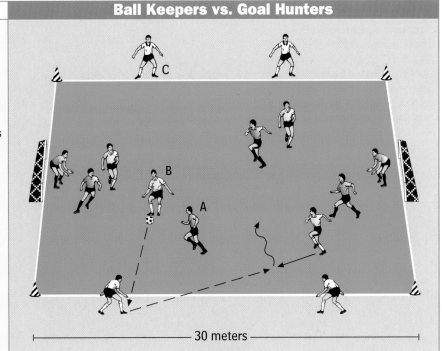

— 30 meters —

Focus On:

- Playing decisive, confident combinations
- Creating opportunities to pass
- Passing accurately

Tips for Coaches

- Have extra balls ready at the goals.

Tips for Players

- Use the entire field! This makes it harder for the opposition to get to the ball.
- Play combinations with the passers whenever possible.

Variations

Level I	Level II	Level III
• Team A can also use the passers to build its attack. • Team B can also use the goalkeepers, in addition to the passers.	• Team B and the passers are limited to a maximum of two touches. • Team A cannot attack the same goal twice in a row.	• Team B and the passers are limited to one touch. • 4 v. 4 + 4 on two goals: The passers help the team with the ball. If defenders win the ball in the opposition's half, they try to score. In their own half, they have to finish three passes in a row (with the help of the passers) before countering.

Setup/Sequence

Two teams play 4 v. 4 in a 35 x 25-meter field. A passer stands behind each endline.

The team that has the ball tries to complete as many combinations as possible from one passer to the other. They score one point for each one.

Passer to Passer

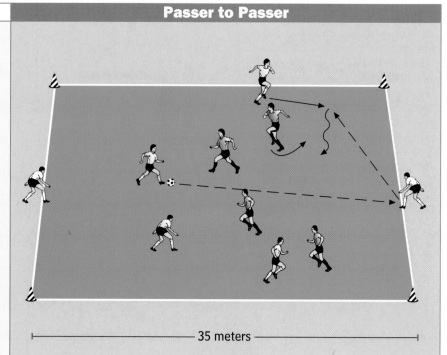

35 meters

Focus On:

- Passing safely
- Getting open

Tips for Coaches

- Mark field boundaries clearly.

Tips for Players

- Spread out across the field, so that if the direction of play switches, you'll have opportunities to pass immediately.
- After you pass, get open again immediately.

Variations

Level I	Level II	Level III
• An extra (neutral) player helps the attackers, to make combination play easier. • 5 v. 5: One player from each team takes on the role of passer. If opponents pass to them, they pass back to their teammates. If teammates pass to them, passer and receiver immediately switch positions.	• Passers are limited to two touches. • 5 v. 5 (6 v. 6) from one passer to the other. • Play to maintain possession. Attackers can also pass to the same passer a number of times in a row. 10 passes in a row = one point. • Goalkeepers act as passers.	• One touch for passers. • 5 v. 5 (6 v. 6) from one passer to the other in a 40 x 30-meter field . • All players inside the field are limited to two touches in a row. • The passers are the goalkeepers: Passing in the air to a goalkeeper = one point.

Setup/Sequence

Three teams of four players each play in a marked 30 x 20-meter field.

Teams A and B play 4 v. 4. One passer from C stands behind each endline or sideline.

A and B, with the help of the passers, both try to maintain possession as long as possible. 10 passes in a row = one point. Which team can score the most points?

Every five minutes, one of the teams on the field switches positions with the passers.

4 v. 4 + 4 Passers

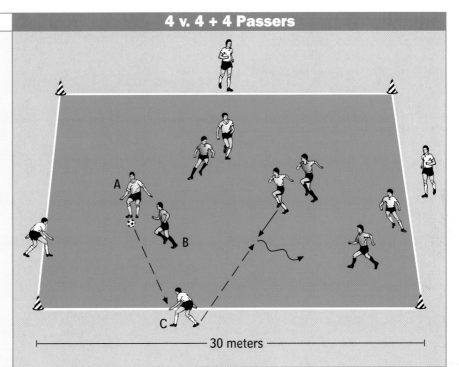

— 30 meters —

Variations

Focus On:

- Building confident combination plays with safe passes
- Passing accurately
- Creating passing opportunities

Tips for Coaches

- Mark field boundaries clearly.

Tips for Players

- Get clear to create passing opportunities for your teammates.
- Spread the field.
- If possible, look for open teammates before you receive the ball.

Level I	Level II	Level III
• An extra (neutral) player helps whichever team has the ball. • The passers can also pass among themselves. • Five passes in a row = one point.	• Passers are limited to two touches in a row. • All players must pass low (below the hips) or else they lose the ball. • 5 v. 5 + 4 passers. • All players must control the ball before passing it on.	• Passers must pass directly. • 6 v. 6 + 4 passers: If a team completes 10 passes in a row before losing the ball, they get it back. • 15 passes in a row = one point. • Passers are limited to two touches in a row, and the players inside the field get one touch.

Setup/Sequence

Field size is 40 x 30 meters. Team A (six players) and Team B (four players) both try to maintain possession as long as possible.

The players from A are limited to two touches in a row, but B has unlimited touches.

After two to four minutes and an active break, reorganize the teams.

6 v. 4 to Maintain Possession

— 40 meters —

Variations

Focus On:

- Confident combination play with opposition outnumbered.
- Maintaining possession when you're outnumbered.

Tips for Players

- When you outnumber the opposition: Confident combination play is easier at a moderate pace, so don't pass too soon. Spread the field.
- When you're outnumbered: Dribble with lots of changes of direction, and use dribbling, wall passes and takeovers to get out of tight situations.

Level I	Level II	Level III
• Enlarge the field to make combination play easier. • The players from A are limited to three touches.	• 6 v. 4 on two goals with goalkeepers, in a 40 x 30-meter field: Team A is limited to two touches and tries to score on both goals repeatedly. Team B plays for possession (one point every 15 seconds) with unlimited touches. If the goalkeeper gets the ball after an attack from A, he distributes to B.	• Team A must pass directly, while the players from B are limited to three touches. • Make the field smaller: This increases pressure on the player with the ball, making it harder to maintain possession.

Setup/Sequence

Two teams play 7 v. 7 in a field two-thirds the standard length (or in a field half) without goals. Cones mark a 12 x 12-meter goal zone in each corner. Mark a centerline as well.

The team with the ball builds combination plays, ending with a pass to a player who has run/is running into a goal zone (= one point).

Dribbling into the zones is not allowed. Defenders may not enter the zones. After the attackers score, their opponents get the ball but must first dribble across the centerline.

Passing Into Goal Zones

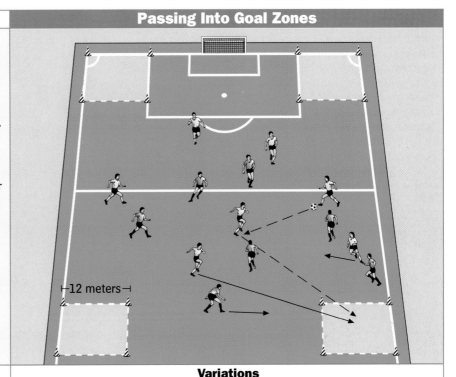

├─12 meters─┤

Variations

Focus On:

- Covering lots of ground with confident combination plays
- Getting open at the right moment
- Shifting the area of play

Tips for Coaches

- Mark the goal zones clearly.

Tips for Players

- Whenever the opposition forms a wall in front of a particular goal zone, change direction.
- Time your runs carefully.
- Create plenty of passing opportunities.

Level I	Level II	Level III
• An extra (neutral) player helps whichever team has the ball. • Enlarge the goal zones.	• All players are limited to two touches in a row. • When the attackers score, they keep the ball but must attack on a different goal zone. • Assign two goal zones to each team.	• Attackers must pass directly. • Defenders may enter the goal zones too. To score, attackers must pass to a teammate in a goal zone as before, but pass receivers must be able to control the ball under pressure from an opponent and then pass back to a teammate outside the zone.

Exercise 1	**5 v. 2**	**Variations**

In a 12 x 12-meter field, five attackers play against two defenders (in the middle). The attackers try to maintain possession by passing as accurately as possible. If a defender wins the ball or the ball goes out of the field, the attacker responsible switches places with whichever defender has been in the middle longer.

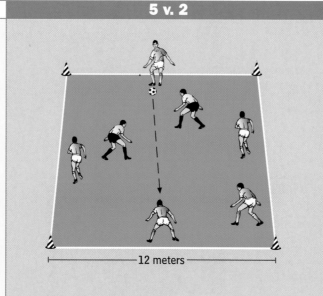

12 meters

- Attackers are limited to two touches.
- Attackers must pass directly.
- Two "required touches" for attackers: They have to control the ball briefly on the first touch before passing it on with the second touch.

Exercise 2	**3 v. 1 + 4 Passers**	**Variations**

5 v. 3 (A vs. B).
Four players from A are passers and stand outside a 15 x 20-meter field, one on each line. The fifth stays in the field and plays against B. The passers try to complete combinations with their teammate in the middle, who must control it and pass it back to them.
Attackers switch roles every 30 seconds. Which attacker can complete the most combinations with the passers?

20 meters

- Passers are limited to two touches.
- Passers can move anywhere along their respective sidelines.
- Low passes in the air to the player in the middle are allowed.
- Same sequence, but with 5 v. 3 + 4 passers: Three attackers and four passers work to keep the ball away from five defenders as long as possible. Don't forget to take breaks!

Exercise 3

Distribute five to seven three-meter wide goals freely about a quarter of a field. Two teams play 5 v. 7. The team of five has unlimited touches and plays to maintain possession. The team of seven attacks on the goals but is limited to two touches in a row; they score one point for each pass through a goal.

5 v. 7 on Cone Goals

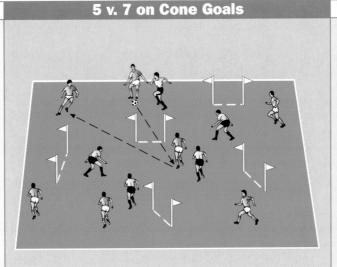

Variations

- Same sequence, but with 5 v. 6 or 5 v. 5 (depending on ability level).
- Attackers must **dribble** through the goals.
- A wall pass through a goal = one point for the attackers.

Exercise 4

In a field quarter, set up three small goals on one endline and a 12-meter wide goal on the other.
The game is 5 v. 5 with an 11th player who helps whichever team has the ball.
Team A attacks on any of the small goals, and Team B must **dribble** across the longer goal line.

5 v. 5 + 1 on Various Goals

Variations

- As above, but with four (or two) small goals.
- As above, but with 5 v. 5 or 6 v. 6 (without the extra player).

Group Tactics: Combination Play to Score

Taking Advantage of Scoring Opportunities

Soccer's biggest attraction has to be the perfectly played goal. However, the more defenders put pressure on attackers and restrict the space available to them in front of the goal, the less chance attackers have to shoot, or even to set up shots. When they do get a chance, they usually have only a split second to make that chance count. But with frequent practice in combination play and shooting, any team can increase its share of shooting opportunities, which leads to an effective attack.

Notes on Shooting Training

Many traditional shooting exercises are poorly adapted (at best) to the demands of today's soccer. Dribbling up to the edge of the penalty area and shooting ignores the element of opposition pressure. But this pressure is precisely what players need to be prepared for, if they want to be able to score in a match situation.

Therefore, shooting training should consist of exercises that reproduce match conditions in and around the penalty area, alternating between simple exercises and others that are more complex. Why the penalty area? Because for the majority of goals, the shot comes from within the penalty zone –

and many times, so does the last pass before the shot.

Beyond that, there are a few important principles for efficient, match-character shooting training:

1. First of all, the general principles of soccer training:

– Move from the simple to the complex.

– Repeat exercises often, occasionally varying the basic sequence (e.g. making it slightly harder).

– Balance periods of exertion and rest.

– Demonstrate!

– Practice each concept regularly for a relatively long period of time.

2. Shooting training must specifically address the demands of match play. This

---

Shooting Training Tips

● The mix of simple exercises, more complex and demanding exercises, and match-oriented games should vary according to ability level, season and team standing.

● Form small groups for shooting exercises. If possible, practice on two goals at once, or else keep one of the groups busy doing something else.

● To master the concepts involved, players must practice shooting over a long period of time, working on it in each session.

● Each session should follow a systematic progression from one exercise to the next, with the objective of arriving at match con-

ditions as quickly as possible.

● Shooting training should always be characterized by variety, match character and fun.

means that time and opposition pressure should be a part of most exercises. You should also encourage players to shoot directly whenever possible, because in today's game, a shooter rarely has time to control the ball before shooting.

3. Offer exercises that cover a wide range of techniques: shots on the ground and in the air, soft shots and hard shots, short-range and long-range shots, etc.

4. The objective of all attack tactics should be to put players in good positions to shoot. Ideally, attackers should be able to get as close as possible to the goal and shoot with little or no interference from opponents. Don't forget to practice this scenario too!

Illustration 11

Objectives

General

- Setting up shooting opportunities with safe but versatile combination play.
- Taking advantage of every shooting opportunity, with daring and determination.
- Passing whenever a teammate is in a good position to shoot.

Shooting Training Tips

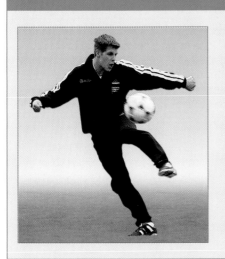

- Keep encouraging players to take shots, even risky ones. Comparatively simple exercises are ideal situations for them to practice determined, aggressive shooting, so that they develop familiarity and self-confidence for similar match situations.
- The difficulty of any exercise should always match the current ability level of the team (and of individual players whenever possible). This is the only way to keep practice productive and players motivated.
- Use equipment (like poles, pins, etc.) judiciously to simulate the opposition, mark field boundaries more clearly and create goal zones for crosses.
- Position may or may not be important, depending on age and ability level. At the lower levels, all players should spend equal time on all aspects of attack and defense.

Setup/Sequence

Set up two goals with goalkeepers on a 40 x 30-meter field.

Two teams play 5 v. 5, focusing on combination play and shooting.

Which team can score more goals in five minutes?

Two Teams on Two Goals

|← 40 meters →|

Focus On:

- Safe combination play
- Executing shots
- Taking advantage of opportunities to score

Tips for Coaches

- Alternate this exercise and simple shooting exercises.
- Keep extra balls at both goals.

Tips for Players

- Make your passes precise and shoot directly whenever possible: It saves time and surprises opponents.
- Shoot with determination.

Variations

Level I	Level II	Level III
• Two neutral players help whichever team has the ball, but they themselves are not allowed to shoot. • As above, but neutral players are allowed to shoot. • As above, but neutral players are limited to one touch (or two). • As above, but with only one neutral player.	• Mark the centerline: Players are limited to three touches in their own half but have unlimited touches in the opposition's half. • Long shots from your own half count double.	• Attackers are limited to three (or two) touches. • The only shots that count are direct shots after back passes. (This encourages attackers to spread out and move up immediately to follow the ball). • As above, but goals scored on volleys count too.

Setup/Sequence

Three teams of four to seven players play on two goals with goalkeepers in a 45 x 35-meter field.

At any given time, two teams play against each other while the third team rests.

Teams switch every five minutes.

Three Teams on Two Goals

Focus On:

- Fast, confident attacks
- Switching quickly to the attack
- Spreading the field

Tips for Coaches

- The team that's not paying should stay active.
- Keep extra balls at both goals.

Tips for Players

- Spread out in all directions; you can cover more ground with your combination plays.
- Always try to form "attack triangles."
- Shoot decisively.

Variations

Level I	Level II	Level III
• Two neutral players help whichever team has the ball, and they are also allowed to shoot. • As above, but neutral players are limited to two touches in a row. • As above, but with only one neutral player.	• Whenever a team scores, their opponents switch with the third team. The goalkeeper throws the ball to the new team. Which team can score 10 goals first? • As above, but attackers are limited to three (or two) touches.	• Enlarge the field to 50 x 40 meters; all three teams play at the same time. B defends one goal, C defends the other, and A attacks continuously on both. After scoring or losing the ball, A gets the ball back immediately and attacks on the other goal. Teams switch every five minutes.

Setup/Sequence

Mark a 30-meter-long "counterline" about 35 meters away from a goal with goalkeeper. Two teams of five play between goal and counterline.

Team A focuses on combination play and shooting. B attempts to disrupt the attack, and attacks on the counterline if they win the ball.

A starts a new attack after each counter-attack. Teams switch roles every five minutes. Which team can score more goals?

Goal vs. Counterline

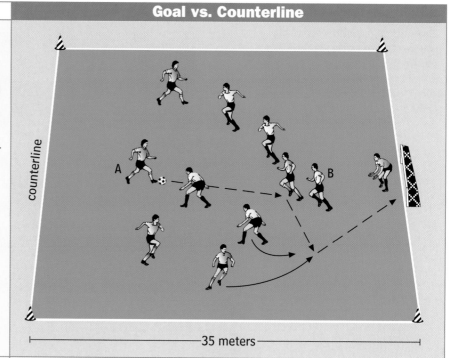

counterline

A   B

← 35 meters →

Focus On:

- Executing shots
- Recognizing shooting opportunities
- Switching quickly to the attack

Tips for Coaches

- Mark the counterline clearly.

Tips for Players

- Be sure to spread the field.
- There should always be a pass receiver open in the middle.
- Forwards can play wall passes or carry the attack ahead on their own.

Variations

Level I	Level II	Level III
• One neutral player (e.g. the coach) helps whichever team has the ball. • As above, but with two neutral players.	• Teams switch roles and directions of attack whenever a defender succeeds in dribbling across the counterline. • Replace the counterline with two small goals (each about three meters wide).	• Instead of one goal, set up two goals with goalkeepers on the same endline (keep the counterline on the other side). A can attack on either goal. • A attacks on both goal and counterline for five minutes. If B wins the ball, they (and the goalkeeper) play to maintain possession. Switch after five minutes.

Setup/Sequence

The playing field is the penalty area. Three teams of four are assigned as follows:

Two teams play 4 v. 4 inside the penalty area on one goal with goalkeeper. The players from the third team are passers who help whichever team has the ball. They are positioned around the penalty area: Two stand behind the endline (one on either side of the goal), and one stands on each sideline. Defenders may not attack passers.

Attackers focus on combination play (involving the passers) and shooting. If the defenders win the ball, they must first complete a combination with a passer before attacking the goal.

Teams switch roles every five minutes.

Game in the Penalty Area on One Goal

Focus On:

- Quickly recognizing shooting opportunities near the goal
- Improving shooting technique
- Shooting accurately and precisely

Tips for Coaches

- If necessary, mark the penalty area boundaries with cones.

Tips for Players

- Set up shooting opportunities with fast but precise passes.
- Aim your passes so that your team mates can move to meet them and shoot off one touch.

Variations

Level I	Level II	Level III
• Attackers may dribble out of the penalty area to control the ball. They may not be attacked while they're outside. • After a goal, the ball goes back to the attackers.	• Passers are limited to two touches in a row. • The two passers on the sidelines are allowed to shoot from outside the penalty area. • Only one-touch shots count.	• Passers must pass directly. • Defenders can attack passers as well. • If defenders win the ball, they must score within the next five touches. • The only shots that count are headers and direct shots set up by a passer.

Setup/Sequence

Set up two goals with goalkeepers on a 40 x 30-meter field.

Two teams play 5 v. 5, but with players assigned to specific halves: 3 v. 3 in one half, 2 v. 2 in the other. Players may not leave their assigned halves.

Two Zones

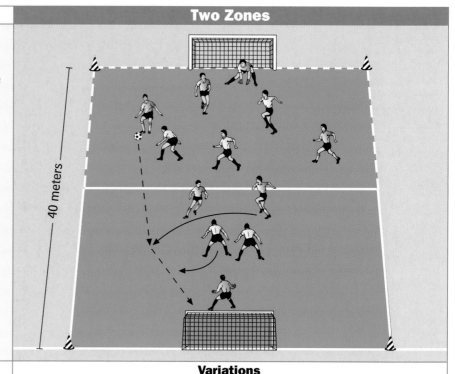

40 meters

Focus On:
- Recognizing shooting opportunities quickly
- Long passes to set up shots
- Showing for passes at the right moment

Tips for Coaches
- Mark the centerline clearly.

Tips for Players
- Don't get clear of your opponent and show for a pass until your teammate sees you and is able to pass.
- Work aggressively for the shot.

Variations

Level I	Level II	Level III
• One unrestricted neutral player helps whichever team has the ball. • Redistribute players: In each half, three attackers play against two defenders. • One defender is allowed to follow attackers into the other half, so that attackers are always outnumbered.	• As above, but with 3 v. 3 + 3 v. 3. • 6 v. 6 in a field half: Team A attacks on a goal with goalkeeper; Team B attacks on two small goals (marked with cones or poles). As before, players are assigned to specific zones: 2 v. 2 in the penalty area, 4 v. 4 in the rest of the field.	• In each half, two attackers play against three defenders. This makes attack building and shooting more difficult. • Restrict touches for attackers during the early attack building phase.

Setup/Sequence

Three teams of four play on two goals with goalkeepers in a 35 x 25-meter field.

Teams A and B play 4 v. 4, while the players from C stand on the sidelines and act as passers, helping whichever team has the ball.

4 v. 4 + 4 Passers on the Sidelines

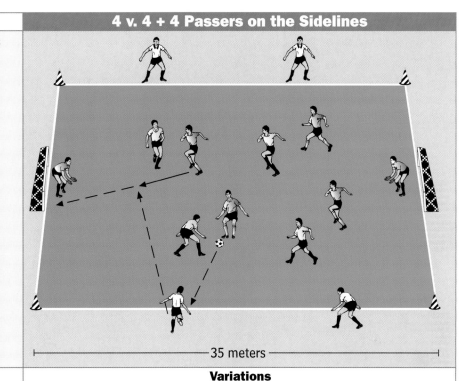

35 meters

Focus On:

- Using accurate passes to set up shots
- Improving passing technique and accuracy

Tips for Coaches

- Have extra balls ready.

Tips for Players

- Set up shooting opportunities with precise passes.
- Aim your passes so that your team mates can shoot off one touch.
- When you have a shooting opportunity, take it!

Variations

Level I	Level II	Level III
• Passers have unlimited touches. • 3 v. 3 + 2 (or 3) passers on the sidelines.	• Passers are limited to two touches. • Passers only help when Team A has the ball, but Team A's players are limited to two touches. Team B, on the other hand, has unlimited touches. Teams switch roles after three minutes. Which team can score more goals?	• Passers must pass directly. • Attackers must score within six touches (including touches by passers). • Attackers must either shoot or pass to a passer after a maximum of three touches. • Only one-touch shots count.

Setup/Sequence

Three teams of four play on two goals with goalkeepers in a 35 x 25-meter field.

Teams A and B play 4 v. 4, while the players from C stand on the endlines, one on either side of the goal, and act as passers, helping whichever team has the ball.

4 v. 4 + 2 Passers Beside Each Goal

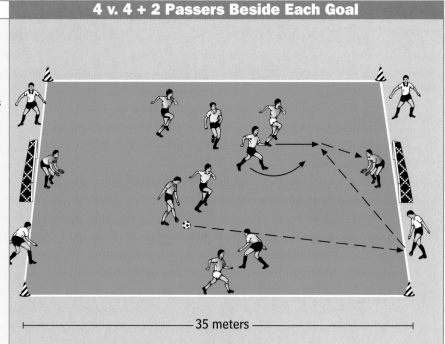

|—————————— 35 meters ——————————|

Focus On:

- Accurate long passes.
- Attacking with numbers.
- Changing pace.

Tips for Coaches

- Have the field boundaries marked and the goals set up before practice starts; this saves valuable practice time.

Tips for Players

- After passing, start after the ball immediately and get open to receive the ball and shoot.
- Look up from the ball one last time before shooting.

Variations

Level I	Level II	Level III
• Passers have unlimited touches. • Any goal scored on a direct shot after a back pass from a passer counts double. • An extra neutral player helps whichever team has the ball.	• Passers are limited to two touches. Shots must follow a back pass from a passer. • All four passers stand around one of the halves: two behind the endline, and one on each sideline. Team A attacks on Goal 1. Team B attacks on Goal 2 but can only score on one-touch shots set up by the passers.	• Passers restricted to one touch. Shots must follow a back pass from a passer. • The only shots that count are headers and volleys set up by the passers. Attackers try to complete a long pass to one of the passers next to the goal, who must then pass it back in front of the goal after no more than two touches.

Setup/Sequence

Set up a seven-meter-wide goal in the middle of a field half. One goalkeeper stands in the goal. Attackers can score from either side.

Form two teams of eight. Two players from each team stand in the corners of the field diagonally opposite one another and act as passers, creating a 6 v. 6 situation. If an attacker plays a combination with one of his team's passers, he immediately switches positions with that player. The player who had been the passer dribbles onto the field and joins the attack on the goal.

One Open Goal With Goalkeeper

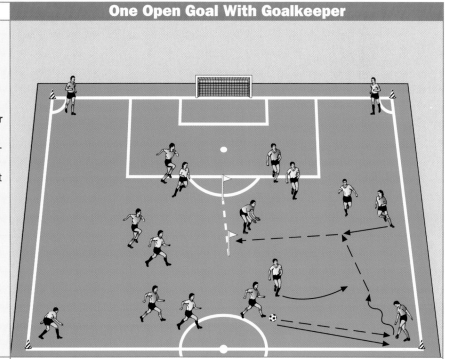

Variations

Focus On:
- Using safe, long-range combinations to set up shots
- Shifting the area of play
- Developing field vision

Tips for Players
- Getting clear and showing for passes on both sides of the goal makes it easier to shift the area of play.
- Switch the direction of your attack suddenly, then go for the goal.

Level I	Level II	Level III
• Attackers can pass to all four passers, but they only switch positions with passers from their own team. • The game continues after goals. Players can't run through the goal. • If the goalkeeper gets possession, he throws it to a passer from the team that had been on defense.	• If defenders win the ball, they have to play a combination with a passer before starting their attack. • Passers only help when Team A has the ball, but Team A's players are limited to two touches. Team B cannot use the passers but has unlimited touches. Teams switch roles after three minutes.	• Attackers are limited to two touches. • The only shots that count are headers and volleys. • Team A tries to score as many goals as possible in seven to 10 minutes, while Team B's objective is simply to maintain possession. Afterwards, teams switch roles.

Exercise 1	Warm-Up: Shooting With Precision	Variations
Set up two goals with goal-keepers about 30 meters apart. Three to five players stand beside each goal with a ball. The first players from the two right-hand groups dribble to the centerline and shoot with the right foot, then join the group on the right side of the opposite goal. When both right-hand groups have finished, the first players from the left dribble onto the field and shoot with the left.	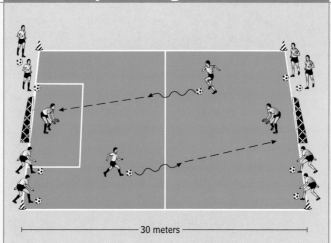 30 meters	• Each player kicks the ball toward the centerline, then shoots on the second touch. • Each player dribbles diagonally to the far end of the centerline and shoots from there. • Two players from each group start at the same time. They dribble five to eight meters, then each passes into the other's path, so that each player can shoot off one touch (or on the second touch).

Exercise 2	Shooting After 1 v. 1 Play	Variations
Setup is the same as Exercise 1, except only the players on the right side have balls. The first player from one right-hand group dribbles a short distance and passes to the first player on the other side, who moves to meet the ball. The passer becomes a defender; the receiver plays 1 v. 1 to score. Afterwards, both players switch positions, and the first two players on the left side start, etc.	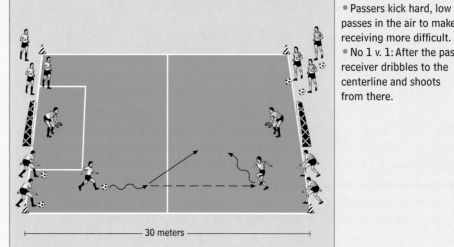 30 meters	• Passers kick hard, low passes in the air to make receiving more difficult. • No 1 v. 1: After the pass, the receiver dribbles to the centerline and shoots from there.

Exercise 3	Shooting From Goal to Goal	Variations

Set up two goals with goal-keepers about 30 meters apart. Form two groups of equal size; each group stands at one end of the centerline. One extra player, with a number of balls, stands to the left of each goal. Each one passes toward the penalty spot; the other players take turns shooting from there.

- Players are allowed to control the ball briefly before shooting.
- Passers kick low passes in the air; shooters can only score on a header or volley.
- Each shooter must complete a short sprint before receiving a pass; the height and force of passes may vary.

Exercise 4	2 v. 2 Rotation	Variations

Players form pairs: Some pairs have one ball each and stand next to the goal; the others stand in front of the center circle.
One player from the first pair on the endline kicks a pass in the air to the first pair in the midfield, then both players sprint from the endline to the penalty area line to defend. The pass receivers play 2 v. 2 against these defenders to score. Each pair then moves to the other group.

- If the defenders win the ball, they can counterattack on two small goals about 35 meters in front of the goal.
- As above, but with groups of three: 3 v. 3 rotation.

Exercise 5	3 v. 2 Outside the Penalty Area	Variations
Three attackers play against two defenders on one goal with goalkeeper in a 40 x 30-meter field. A single passer, with a number of balls, stands on the opposite endline. The passer begins each play with a pass to whichever attacker is open. The attackers play combinations to score If the defenders win the ball, they pass to the passer, who starts the next attack.	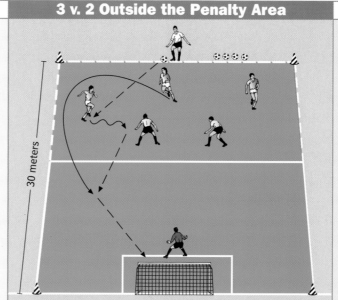	• If the attackers cannot break through, they can pass back to the passer. • Enlarge the field to 40 x 40 meters: Five attackers (with one passer) play against three defenders. • Attackers must complete a pass to a teammate in the penalty area before shooting.

Exercise 6	2 v. 2 in Rapid Succession	Variations
Set up two goals with goal-keepers about 25 meters apart. The players form pairs. The pairs from A stand on the sides of one goal; the pairs from B stand on the other side of the field. The first pair from A plays against the first pair from B. After the end of the play (goal or ball out of touch), the next two pairs take the field. The ball goes to the pair whose teammates scored on the last play.	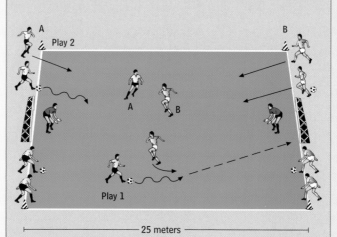	• Each pair's goals count toward a team total. Which team can score more goals? • Distribute the pairs from both teams evenly on both sides of both goals. After each goal, the defenders drop out. A pair of their teammates dribbles onto the field and attacks on the opposite goal, while the pair that scored on the last play defends.

Exercise 7

Set up one goal with goal-keeper on each endline of a 30 x 40-meter field. The center-line must be clearly marked. Two teams play 3 v. 3. A neutral "wall passer" is positioned in front of each goal help the attackers. Every goal following a wall pass with one of these players counts double.

Which team can score more goals in four minutes?

3 v. 3 With "Wall Passers"

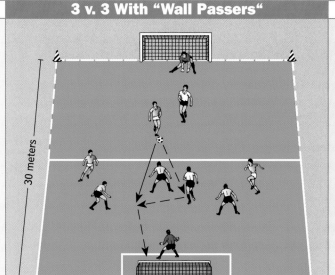

30 meters

Variations

• As above, but with 4 v. 4 plus two "wall passers."
• The "wall passers" can fake a wall pass, then pass directly to a different attacker.

Exercise 8

Players form pairs. One pair starts out on defense: One player stands in front of the goal (with goalkeeper), another stands behind the endline. The other pairs have one ball each and take posi-tions about 30 meters away from the goal. The first pair starts toward the goal and plays 2 v. 1 to score. If they succeed, the defenders switch positions and stay on defense; otherwise, attackers and defenders switch roles.

2 v. 1 on One Goal

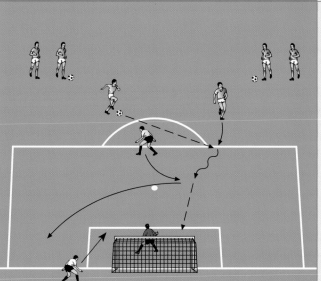

Variations

• Any defender who wins the ball passes it back, either to the goalkeeper or to the other defender, who moves to meet it.
• Any defender who wins the ball counterattacks on two small goals.

Group Tactics: Ball-Oriented Defense

What Is "Ball-Oriented Defense?"

In the past, defense was almost always a matter of man-marking, regardless of position. All defenders had to do was to attack their closest opponents, pursue them all over the field, and shut them down whenever possible. In this system, each individual defender was always responsible for the same attacker. In unusual situations, minor deviations from this strict policy were allowed: For example, if an attacker got past his defender, another defender could cover for a short period of time.

However, as a concept of team defense tactics, man-marking became obsolete long ago. Its disadvantages are all too clear:

By coordinating their opening runs, and especially by "pulling back" defenders, attackers can easily create wide-open spaces to build their attack. All individual attackers have to do is win a 1 v. 1 and follow it with another play (cross, dribbling, pass)¯assuming they're not already in a good position to shoot.

Today, things are much harder for attackers, because the player with the ball is often attacked by two or three defenders simultaneously. Defenders are rarely assigned to individual attackers anymore.

Instead, they're assigned to specific zones, according to the starting formation, and they attack whichever opponents happen to be nearby. And these zones are not rigidly defined; they all overlap and shift, depen-

Ball-oriented defense: Defend actively; put pressure on the attacker!

Basic Plays	**Defending Against Attacks on the Outside**
• In an attack on the outside, the closest outside defender attacks the player with the ball while the other defenders move slightly closer to them. • Using positional play, the outside defender tries to force the attacker outward and prevent a direct attack on the goal. • The other defenders orient themselves toward their teammate: They move toward the ball and cover one another.	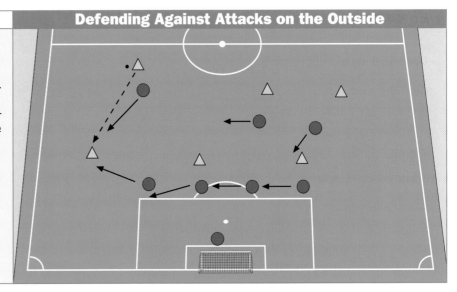

ding on the current position of the player with the ball and the running paths of the other attackers. Defenders near the ball always move quickly to attack the player who has it. Any other attackers nearby are closely covered by other defenders. Defenders also use intelligent positional play to block passing lanes, close down the playing space and disrupt or even stop attackers' combination plays.

That means that all defenders are constantly reorienting themselves toward the ball; the defenders closest to it cover attackers closely while their teammates farther away defend their zones. By moving as a unit to follow the ball, defenders close in on the ball, surround it and make it impossible for the opposition to avoid losing it.

Teaching Ball-Oriented Defense

While players are working to develop their ball-oriented defense skills, it's important to keep emphasizing the importance of good positional play and moving with the ball.

One way to do this at the beginning is with small-sided games on goals, in which attackers outnumber defenders, e.g. 5 v. 4 or 4 v. 3.

In this type of situation, players learn very quickly that they're not just responsible for one opponent, and that they have to help each other if they want to defend successfully.

In the past, soccer training focused on "man-marking;" today, on the other hand, we focus on good zone defense. In other

The Basics

Players must be able to:

- Play a solid 1 v. 1 in all basic situations.
- Follow a constantly changing game situation.
- See "the big picture" and adapt their own individual positions optimally to the positions of the ball, teammates and opponents.
- Learn and discipline themselves.
- Exercise self-criticism in order to learn from situations in practice and match play.
- Think and act as part of a team.

Basic Plays

- In an attack in the middle, the closest inside defender (or center midfielder) moves to meet the attacker.
- The other defenders move slightly inward and cover their teammate's back.
- Important: Not only should defenders stop attackers, they should also put pressure on them with a careful, intelligent attack.

Defending Against Attacks in the Middle

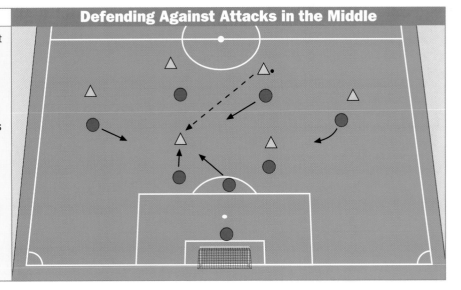

Training Methods

Age-appropriate teaching methods for ball-oriented defense:

● With games on small fields, 6- to 10-year-olds can already start picking up the basics of active, coordinated defense and learn to think, "We want the ball!"

● Ages 10 through 12 are the time to start systematic 1 v. 1 training, because good 1 v. 1 play is the foundation of good performance.

● After age 12, we can start building the basic tactics of ball-oriented defense on this foundation.

words, players defend in predetermined zones, engaging and attacking any attackers who enter these zones.

Players' zones are determined by their positional groups (defenders, midfielders, forwards).

Young players must learn to orient themselves toward the ball, put pressure on the player with the ball and restrict the space around the ball. If the ball is passed, they reorient themselves to it and to the new game situation.

Training 6- to 10-Year-Olds

With small-sided games on small fields, 6- to 10-year-olds can already start learning the basic skills necessary for defending as a unit and thinking in terms of winning the ball quickly.

The basic approach is not just to passively disrupt the opposition's game, but to

defend actively ("We want the ball!"). Never assign destructive tactics (e.g. "shutting down" a specific opponent). Youth coaches should start teaching active defense from the very beginning.

Training 10- to 12-Year-Olds

10- to 12-year-olds are ready to start systematic training in individual tactics, focusing on 1 v. 1 play. After all, even the most carefully planned defense strategies will only work if each player involved possesses the necessary tactical skills. Since 1 v. 1 skills are so important for all other tactics, every player needs to learn proper 1 v. 1 behavior, step by step. Patience and a methodical approach are essential.

Training 12- to 14-Year-Olds

At the same time, or by ages 12 to 14 at the latest, players should start learning the

---

Right

● After a pass, the closest defender immediately puts pressure on the pass receiver.

● All other defenders move toward the ball as well and into compact formation. Important: Each player in the formation should be able to help the others and cover their backs.

● Attackers farther away from the ball are covered from a distance. The backfield is defended by whichever players have moved in toward the middle.

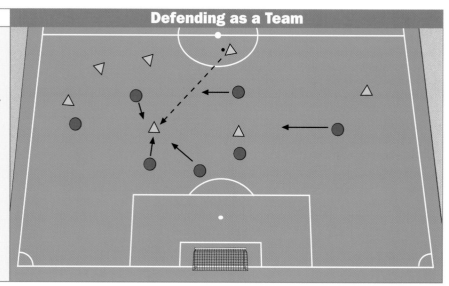

Defending as a Team

basic group and team tactics involved in ball-oriented defense.

Here again, small-sided games are the focus of practice, but unlike basic training, they focus on specific **technical-tactical** concepts.

Practice games on small goals, in which attackers outnumber defenders (3 v. 2, 4 v. 3, 5 v. 4 etc.) are helpful for teaching ball-oriented defense.

These exercises teach defenders to orient themselves toward the player with the ball. One defender attacks, and the others cover the space around the ball. After a pass, the closest defender engages the pass receiver while the other defenders cover the space nearby as before

An effective alternative for teaching the principles of ball-oriented defense is to play on four small goals.

In this case, you should focus on:

1. moving with the ball as a unit
2. restricting the space available to attackers
3. protecting whichever goal the opposition is attacking.

Tactics exercises can only be productive if players regularly receive **corrections** and **advice** from the coach. The coach asks questions and explains and justifies the principles involved, using the current game situation as an example. For youth players, this type of **immediate** feedback is exceptionally helpful and productive.

Active, ball-oriented defense is indispensable for a successful and attractive game. The individual and group tactics involved should be taken one step at a time until they've been perfected.

Any team can learn ball-oriented defense, regardless of its preferred playing system. And in match play, you can adapt it to match

Ball-oriented defense: Don't switch; keep moving with the ball!

Wrong	**Defending as a Team**
• Only a few defenders are involved in the attempt to win the ball. The pass receiver is only under attack from one nearby defender. • Potential pass receivers in the backfield are not covered, so that the player with the ball can easily make a back pass. • Defenders are not moving toward the ball and pressuring the opposition, making it easy for attackers to maintain possession. • Defenders away from the ball are closely marking attackers.	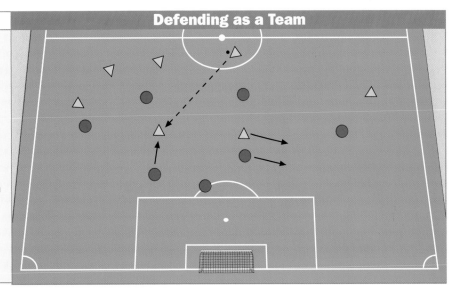

your formation, your positional roles, and the opposition's playing style.

For optimal youth development, practice and match play must form an interconnected whole. That's why training is more than just a set of age-appropriate exercises; it also teaches positional roles, playing systems and a concept of the game – including up-to-date defense concepts, and the principles and skills they involve.

A few basic principles:

1. No more assignments to individual opponents. Players have specific zones to defend, and they engage and attack all opponents who enter those zones.

2. No more formations that keep the sweeper far back behind the defense. The sweeper should be able to adapt to any game situation, while still remaining in charge of the defense.

Essential Skills

• Defenders must constantly reevaluate their positions with regard to the position of the ball, teammates and opponents, and correct as necessary. They should always be moving with the ball.

• Be able to instantly evaluate game situations.

• Know the possible solutions for a variety of situations.

• All defenders must take part in the defense; this requires intense concentration and good discipline.

• Be able to anticipate the opposition's plays.

• They must keep motivating themselves and never let themselves get careless.

• Defend actively and avoid falling for fakes.

• Use pressure to force the player with the ball to make mistakes.

• When a nearby teammate is involved in a 1 v. 1, defenders have to do more than just watch: they must help win the ball.

Ball-oriented defense: Move in close and stay with your opponent!

Illustration 12

Training Objectives

General

Skillful 1 v. 1 Defense

- If the attacker approaches directly from the front:

  1. Engage the attacker, then move gradually backwards.
  2. Face the attacker diagonally, offering a breakthrough on the less dangerous side (outside).
  3. While moving backwards, wait for a good chance to attack the ball.
  4. When attacking the ball, move in the same direction as the attacker and "sneak" it away.

- If the attacker is facing away from the goal and showing for a pass (especially in the middle):

  1. Get into position to intercept a pass.
  2. Always keep an eye on the ball and your opponent. Pay attention to all of the opposition's plays.
  3. Stay goalside of your opponent.

General

Defending as a Group

- Don't just react to the opposition's plays; defend actively.
- Always try to force opponents into 1 v. 1's where they might make mistakes and lose the ball.
- Stay in communication with your teammates at all times. This is especially important for switching with teammates and is the only way to achieve an organized and integrated defense formation.
- Move to the ball and outnumber the attackers around it. This makes it easier to win the ball.
- Block potential pass receivers. Don't let attackers use combination plays to get out of tight situations.
- If they complete a pass anyway, readjust immediately to the new situation. Move to the ball and put pressure on the player who has it.

General

Defenders Outnumbered

- The defender closest to the ball moves in to disrupt the attack.
- The other defenders move slightly toward the player with the ball, in order to prevent a breakthrough, and watch the other attackers as well.
- After a pass, the player with the ball is again carefully attacked by the closest defender. The other defenders move toward the ball again.
- In the midfield or in the opposition's half, an outnumbered group of defenders should try to slow down the attack by moving backwards slowly. The objective: to gain time for other defenders to arrive.
- When defenders are outnumbered near their own penalty area, one of them should mark the player with the ball closely and keep him from shooting. The others form a line with their teammate. If attackers start moving toward the goal without the ball, force them offsides.

Setup/Sequence	4 v. 4 on Three Goals Each
Set up three small goals on each endline of a 20 x 30-meter field. Two teams play 4 v. 4. Each team defends the three goals on its own endline and attacks on the other three. Playing time is five minutes.	

Variations

Focus On:	Level I	Level II	Level III
• Practicing zone defense • Ball-oriented play **Tips for Coaches** • Place extra balls at each goal. **Tips for Players** • Orient your defense formation toward the ball and spread out in all directions. • Whenever possible, two defenders should attack the player with the ball. • Watch for the opposition's passing opportunities and intercept their passes.	• A neutral player helps whichever team has the ball, to make combination play easier. • After a goal, the attackers keep the ball but attack on the other three goals. • The coach participates as a neutral player.	• Divide each endline into three equal sections. Each team tries to dribble across the opposition's endline. Attackers score two points for dribbling across the center section, one point for either end section. • 5 v. 5 (6 v. 6) on three small goals each.	• 5 v. 4 in a field half, from sideline to sideline. The team of five defends four small goals, the team of four defends three. To make it harder for the team of five, they're limited to two touches.

Setup/Sequence

Two teams play 4 v. 4 in a 20 x 30-meter field.

Attackers practice combination play and try to dribble across the opposition's endline (the long side).

If defenders win the ball, they counter-attack in the opposite direction.

Playing time is four minutes.

4 v. 4 on Goal Lines

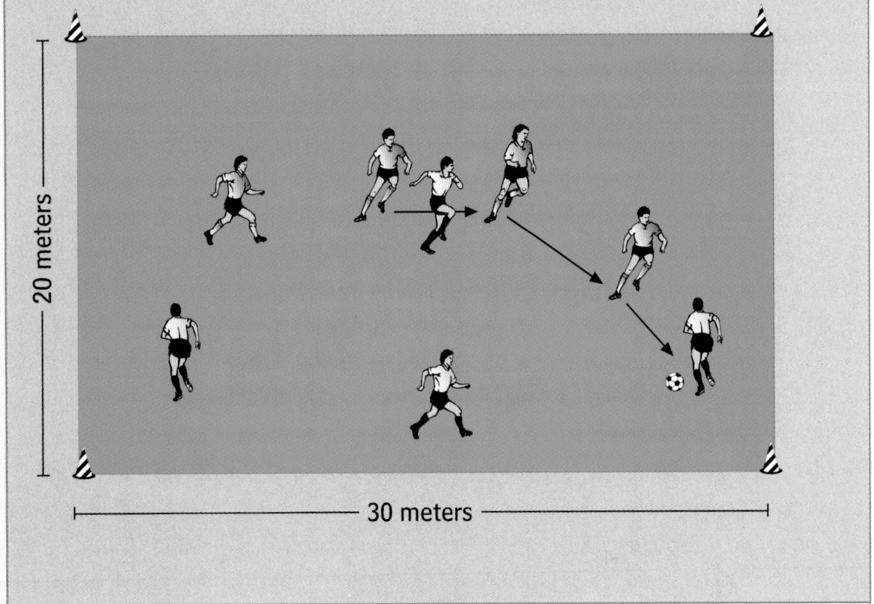

20 meters

30 meters

Variations

Focus On:	Level I	Level II	Level III
• Mutual support on defense • Switching quickly from defense to attack	• An extra player (or the coach) helps whichever team has the ball. • The endlines are the short sides of the field (to make it easier for defenders).	• Make the endlines longer (to make it harder for defenders). • Mark a three-meter deep zone on each endline; attackers must dribble into this zone (one point).	• 4 v. 4 (or 5 v. 5): Each player must complete three touches before passing the ball. Objective: Defenders should orient themselves toward the ball and actively attack opponents before they can pass.

Focus On:
- Mutual support on defense
- Switching quickly from defense to attack

Tips for Coaches
- Train in positional groups, e.g. one team could be the midfield from the starting lineup.

Tips for Players
- Close down the space available to attackers by moving with the ball.
- When attackers change positions, you should usually "trade" them with your teammates. However, if there's any chance they might break through, stay with your original opponents.

Setup/Sequence

Mark out a 20 x 30-meter center zone inside a 40-meter-long field and place two small goals on each endline. Two teams play 4 v. 4 within the center zone. One attacker must dribble across the opposite "endline" of the center zone before the rest of the team can follow and attack on the goals.

Playing time is five minutes.

4 v. 4 on Two Goals Each, Starting in the Middle

|← —————————— 40 meters —————————— →|

Focus On:

- 1 v. 1 defensive play
- Mutual support on defense

Tips for Coaches

- Run through the exercise once with a demonstration group.

Tips for Players

- Orient your defense formation toward the ball and spread out in all directions.
- Whenever possible, two defenders should attack the player with the ball simultaneously

Variations

Level I	Level II	Level III
• A neutral player helps whichever team has the ball, to make breakthroughs and combination plays easier. • After scoring, the attackers keep the ball but attack on the other two goals. • The coach participates as a neutral player.	• 5 v. 5 in a marked zone in the middle of the field. A normal goal with goalkeeper stands about 20 meters past each endline. Any attacker who dribbles across the opposition's endline can shoot without interference. • As above, but attackers must play 1 v. 1 against the goalkeeper to score.	• Same setup as in Level II, but attackers must complete a wall pass across the opposition's endline before shooting. • As above, but after crossing the endline, attackers must play a second wall pass with a forward before shooting. • 6 v. 6 in the center zone (increased opposition pressure).

Setup/Sequence

Two teams play 4 v. 4 in a 40 x 30-meter field. Three small goals stand two meters past each endline. The outside goals are two meters wide, and the middle goals are three. Attackers practice combination play and try to score on one of the opposition's goals. Players are not allowed to leave the field.

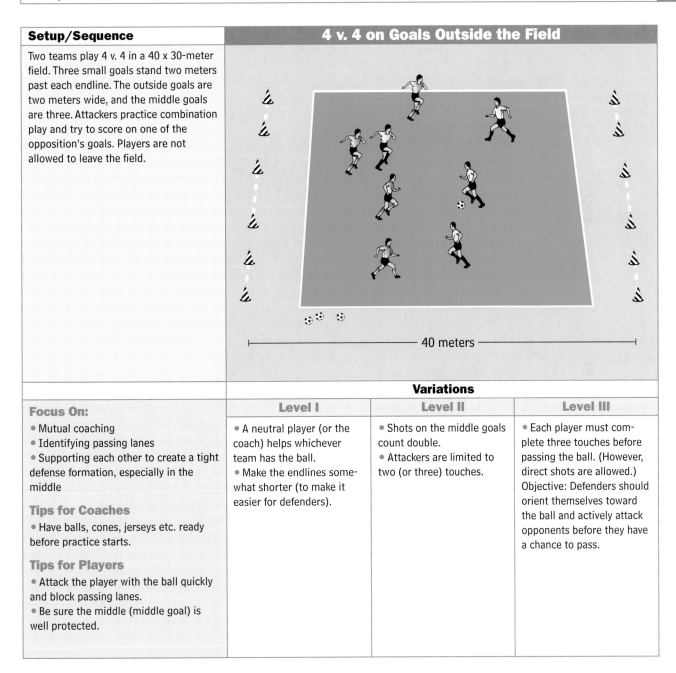

4 v. 4 on Goals Outside the Field

40 meters

Focus On:

- Mutual coaching
- Identifying passing lanes
- Supporting each other to create a tight defense formation, especially in the middle

Tips for Coaches

- Have balls, cones, jerseys etc. ready before practice starts.

Tips for Players

- Attack the player with the ball quickly and block passing lanes.
- Be sure the middle (middle goal) is well protected.

Variations

Level I	Level II	Level III
• A neutral player (or the coach) helps whichever team has the ball. • Make the endlines somewhat shorter (to make it easier for defenders).	• Shots on the middle goals count double. • Attackers are limited to two (or three) touches.	• Each player must complete three touches before passing the ball. (However, direct shots are allowed.) Objective: Defenders should orient themselves toward the ball and actively attack opponents before they have a chance to pass.

Setup/Sequence

Set up a goal with goalkeeper and two small goals (two meters wide) on each endline of a field half. Use cones to divide the field into three equal zones. Two teams play 6 v. 6: Each team defends all the goals on its own endline and can attack on any of the other three. If any defenders are still in the opposite wing zone when attackers shoot, the goal counts double.

Playing time is seven minutes.

Six-Goal Game

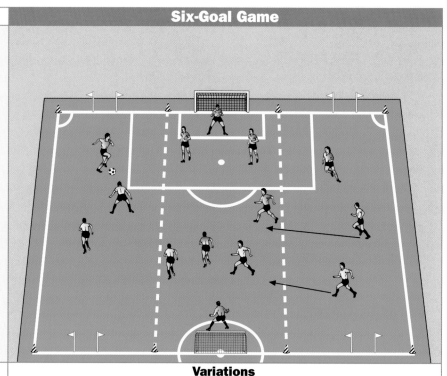

Focus On:

- Moving with the ball as the situation requires
- Constant communication

Tips for Coaches

- Have balls, cones, jerseys etc. ready before practice starts.

Tips for Players

- Orient your defense formation toward the ball and spread out in all directions.
- Move with the ball and defend actively. Don't just react to the opposition's attack.

Variations

Level I	Level II	Level III
• A neutral player (e.g. the coach) helps whichever team has the ball, to make shots and combination plays easier. • After a goal, the attackers keep the ball but attack on the other three goals.	• Same sequence, but with 7 v. 7 (increased opposition pressure, more restricted space). • Instead of small goals, attackers have to dribble across the endlines of the wing zones. • Same sequence, but on three small goals.	• Attackers are limited to two (or three) touches.

Setup/Sequence

Mark out a 20 x 35-meter center zone inside a 50-meter field. Two teams of five play 4 v. 4 within the center zone. One goal with goalkeeper about 15 meters past each endline.

The fifth player from each team stands next to a goal. Any attacker who dribbles across the opposite "endline" of the center zone can shoot without interference. After scoring, the attackers keep the ball and attack the other goal, starting their attack in one of two ways: If they score on their own goal, their extra player switches places with the shooter. If they score on the other goal, then the opposition's extra player passes the ball back to them to attack in the opposite direction.

4 v. 4 On Two Goals, Starting in the Middle

Play 1

Play 2

50 meters

Focus On:

- 1 v. 1 defensive play
- Switching quickly from defense to attack and vice versa

Tips for Coaches

- Have plenty of extra balls ready by the goals.
- Run through the exercise once with a demonstration group.

Tips for Players

- Attack the player with the ball quickly and work actively to prevent solo runs.
- Fight hard for the ball whenever you get a good opportunity.

Variations

Level I	Level II	Level III
• Make the endlines somewhat shorter (to make it easier for defenders). • A neutral player helps whichever team has the ball, to make breakthroughs and combination plays easier. • Same sequence, but with 3 v. 3 in the center zone.	• Same sequence, but with 5 v. 5 in the center zone (increased opposition pressure, more restricted space). • As above, but attackers must play 1 v. 1 against the goalkeeper to score.	• After a goal, two active players switch places with two substitutes.

Setup/Sequence

Set up two standard goals with goal-keepers side by side on the same end-line, about 15 meters apart. Mark a 35-meter long counterline about 15 meters away.

Two teams play 4 v. 4: A attacks on both goals; if B wins the ball, they start a counterattack. If they succeed in dribbling across the counterline, the two teams immediately switch roles and directions of attack.

Playing time is five minutes.

4 v. 4 on Two Side-by-Side Goals

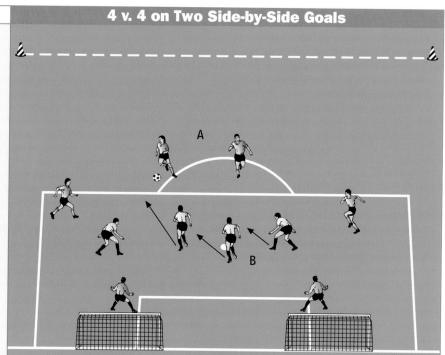

Focus On:
- Active defense
- Preventing shots

Tips for Coaches
- To save practice time, set up the goals before practice starts.

Tips for Players
- Engage the attacker with the ball at the right moment.
- Whenever possible, two defenders should attack the player with the ball simultaneously.
- Block the attacker's "strong leg."

Variations

Level I	Level II	Level III
• Teams don't switch roles: Team A attacks on the goals for five minutes, B on the counterline (dribbling across = a "goal"). • If the defenders win the ball, they attack on three small goals instead of a counterline.	• Same sequence, but with 5 v. 5 (increased opposition pressure). • To counterattack, Team B must dribble through either of two two-meter-wide countergoals.	• Team A attacks on the goals for five minutes. If B wins the ball, they are joined by one goalkeeper and play to maintain possession within the field. After the end of the playing time and an active rest period, the teams switch roles. Which team can score more goals?

Setup/Sequence

Place a goal with goalkeeper on each endline of a 40 x 25-meter field. Divide the field into three zones, the end zones narrower than the center zone. Two teams play 4 v. 4.

To score, attackers must shoot **directly** after a pass and be inside the opposition's end zone. Furthermore, all other attackers must be out of their own end zone.

Playing time is four minutes.

4 v. 4 in Three Zones

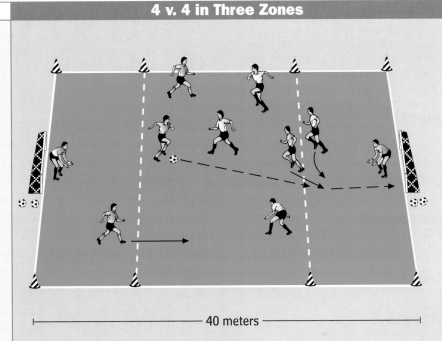

├─────────── 40 meters ───────────┤

Focus On:

- Monitoring teammates and opponents
- Blocking passing lanes
- Clearing your own end zone

Tips for Coaches

- Mark the field and the zones clearly.
- Pay attention to playing times and rest periods.

Tips for Players

- Position yourselves along the inside line diagonally behind the player with the ball.
- Intercept passes if possible.

Variations

Level I	Level II	Level III
• Attackers are allowed to shoot from the center zone, and shots do not have to be direct or follow a pass, but attackers still have to clear their own end zone first. • A neutral player helps whichever team has the ball, to make shots and combination plays easier.	• The offsides rule applies when attackers are in the opposition's end zone. • After scoring, the attackers keep the ball and attack immediately on the other goal.	• To score, attackers must shoot directly after a pass and be in the center zone. • Attackers are limited to two (or three) touches.

Setup/Sequence	6 v. 4 on Two Goals

Form two teams of six. Six attackers play against four defenders on two goals with goalkeepers in a field half; the two "free" defenders jog two laps around the field.

As soon as they finish their laps: They rejoin their team, two attackers drop out and start jogging, and both teams switch roles, creating a 6 v. 4 situation again. Attackers try to take advantage of their superior numbers and score as many goals as possible. Which team can score more goals in the time it takes for all the players to jog two laps?

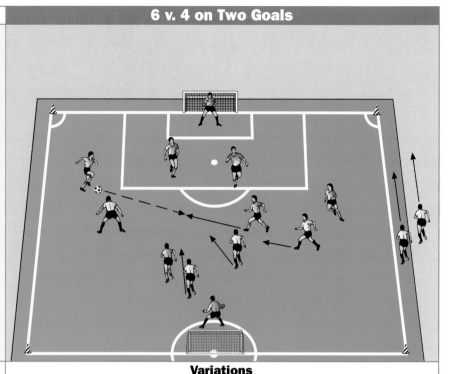

Variations

Focus On:	Level I	Level II	Level III
• Defending while outnumbered • Learning pressing **Tips for Coaches** • You can also add extra challenges for the "free" defenders (e.g. a slalom course or hurdles). **Tips for Players** • Two defenders should attack the player with the ball simultaneously. • Keep attackers from completing combination plays.	• Make the field smaller, to make it easier for defenders to win the ball. • Same sequence, but on two (or three) small goals set up side by side on each endline.	• Attackers must pass the ball after two touches. • Attackers can only score on direct shots. • Make the field shorter and narrower: Attackers can attack on both goals, and if defenders win the ball, they (and the goalkeeper) try to maintain possession as long as possible (five passes = one point).	• Attackers must play one touch and defenders are limited to three touches. • Same sequence, but with only one goal. "Free" pairs have to jog four laps around the field. Attackers try to score , while defenders (and the goalkeeper) play to maintain possession until they have to switch roles.

Setup/Sequence

4 v. 4: Pressing After a Pass From the Goalkeeper

The field is twice the size of a penalty zone and has just one goal with goal-keeper. Groups A and B play 4 v. 4. Each group starts out in its own half; Group A starts out on defense.

The goalkeeper starts each round by passing to a defender inside the defenders' half. The attackers then enter the defense half and immediately attack to win the ball quickly and shoot. The defenders' objective is to escape the press and dribble across the endline of the attackers' half.

Teams switch roles after 10 rounds.

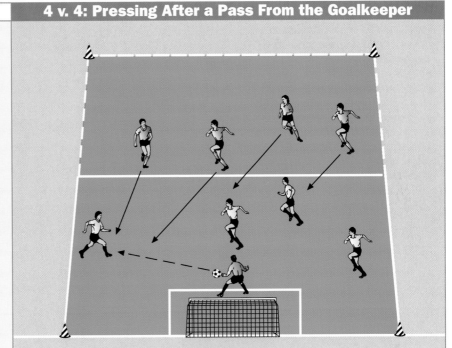

Variations

Focus On:
- Recognizing pressing situations
- Approaching the player with the ball correctly

Tips for Coaches
- Make sure the breaks between rounds are sufficient.

Tips for Players
- Two defenders should attack the player with the ball on the sideline and block inside passing lanes. This makes it harder to pass and forces the attacker to risk dribbling against two opponents.

Level I	Level II	Level III
• Four attackers play against three defenders. • Defenders are not allowed to secure the ball by passing it to the goalkeeper (making pressing easier). • The goalkeeper starts each play by throwing the ball (low) to a defender (making pressing easier).	• Defenders are allowed to pass to the goalkeeper (making pressing harder). • Defenders attack on two small goals on the opposite endline. • Defenders must complete five passes in a row before starting their attack on the endline.	• If the attackers win the ball, they have to complete five passes in a row before they're allowed to shoot.

Setup/Sequence

Set up a 40 x 30-meter field and two goals with goalkeepers.
Form three teams of four (A, B, C).
First, A attacks on Goal 1 (B's goal), while Team C waits its turn by Goal 2. If B wins the ball, they attack on Goal 2, and Team C defends. However, Team C is not allowed to take the field until the ball crosses the centerline. Team A can follow B as far as the centerline and try to win the ball back for a new attack of its own.

Playing time is seven minutes.

"Brazilian Game"

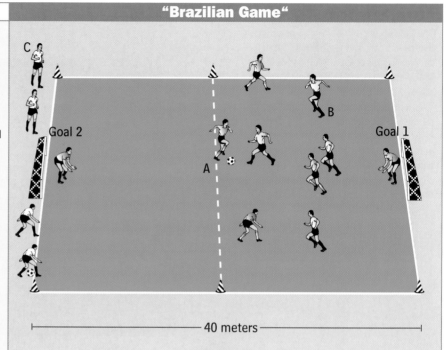

Goal 2

Goal 1

A

B

C

⊢————— 40 meters —————⊣

Variations

Focus On:
• Switching quickly to defense after losing the ball.

Tips for Coaches
• Don't let the third team start their attack too soon.

Tips for Players
• Reorient yourself to new situations immediately.
• The closest defender should immediately put pressure on the player with the ball.
• All other defenders should cover nearby opponents and potential pass receivers.

Level I	Level II	Level III
• A neutral player helps whichever team has the ball. • Same sequence, but with two small goals (two meters wide) per team.	• Same sequence, but with teams of five. • If defenders win the ball, they have to complete five passes in a row before they're allowed to cross the centerline.	• Attackers are limited to two touches. • Same sequence, but with 6 v. 6 v. 6 (enlarge the field slightly). • Attackers can only score on direct shots.

Setup/Sequence

Two teams of six play on a 40 x 30-meter field. Two players from Team A stand outside the field, one behind each endline. This creates a 6 v. 4 situation.
Both teams play to maintain possession. Team A tries to pass to the two outside players as often as possible, scoring one point for each pass.
Team B scores one point for every 10 passes in a row.

6 v. 4 + 2 Passers

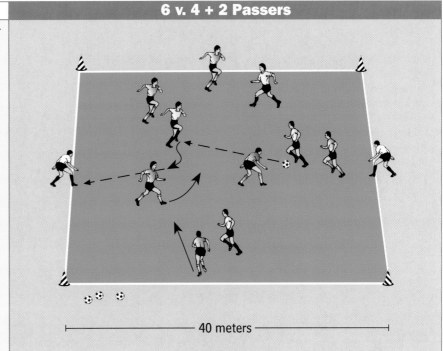

— 40 meters —

Variations

Focus On:
- Recognizing pressing situations

Tips for Coaches
- Substitute the outside players regularly.

Tips for Players
- Win the ball back quickly.
- Whenever possible, two defenders should attack the player with the ball.
- If your team wins the ball, open the game up immediately and cover as much ground with your combinations as possible.

Level I	Level II	Level III
• Whenever the outside players receive passes, they switch places with the passers immediately by dribbling onto the field and continuing the game. • The coach stands on one of the unoccupied sides of the field and acts as a third pass receiver for A.	• Players from the team of six are limited to two touches. • The two passers are limited to two touches. • Same sequence, but with 7 v. 5 + 2 outside passers.	• Players from the team of six must pass directly. • The two passers must pass directly.

| Exercise 1 | 1 + 2 v. 3 on Two Goals | Variations |

Two teams of three on a 20 x 25-meter field with three-meter-wide goals.
Three attackers play against two defenders. The third defender stands on one sideline and calls offsides. If the defenders win the ball, the line judge joins them immediately while their opponents supply a new line judge. The new attackers must then complete three passes in a row before they're allowed to shoot.

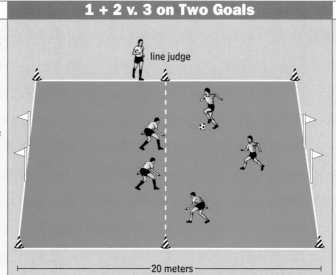

- No offsides: The "free" defender stands in the goal, which is widened to five meters.
- Reward active defense with bonus points for winning the ball from the opposition.

| Exercise 2 | 4 v. 3 With Three Groups | Variations |

Set up two five-meter-wide goals on a 25 x 20-meter field. Two out of three teams play 4 v. 4 (teams rotate). First, team A attacks on Goal 1 (B's goal). One player from B has to stand in the goal, which creates a 4 v. 3 situation. Team C (three defenders and one goalkeeper) waits by Goal 2. If Team B succeeds in winning the ball, all four attack on Goal 2 while A waits behind Goal 1.

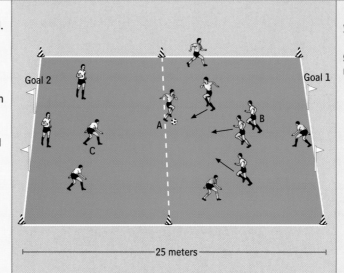

- Limit touches according to your preference.
- Each team has a permanent goalkeeper (no switching roles).
- 3 v. 2 instead of 4 v. 3.

Exercise 3

Set up a five-meter-wide goal on one of the long sides of a 20 x 30-meter field. On the other endline, set up two three-meter-wide goals 10 meters apart.

Two teams play 4 v. 3 on this field. The group of four defends the two smaller goals.

4 v. 3 on Three Small Goals

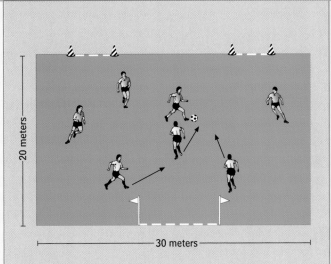

20 meters

30 meters

Variations

- Instead of marking the larger goal with poles, use a portable standard goal with goalkeeper.
- Limit touches for the team of four.

Exercise 4

Mark out two 20 x 30-meter fields separated by a five-meter wide "free zone."

Set up a three-meter-wide goal on each of the four end-lines.

Team A (attackers) has six players (three in each field), and Team B has four (two per field). Each round starts with a 3 v. 2 in one of the fields. Attackers must pass across the free zone to their teammates in the other field, while defenders can cross the zone.

3 v. 2 + 3 v. 2 on Two Goals Each

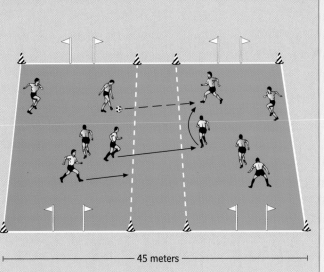

45 meters

Variations

- Mark a centerline in each field and enforce the offsides rule.
- Passes have to be below knee level.

Exercise 5	Defending as a Group 1 (2 v. 3)	Variations
Mark a goal line about 35 meters in front of a goal with goalkeeper. Four defenders form two pairs (switch frequently). Pair A stands in front of the line, and Pair B waits to one side. The rest of the team forms groups of three. Pair A plays 2 v. 3 to defend the line. Any attacker who succeeds in breaking through (i.e. dribbling across the line) can shoot without interference.	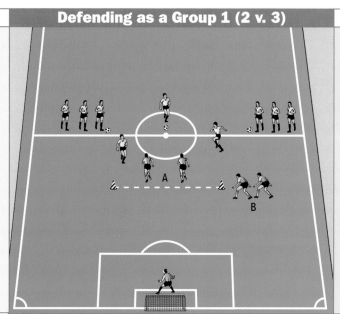	• After breaking through, attackers play 1 v. 1 against the goalkeeper. • Pairs A and B don't switch places until the active defenders win the ball.

Exercise 6	Defending as a Group 2 (2 v. 3)	Variations
Mark two 15-meter-long goal lines. Four defenders form two pairs. Each pair stands in front of a goal line. The rest of the team forms groups of three and lines up on both goal lines. Each pair of defenders has two plays in a row: First they play 2 v. 3 to defend the line from one side, then the other side. One pair plays while the other pair rests. The attackers try to dribble across the line.	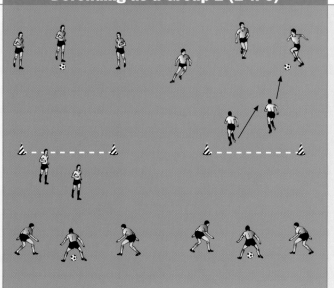	• Adjust the length of the goal lines according to players' ability level. • Attackers have to pass the ball through two small goals placed side by side, ten meters apart.

Exercise 7

Mark two six-meter goal lines. Three defenders stand on one side of the lines, and two or three substitutes wait on one side. The rest of the players form groups of four attackers each and distribute themselves on both sides. Defenders play 3 v. 4 to keep attackers from dribbling across either line. After each round, a new attack starts on the other side. Substitute two to three defenders every two rounds.

Defending as a Group 3 (3 v. 4)

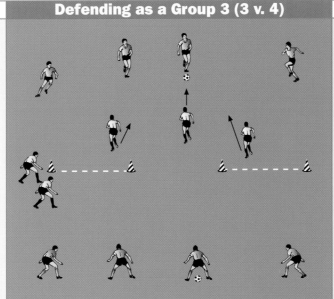

Variations

- Adjust the length of the goal lines according to players' ability level.
- Attackers have to pass the ball through any of three small goals placed in a row, 10 meters apart.

Exercise 8

Set up three small goals (about two meters wide) in a row on each endline of a 30 x 40-meter field. Form two groups of four. The four attackers from A try to dribble through one of the opposition's goals. Three players from B defend; the fourth waits behind the endline. Either A scores or B wins the ball and passes it back to the fourth player; afterwards, both teams switch roles.

Defending as a Group 4 (3 v. 4)

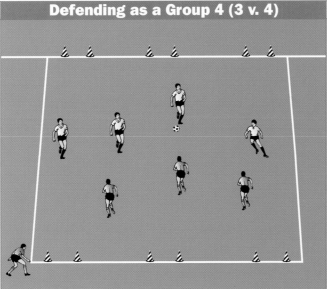

Variations

- Adjust the size of the goals according to players' ability level.
- Same sequence, but with only two small goals.
- One team attacks on three small goals, while the other attempts to dribble across the opposition's endline.

Exercise 9	Defensive Support 1 (1 v. 2)	Variations

Mark a line 35 meters in front of the goal. Using cones, divide it into thirds. One attacker (with ball) stands behind each section, 20 meters away. Attacker A dribbles toward the line and tries to dribble across his section. If he succeeds, he can shoot without interference. However, Defenders 1 and 2 work together to stop him. Afterwards, B plays against 2 and 3, then C against 3 and 4, etc.

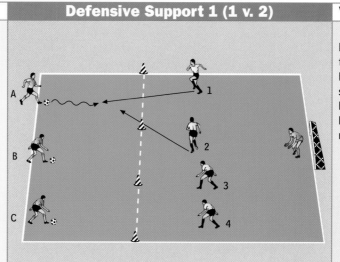

• The three attackers pass the ball back and forth among themselves until one of them breaks toward the nearest line section and attempts to dribble across. Defenders move to help their neighbors as necessary.

Exercise 10	Defensive Support 2 (1 v. 2)	Variations

Four players play 1 + 1 v. 2 between two small goals (three meters wide) and a counterline (15 meters long). One attacker plays against both defenders to score. The attacker can always play a back pass to get out of trouble; in which case the pass receiver starts a new 1 v. 2 attack. If the defenders win the ball, they start a counterattack (dribbling across the counterline).

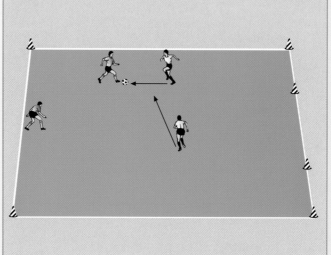

• The game periodically switches to 2 v. 2.
• Same sequence, but as 1 + 2 v. 3.

Exercise 11	Flat Four: Moving Sideways	Variations

Two teams of four play in assigned formations: Group A forms a flat four about 15 meters in front of the penalty area, and Group B starts its attacks with three forwards and a passer. The passer starts each round with a pass to a forward, who works to set up a shot. The four defenders move sideways to force 1 v. 1's for the ball. If they win it, they pass to the passer. Offsides rule applies.

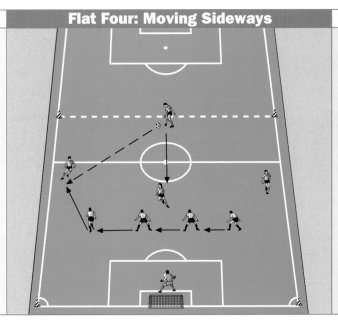

• Same sequence, but the flat four can also fall back if necessary. If the defenders win the ball, they shoot as quickly and accurately as possible at a goal on the opposite penalty area line (they become attacking forwards). Afterwards, all players return to their original positions.

Exercise 12	Moving Forward and Back	Variations

Same setup as Exercise 11, but now the passer can also move up to the front of the attack. Depending on the situation, the flat four may move sideways, back or forward. If the attackers pass the ball back, defenders should move forward immediately, without losing the flat four structure.

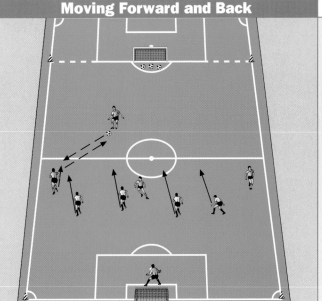

• Team A (attackers) has two forwards, two outside midfielders, one offensive and one defensive midfielder. Team B is a flat four plus goalkeeper. The goalkeeper starts each play with a long pass to Team A's defensive midfielder. The flat four breaks up and the two teams play freely. If Team B wins the ball, they shoot at the opposite goal as quickly as possible.

Team Tactics: Solid Attack-Building

The Wing Attack: Advantages and Objectives

Building a solid attack in your own half, with lots of pass sequences, often gives the opposition a chance to fall back to its own half and get into formation in front of its goal.

When you're facing this kind of compact defense, it takes versatility, patience and confident combination play to set up a shot. When the opposition falls back deep in its own half and forms up around the penalty area, a versatile attack on the wings, followed by crosses or back passes, can be an effective tactic. Attacks in the middle involving wall passes and three-player combinations (for example) are often promising as well.

However, these plays require good individual ability and fast, confident combination play. The advantages of the wing attack are:
- Since the wings are not so heavily defended, attackers have a better chance of breaking through.
- Solo or combination plays on the wings lure defenders out of the middle, which opens up space in front of the goal.
- Crosses, back passes and other types of passes to teammates in front of the goal are a good way to set up shots, no matter how well the opposition positions its defenders. This means that attackers in the middle have to be ready to shoot at any moment.

The Wing Attack: Execution

A versatile wing attack is characterized by:
- solo dribbling
- creative, versatile combination play focusing on the outside positions
- the following combinations: wall passes (with variations), takeovers, and above all, overlapping
- carefully aimed crosses and/or other passes to attackers in front of the goal, depending on the situation.

Basic Sequence	Attack Building: Possibilities

Passing in Front of the Goal
- When attackers are on the wing and defenders are relatively far from their goal, a good tactic is to cross or pass behind the defensive line and in front of the goal.
- This gives teammates a chance to get a running start on the ball, which gives them the advantage of momentum over their opponents.
- Attackers in the middle should move decisively to meet the cross and finish, regardless of the risks.

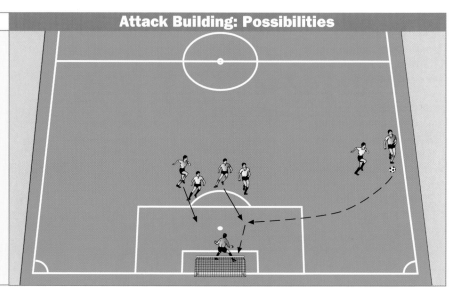

Solid Attack Building: General Characteristics

When the defense is compact, all good attacks have certain characteristics in common:
- Passing is safe, versatile and precise, including square, back, diagonal and deep passes.
- Receivers show for passes at various positions all over the field.
- Play shifts from one side of the field to the other.
- Attackers protect the ball, even under intense opposition pressure.
- Shooting is the main objective.
- Attackers change the rhythm of the attack frequently.

Attack Training: Basic Principles

- First, players have to learn a variety of individual and group attack tactics, in the context of a long-term training process. It's important to teach the tactical elements in sequence and to spend plenty of time on each one.
- The next step is to tailor these tactical elements specifically to the roles of individual players and groups, as well as the team's overall attack plan.

Illustration 13

Objectives

General

- A solid building phase followed by fast, effective combinations in the middle
- A versatile game on the wings based on solo plays and precise combinations
- Precise crosses, back passes and other passes to players in front of the goal

Basic Sequence

Crossing in Front of the Goal
- The primary objective of every attack on the wings is to get as close as possible to the opposition's goal line and then cross in front of the goal.
- To prevent the goalkeeper from interfering (or even intercepting the cross), spin the ball away from the goal and toward a teammate or a specific attack zone away from defenders.
- Passes that curve toward attackers are easier to head at the goal.

Attack Building: Possibilities

Setup/Sequence

Divide a standard field into two zones of different sizes: Zone A stretches from the goal (with goalkeeper) to ten meters away from the centerline; two teams of three play in this zone. Zone B (the rest of the field) has two teams of six plus one neutral player.

Each team in Zone B plays with one of the teams in Zone A. The game starts in Zone B; the attackers there play combinations with the help of the neutral player. At the right moment, they shift the attack to Zone A; the attackers there play 3 v. 3 to score.

Playing time is 15 minutes.

Two-Zone Game

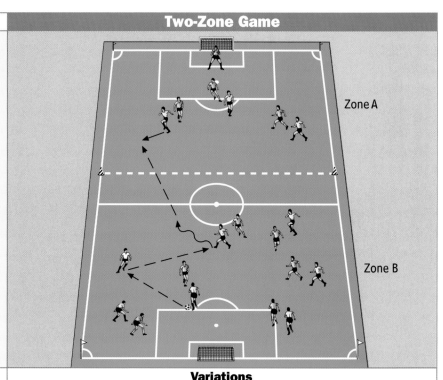

Zone A

Zone B

Focus On:

- Setting up shots with safe passes
- Accurate passing in the front of the attack

Tips for Coaches

- Assign players to groups according to their positions.

Tips for Players

- Be sure to kick safe passes to your teammates, either to their feet or into their running paths.
- Get out of tight situations by shifting the area of play.

Variations

Level I	Level II	Level III
• In Zone B, two neutral players help whichever team has the ball, to make it easier to maintain possession. • Neutral players are limited to two touches in a row (or only one). • Same sequence, but with 4 v. 4 or 5 v. 5 + 2 neutral players in Zone B. • The neutral player is the coach.	• The "attack builders" in Zone B are limited to two touches. • In Zone B, 10 passes in a row score one bonus point. • The players in Zone B have unlimited touches – but no neutral players. • After the pass into Zone A, one attacker can cross the line until the attackers finish.	• The "attack builders" in Zone B are limited to two touches. • In Zone B, 10 passes in a row score one bonus point. • The players in Zone B have unlimited touches – but no neutral players. • After the pass into Zone A, one attacker can cross the line until the attackers finish.

Setup/Sequence

Two teams play 6 v. 6 in a field half on two standard goals with goalkeepers. Three neutral players help whichever team has the ball. Attackers are limited to two touches in a row, while the three neutral players must pass directly and are not allowed to shoot.

Playing time is 10 minutes.

6 v. 6 + 3 Neutral Players on Two Goals

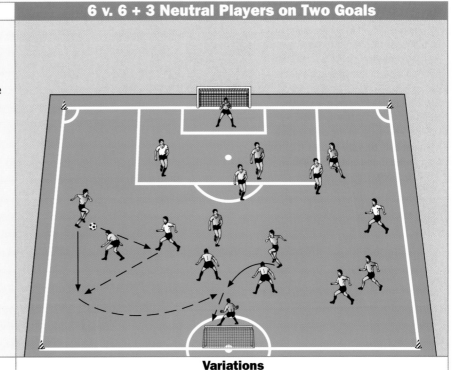

Variations

Focus On:
- Setting up shooting opportunities with safe, far-ranging combination plays
- Scoring opportunities

Tips for Coaches
- Set up the goals before practice starts; it saves valuable practice time.
- Include motivational shooting exercises during the active rest periods between rounds.

Tips for Players
- Your combinations should cover the entire field.

Level I	Level II	Level III
• Both teams have unlimited touches, while the neutral players are limited to two touches in a row. • Enlarge the field: The bigger it is, the easier it is to control the ball and play combinations.	• Only two neutral players help the attackers. • Attackers can only score: • on direct shots. • after 10 passes in a row (not including neutral players).	• Attackers can only score: – immediately after a wall pass. – on a volley or header following a cross. – after all the neutral players (or attackers) have touched the ball. • Make the field smaller.

Setup/Sequence

Two teams play 6 v. 6 on two goals with goalkeepers in a field half. Mark two five-meter goal lines 15 meters in front of each goal, one on each wing. Attackers must use these wing goals to set up their shots; i.e. goals do not count unless attackers have just dribbled or passed through one of the wing goals.

Playing time is 10 minutes.

Using the Wings

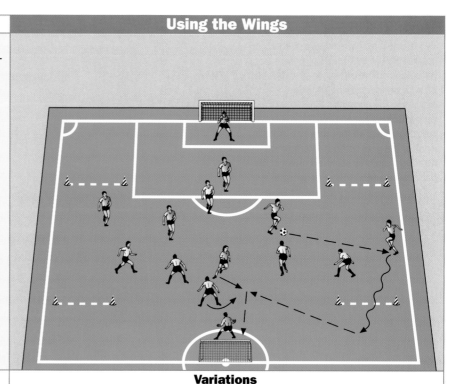

Focus On:

- Solo plays on the wings
- Combinations on the wings
- Scoring on crosses
- Shifting the area of play appropriately

Tips for Coaches

- Have balls, cones, jerseys etc. close at hand.
- Include crossing and shooting exercises between rounds.

Tips for Players

- Create a breakthrough on one of the wings by suddenly shifting the attack.

Variations

Level I	Level II	Level III
• A neutral player helps the attackers. • Make the wing goals wider. • Attackers are allowed to attack in the middle, but shots following passes through the wing goals count double.	• Shots must follow specific plays: 1. Far-post cross. 2. A back pass toward the penalty spot. 3. Near post cross. • Attackers are limited to two touches until they get the ball through a wing goal; then touches are unlimited. • After a goal, the attackers attack in the opposite direction.	• Attackers limited to one touch until they break through a wing goal; then they're limited to two (or three) touches. • Instead of the wing goals, set up a 25-meter "taboo line" in the center of the field. Players are allowed to run across this line, but not to dribble or pass across it.

Setup/Sequence

Two teams play 7 v. 7 on two goals with goalkeepers in two-thirds of a field.
Mark a 10- to 15-meter-wide zone along each sideline. Players have unlimited touches in these zones but are limited to three touches between them.
The objective is to focus on attacking on the wings.
Direct shots following passes from the wing zones count double.
Playing time is 12 minutes.

7 v. 7 With Three-Touch Rule

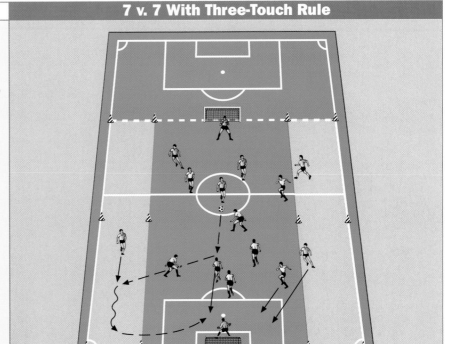

Variations

Focus On:	Level I	Level II	Level III
• Safe combination play in the middle, shifting the attack to the wings when appropriate • Precise crosses in front of the goal • Scoring on crosses • Shifting the area of play **Tips for Coaches** • Mark the wing zones clearly. **Tips for Players** • Crosses should be hard and accurate. • Be versatile in setting up shots.	• Add an extra neutral player. • Enlarge the wing zones. • Touches are unlimited only in the middle zone. Each team has two wing players, one on each side, who cannot leave their zones. They can cross to teammates in front of the goal without interference.	• Players are limited to two touches in the middle zone. • 8 v. 7: The team of seven has unlimited touches everywhere, the team of eight has unlimited touches in the wing zones and two touches in the middle. • Each team has two wing players who can cross without interference.	• One touch in the middle zone. • Smaller field . • Shots must follow specific plays: 1. A cross behind the defense and toward the rear post. 2. A back pass toward the penalty spot. 3. A hard cross toward the front post. • Shots from the wing zones count double.

Exercise 1

Crossing From a 3 v. 1 on the Wing

Mark out a 15 x 15-meter zone on each sideline, 15 meters away from the centerline. Four players (three attackers and one defender) play in each zone. A third group of four waits in front of the goal.
Play alternates:
Attackers try to dribble across the endline and toward the goal. One attacker is allowed to cross. The four players waiting there play 3 v. 1 to score.

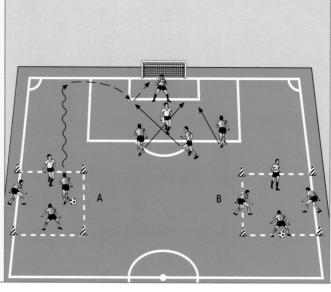

Variations

- 2 v. 2 on the wings and 2 v. 2 in front of the goal.
- 3 v. 2 (2 v. 1) on the wings and 3 v. 2 (2 v. 1) in front of the goal.
- A passer stands behind each wing zone and start each play by passing to an attacker.
- 3 v. 2 on the wings and 1 v. 1 in front of the goal. The wing attackers try to pass to the attacker at the goal. After the pass, the wing players join and play 4 v. 3 to score.

Exercise 2

Combination Play on the Wing

Divide players into groups of three and position half of the groups at one corner of a field half, half at the corner diagonally opposite.
Groups take turns attacking, focusing on fluid combination play. When they reach the endline, the player with the ball crosses to a teammate in front of the goal, who tries to score on a header.
Afterwards, a group on the other side of the field attacks.

Variations

- The shooter receives a back pass on the ground from the endline and shoots directly.
- Attackers are limited to two touches.
- Attackers must pass directly up until the cross.
- Same sequence, but using the entire field.

Exercise 3	Crossing After a Pass in the Air	Variations

Passer A has a number of balls and stands about 35 meters in front of a goal with goal-keeper. Two attackers play against two defenders in the penalty area.

A passes in the air to B, who receives the ball from the side and immediately tries to cross in front of the goal. As soon as A passes, one defender runs out of the penalty area to B and tries to interfere with the cross.

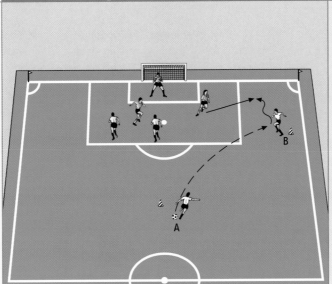

- B receives the pass in motion.
- The defender can't leave the penalty area until B touches the ball.
- Set up different configurations of players in front of the goal.
- After passing, A is allowed to open for passes in the back-field.
- Set different requirements for the pass to B.

Exercise 4	1 v. 1 on the Wings / 2 v. 2 in Front of Goal	Variations

Two goals with goalkeepers where the penalty area side-lines meet the endline. The area in front of the goals is divided into a middle zone and wings.

Two teams of four are assigned as follows: 1 v. 1 on each wing and 2 v. 2 in the middle zone. A passer in the center circle passes to an open wing player, and players play 4 v. 4 on both goals. Afterwards, the passer passes to the other wing, etc.

- After passing, the passer is allowed to join the wing attack. (In this case, assign three or four passers.)
- If the defenders win the ball, they can start a counter-attack on two marked counter-lines.
- Assign 1 v. 1 on each wing and 3 v. 3 in the middle.

Team Tactics: The Speed Attack

The Speed Attack: Advantages and Objectives

The speed attack is a tactical response to a defense that's disorganized or has moved too far forward. It makes use of the wide-open spaces in the opposition's half with a fast, determined attack that's totally directed toward setting up shots and scoring. It requires every player's actions to be perfectly coordinated with the rest of the team's.

Certain conditions are optimal for a speed attack:
• If you're planning a speed attack, pull back into your own half: This restricts the space available to opponents for attacking the ball, and often causes the opposition to intensify its attack by moving farther forward and switching defenders to the attack. This creates open spaces in the opposition's half, which you can then take advantage of with a speed attack.

• When the opposition temporarily out-numbers you, they often put their defenders on the attack and move their entire defensive line up to the centerline.

• When the opposition is behind, for example in the second half, they often break up their defensive formation and let the sweeper or another defender play as an attacker. The speed attack can expose a weakened defense.

• When the opposition has a set play in front of your goal, they tend to let defenders move up to the front row if they're big and are good at heading. If you can win the ball, you have a perfect chance for a speed attack.

• If you're down by one player (or more), the opposition tends to attack you more. They loosen up their defensive line, which opens up space for a speed attack.

Basic Sequence	The Speed Attack
Switch From Defense to Attack • As soon as you win the ball, move actively forward as a large unit, at top speed. • Defenders and defensive midfielders may move forward as well, depending on the situation. Important: Passers and receivers should all coordinate their actions. Try for long-range combinations. • Also: Don't let your defenders move up so far that your back is unprotected. • Start the speed attack with a safe pass.	Winning of the ball

The Speed Attack: Execution

A successful speed attack relies on certain tactics and actions:

1. Combination plays and dribbling must be **fast**.

2. Long diagonal and through passes to open teammates are ideal combinations for covering lots of ground.

3. Combination plays must be safe, so that you don't lose a promising opportunity. Above all, it's important not to slow down the pace, e.g. by passing behind the receiver.

4. You can't make it all the way to the goal unless you start the attack by moving forward as a large group, at top speed. Whichever players are in the best positions (including defenders!) should move forward with the group.

5. Pass receivers have to coordinate their running paths with one another, even at top speed. This also includes forwards who switch places.

6. Always look for the most direct path to the goal, and finish with a shot or a header. Be aggressive, confident and willing to take risks.

7. When you're opening for passes, always remember the offsides rule, even at top speed. This is just one reason why concentration is so important!

Illustration 14

Objectives

General

- **Acting as a compact defensive unit**
- **Recognizing speed attack situations quickly**
- **Opening for passes in a way that fits the situation, and moving defenders forward quickly**
- **Building a fast, determined attack**

Basic Sequence	The Speed Attack

Coordinating Showing Runs

- Fast dribbling will get you across the midfield quickly in many situations.
- If defensive players (such as the sweeper) move forward to stop the player with the ball, options for forwards include quickly switching places and/or quick combinations with other teammates, such as overlapping.
- Afterwards, go for the goal!

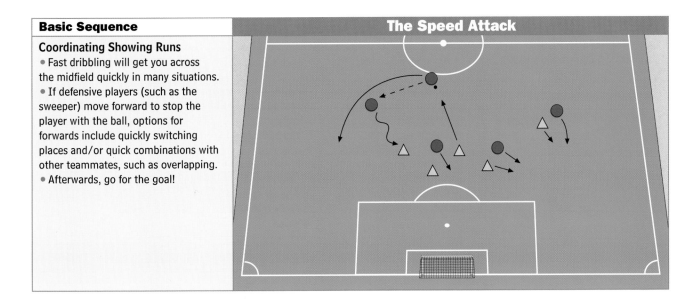

Setup/Sequence

6 v. 6 on Goal With Goalkeeper and Two Counter Goals

Set up two small goals (two meters wide) on the centerline, each one 10 meters from a sideline.

Six attackers play against six defenders on a standard goal with goalkeeper. If the defenders win the ball, they counterattack as quickly as possible on one of the small goals.

Playing time is 10 minutes.

Focus On:
- Switching quickly to the attack
- Decisive speed attack

Tips for Coaches
- Assign players to teams according to their positions.

Tips for Players
- The defense should pull far back and stay compact.
- For attackers: When the opposition forms a line in front of the goal, try using diagonal passes.

Variations

Level I	Level II	Level III
• A neutral player helps the attackers. • Set up a third counter goal on the centerline for the defenders. • After finishing, the attackers keep the ball and start a new attack (from the centerline). • The neutral player is the coach.	• Same sequence, but 7 v. 7. • Five (or six) attackers against six (or seven) defenders. • After each shot, the attackers get a corner kick. If the defenders win the ball, they counter, or the goalkeeper starts a counterattack by throwing it to a defender.	• The attackers get free kicks from various positions. They should try to send them in into the penalty area. If the defenders intercept the ball, they counterattack on the small goals. • Defenders must complete each counterattack within 10 seconds, or else they lose the ball.

Setup/Sequence

Two teams play 6 v. 6 in a field half. At the coach's signal, the team that has the ball starts a speed attack on the goal (with goalkeeper) in the opposite half. If they score on one of these attacks, they get two points. If the defenders win the ball, they can also counterattack, but they only score one point.
After the attackers finish, all players return to the original half for a new 6 v. 6.

Switching From Combination Play to Speed Attack

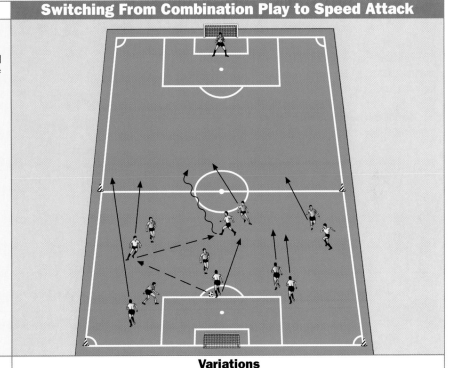

Variations

Focus On:
- Switching quickly from combination play to speed attack
- Combining safe combinations and high-speed play

Tips for Coaches
- Have extra balls ready.
- Take a five-minute break every four to six attacks.

Tips for Players
- When the coach signals, go deep so that the player with the ball can complete a long pass quickly – but watch out for the offsides rule.

Level I	Level II	Level III
• A neutral player helps whichever team has the ball. • Play without the offsides rule.	• Attackers are limited to three touches while securing the ball, unlimited touches if attacking on the goal. • A neutral sweeper in front of the goal assists the defense. • 7 v. 5: The team of five has unlimited touches at all times, while the team of seven is limited to three touches.	• Attackers are limited to two touches while securing the ball. • Defenders must complete each counterattack within 15 seconds, or else they lose the ball. • Make the starting field smaller.

Setup/Sequence

Two teams play 7 v. 7 in a 40-meter-wide zone centered on the centerline. Each team attacks on two small goals on the sidelines. Goalkeepers stand in the normal goals (1 and 2).

Whenever the coach calls out "1" or "2," the team that has the ball has to attack that goal at full speed. If the defenders win the ball, they have to attack on the same goal. Afterwards, a new 7 v. 7 begins in the center zone.

Switching From Small Goals to Normal Goals

Goal 1

Goal 2

Focus On:

- Switching quickly from solid attack building to speed attack
- Combining safe combinations and high-speed play

Tips for Coaches

- Have extra balls ready at the small goals.
- Take a five-minute break every four to six attacks.

Tips for Players

- When the coach signals, go deep so that the player with the ball can complete a long pass.

Variations

Level I	Level II	Level III
• A neutral player in the center zone helps whichever team has the ball. • Same sequence, but 6 v. 6. • Enlarge the center zone and/or the small goals. • The neutral player is the coach.	• Same sequence, but 8 v. 8. • Attackers are limited to three touches when attacking on the small goals. • If the defenders win the ball during a speed attack, they have to attack on the **opposite** goal.	• Team A starts out playing to maintain possession in the center zone. Team B tries to win the ball and counter on the far goal. Teams switch roles after three attacks. • On speed attacks, players have to pass or dribble through one of three small goals in the outside zones.

Setup/Sequence

Two teams play 6 v. 6 on five two-meter-wide goals that are distributed freely throughout a field half.

Attackers score by dribbling through these goals. At the coach's signal, the team that has the ball starts a speed attack on the goal with goalkeeper in the other half, while the other team defends. Finishing = one point, and scoring = two points. Afterwards, players start a new attack on the small goals.

Small Goals / Countergoal With Goalkeeper

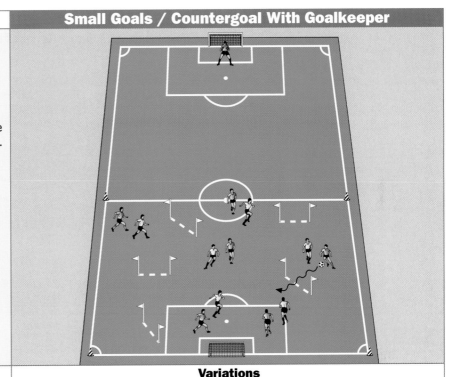

Variations

Focus On:
- Safe combination play on the small goals and quick shifts to high-speed play

Tips for Coaches
- Don't overwork players: Include a relatively long, active rest period every five attacks.
- Have the players set up and take down the small goals.

Tips for Players
- Speed attacks should combine decisive solo plays with long-range combination play.

Level I	Level II	Level III
• A neutral player helps whichever team has the ball. • An extra player stands on the opposite side of the centerline to pass and receive.	• Attackers are limited to three touches while attacking on the small goals, but they have unlimited touches during speed attacks. • On counterattacks, attackers have to get past an extra player ("neutral defender").	• Defenders must complete each counterattack within 15 seconds, or else they lose the ball. • Make the starting field smaller. • One team attacks only on the small goals, while their opponents counter on the goal with goalkeeper. Team switch roles periodically.

Exercise 1	Speed Attack With Forward Pass 1	Variations
Two teams of four play on two goals with goalkeepers. Play begins with a 4 v. 3 on Goal 1. The forward from Team B (defenders) stays in the other half to receive passes. If Team B wins the ball, they pass to their forward and immediately move up to counter. Team A's forward stays behind, creating a new 4 v. 3 in the other half, etc. Forwards are not allowed to shoot.		• Same sequence, but in a larger field with 5 v. 4 + 1 passer. • To score on a speed attack, the forward has to pass to a teammate.

Exercise 2	Speed Attack With Forward Pass 2	Variations
Two teams play 4 v. 4 in a 30 x 40-meter field behind the centerline. One attacker and one defender wait outside the far penalty area. Team A tries to maintain possession. If B wins the ball, they counter-attack on the goal (with goalkeeper) by passing to their teammate at the penalty area line. After the pass, the other attackers move up.	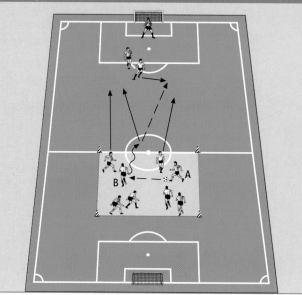	• Same sequence, but with 5 v. 5 at the centerline. • Same sequence, but with 2 v. 2 (or 3 v. 3) in front of the goal. • Team A's objective is to dribble across the rear endline of the marked field (= one point). If they succeed, they keep the ball. If B wins the ball, they attack on the goal with goalkeeper as above.

Exercise 3	4 v. 6 With Pass to Forward	Variations
Two teams play on a normal field with goalkeepers. Players start out in their assigned halves: In one half, four attackers from Team A play against six defenders from B, while two attackers from B and two defenders from A wait in the other half. If the defenders win the ball, they start a counterattack with a long pass to their forwards in the other half.	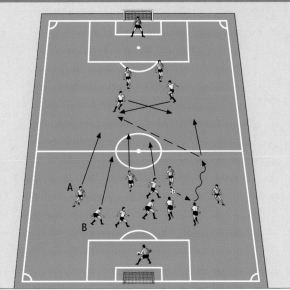	• Same sequence, but with 4 v. 5 (or 4 v. 4) in one half and 2 v. 2 (2 v. 3) in the other. • Make the attack zone in front of the goal smaller (e.g. by extending the penalty area sidelines).

Exercise 4	Speed Attack on a "Goal Field"	Variations
Mark out two 20 x 30-meter fields 15 meters apart. Two teams of four play in one field; Team A's objective is to maintain possession. If B wins the ball, they start a counterattack into the other field, where they try to maintain possession in a new 4 v. 4 situation. Each successful move into the other field scores one point. Include a five-minute break after three to five attacks.	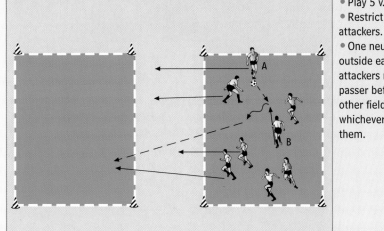	• Play 5 v. 5 in larger fields. • Restrict touches for attackers. • One neutral passer stands outside each endline. Speed attackers must pass to the passer before switching to the other field. Passers help whichever team passes to them.

Team Tactics: Defense Concepts

Playing Systems and Defense Patterns

By the end of the 1990s in Germany, soccer tactics were more in the news than ever before. There was lots of talk about Germany's "antiquated" playing systems, particularly anytime Germany played a disappointing game against an international opponent. The call came for a shift from the "traditional" 3 – 5 – 2 system to the supposedly "modern" 4 – 4 – 2 with flat four.

Many of these tactics debates were unrealistic. Catchphrases like "flat four" and uncritical comparisons of playing systems tended to distract people from the truly significant trends of top soccer.

Playing systems simply determine how many players are assigned to which positional groups (defense, midfield, attack). They have nothing to do with a team's basic tactical approach or the specific actions of individual attackers and defenders. And they're equally uninformative when it comes to a team's defensive strategies or the quality of defensive play by individuals, positional groups or the team as a whole.

So where do we look for answers about the quality of a team's game – possibly even about their success or failure? In individual players' specific roles, regardless of playing system, and the actions of these players. Zone defense works just as well in a 3 – 5 – 2 system as it does in a 4 – 4 – 2 system, and both formations lend themselves equally well to line defense – it all depends on individual players' positional roles.

No matter what playing system you use, it's important to shield the ball so that the opponent can't get at it without fouling.

In the following section, we'll start by defining the basic characteristics of an effective, attractive defensive plan. Next, we'll use modern playing systems to illustrate how the guidelines of modern defense can be applied to a variety of **different** playing systems.

Characteristics of Modern Defense
Ball-Oriented Defense

• Ball-oriented, opponent-oriented defense is the standard tactical plan for all teams. It's the only system that enables a team to defend in compact formation and restrict the opposition's playing space in every direction.

• The individual and group tactics that form the foundation of this playing style have already been explained (see "Group Tactics: Ball-Oriented Defense"). Defenders are not responsible for specific opponents; instead, they should attack all opponents who enter their defensive zones or are already inside them. All players' defensive zones overlap, so that all the players in a given positional group must be constantly moving toward the player with the ball. In other words, they have to move in so that they can all support each other.

• The following rule applies to **all** players on defense (including midfielders and attackers):

In ball-oriented defense, you cover and attack any opponent in your zone. Mount a determined attack on each different opponent: 1 v. 1 or even 2 v. 1 (two defenders attack the same attacker at the same time). The players farther away from the ball move toward it. At the same time, however, they protect the surrounding space from long passes and shifts of play.

• When attacking the player with the ball, every player's objective should be to win the ball. In other words, attack the player with the ball actively. The rule for all defenders is: "Defend actively and take the initiative! Force opponents to make mistakes and lose the ball!"

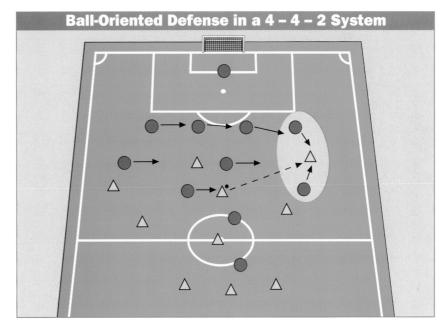

Ball-Oriented Defense in a 4 – 4 – 2 System

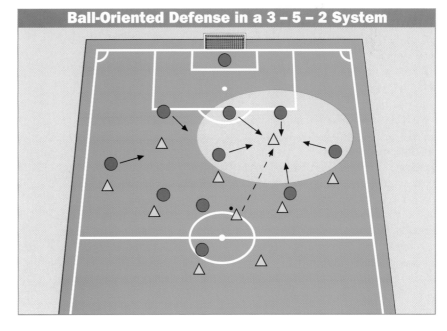

Ball-Oriented Defense in a 3 – 5 – 2 System

Illustration 15

Forms of Pressing

| 1 | Pressing in Front of the Goal | 2 | Pressing in the Midfield |

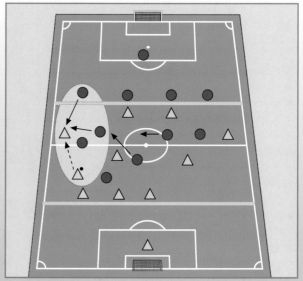

Forms of Pressing

Pressing is a defense tactic in which several defenders put pressure on the player with the ball at the same time. They restrict their opponent's playing space so much that breakthroughs and passes become difficult if not impossible. This improves the defense's chances of winning the ball.

Players have to learn to recognize which situations are favorable for pressing so that they can swing into action in an instant.

There are three basic types of pressing:

1. Pressing in Front of the Goal

In this version, the entire team falls back into its own half. Players wait for the opposition in a tightly arrayed, well-organized formation and attack the player who has the ball with superior numbers of defenders. Their own attack is oriented toward the fast counterattack.

2. Pressing in the Midfield

In this version, the team forms a tight formation in the midfield (about 15 yards in front of the centerline). The objective is to win the ball near the centerline: If the opposition passes into the midfield while building their attack, two or three defenders immediately attack the receiver. All other defenders move toward the ball in order to close down the space around it. The sweeper moves up into the midfield as well.

3	Attacking Pressing	Objectives	Characteristics
	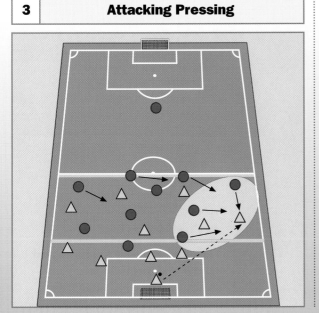	• Using strong defense to make it harder for the opposition to attack • Creating open spaces for counters when the opposition has moved	**1** • Compact defense formations in front of the goal • Quick, uncomplicated counterattacks after winning the ball
		• Winning the ball in the midfield • Switching quickly to the attack after winning the ball	**2** • Solid defense formations in the midfield • Moving with the ball, decisively and in a way that's appropriate to the situation
		• Winning the ball when the opposition is still in its own half • Putting constant pressure on the opposition	**3** • Moving forward as a team deep into the opposition's half • Attacking the opposition while they're still building their attack

All of these actions put a great deal of pressure on the opposition. A team with lots of experience playing together can refine the basic sequence even further: In appropriate situations, key players (sweeper, defensive midfielder) give a signal for a sudden switch to deep pressing. Then the entire team moves decisively and aggressively forward every time the opposition plays a square or back pass, to try to win the ball.

If they succeed, the whole team switches to the attack and tries to get past the opposition's (inevitably disorganized) defense as quickly as possible.

3. Attacking Pressing (Deep Pressing)

This is the most attack-oriented type of pressing: Defenders engage the opposition at the edge of their own penalty zone and try to disrupt their attack building. This requires the entire team to move deep into the opposition's half. Active defense begins at the opposition's penalty area. This move into the opposition's half requires defenders to open up their own formation somewhat, so it is vulnerable to a speed attack from the opposition. Furthermore, this type of pressing is incredibly exhausting: Constant pressure requires a great deal of running, with hardly any time left for regeneration. For these reasons, deep pressing is not a workable option for the length of an entire

This is all the space a top attacker like Ronaldo needs to set up a shot.

match. It should only be used in specific situations or phases, e.g. at the beginning of the match, right after the halftime break, after defenders' own corner kicks or throw-ins, after the opposition's back passes or toward the end of the game when the defenders are behind.

Flexible Defense Instead of Rigid Formations

The basic objectives of modern defense are to build a compact defense formation, create favorable conditions for winning the ball and put players in good positions to start a counterattack. The playing system comes second!

When you're defining positions and assigning roles within positional groups,

you must be able to answer the following questions:

1. What kind of vision or concept of the game do I want to realize? Will we play with or without a sweeper?

2. What kind of duties can my players handle? What kind of talents and experience do they have?

3. What does my concept of the game mean in terms of individual, group and team tactics?

4. Would my players be overwhelmed by this approach to the game initially, even though it might enable them to be more successful and play more attractive soccer in the long run? How can I systematically prepare my players for this approach?

As a coach, your objective should be to achieve maximum flexibility in terms of position assignments and duties within each positional group.

Modern Playing Systems and Defense Formations

The 1998 World Cup in France started a trend toward playing styles and systems that are more versatile and flexible, in terms of both attack and defense.

One important discovery related to defense formations was that most teams broke away from the rigid flat four formation (with two outside and two inside defenders, moving sideways, backward and forward as a solid line) or only practiced it sometimes.

The "classic" compact flat four was almost always a purely defensive formation. However, now that the game is dominated by a more clearly attack-oriented playing style, with flexible outside defenders who can also join the attack, the traditional flat four should be considered obsolete.

Many of the teams in the 1998 World Cup employed a wide variety of basic formations. These formations differed primarily in terms of the role, function and usual position of the sweeper: Many teams played with a sweeper behind the defenders; in others, the sweeper's position was even with the defenders. Still other teams played with a free player in front of two, three or even four defenders. Another variation involved a sweeper behind the defenders and a free central player or "front sweeper" in front of them.

While discussing the "flat four," coaches should always consider the position of the sweeper and pay special attention to trends in international soccer. It should be obvious that changing the sweeper's position, as described above, also changes the sweeper's role.

In any case, one thing is certain: The "playing system" comes second, as a matter of principle. It's much more important to assign players' roles according to their individual talents and your own vision of the game, regardless of the basic formation, so that you can address your team's weaknesses and build a successful, attractive game.

These days, ball-oriented defense should be the obvious choice, so when you're assigning defenders' roles, the first thing to consider is whether you want to play with a sweeper or not.

All players have their own defense zones within their positional groups, and they attack any opponent who enters their zones. Single opponents are frequently attacked by two or more defenders because defenders' zones overlap and because all defenders are

always moving toward the player who has the ball. All of this makes things difficult for attackers.

The sweeper's game depends on the sweeper's roles. Ultimately, it's up to sweepers to evaluate each situation and decide whether they need to play behind, in front of or even with the defense. In any case, sweepers should help their teammates mount effective attacks on the ball. Also, sweepers should be the "boss" of the defense, regardless of where they happen to be at the moment.

Whether you have three or four defenders at your disposal, if you choose to play without a sweeper, you'll have to use a line defense. In terms of their approach to the game, position assignments and role assignments within positional groups, coaches today have to be much more flexible than they did in the past. Today, players who have the technical-tactical ability required to respond flexibly to any and all situations are worth their weight in gold.

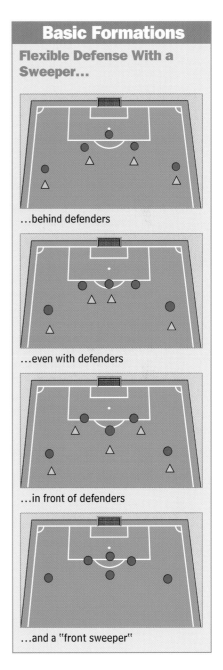

Basic Formations

Flexible Defense With a Sweeper...

...behind defenders

...even with defenders

...in front of defenders

...and a "front sweeper"

Illustration 16

Defending as a Team

GUIDELINES

For the Whole Team

① Don't just react to the opposition's actions; defend actively!
Your desire to win the ball should be obvious in every situation.

② Talk to each other. That's the only way to keep a flexible defense formation organized and coordinated. Communication is especially important for switching opponents to teammates.

③ Move toward the ball. The defense's job is to outnumber the attackers around the ball, so that then they can fight for it aggressively.

④ Always make sure your team stays in compact formation. This means that the individual positional groups have to stay close together. When the opposition has the ball inside their own half, move up and start defending there.

SAMPLE SITUATIONS

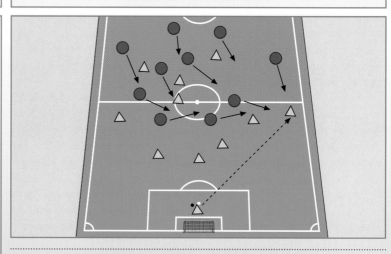

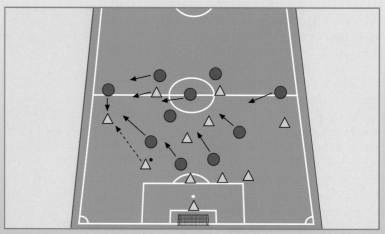

Setup/Sequence

Two teams play 4 v. 4 in a 40 x 15-yard field on the edge of the penalty zone. Two two-yard-wide goals stand on the endline farther away from the goal. Team A focuses on moving with the ball, in order to keep Team B from getting into the penalty area.

If the players from B succeed in dribbling into the penalty area, they're allowed to shoot at the goal (with goalkeeper) without interference. However, they have to dribble across the line; they can't pass across it.

Afterwards, B starts a new attack from the small goals. If A wins the ball, they counterattack on one of the small goals.

4 v. 4 Outside the Penalty Area

B

A

Focus On:
- Moving with the ball
- Defending as a team

Tips for Coaches
- Assign five players to Team B; one player sits out each attack.

Tips for Players
- Move as a unit to follow the ball.
- Make a decisive attack on the player with the ball; prevent shots at all costs.
- When attackers switch positions, "trade" them with your opponents as appropriate.

Variations

Level I	Level II	Level III
• Attackers have to dribble through one of three small goals (two yards wide) on the penalty area line in order to get into the penalty area (to make it easier for defenders).	• When the attackers break through, one defender is allowed to follow into the penalty area and interfere with the shot. Any defender who wins the ball in the penalty area starts a counterattack. • When the attackers break through, all players are allowed to follow them into the penalty area	• Five attackers play against four defenders (to make it harder for defenders). • Instead of a goal with goalkeeper, mark out a three-yard-wide zone just behind the penalty area line. The player with the ball has to pass to a teammate inside this zone (= one point). Attackers can't enter until after the pass.

Setup/Sequence

Mark out an "attack line" 30 meters in front of a goal with goalkeeper. Two teams play 5 v. 5 between the attack line and centerline.

Team A starts by attacking from the centerline; their objective is to dribble across the attack line. If they succeed, they're allowed to shoot without interference. Afterwards, they start another attack.

If Team B wins the ball, they try to dribble across the centerline.

5 v. 5 With an Attack Line

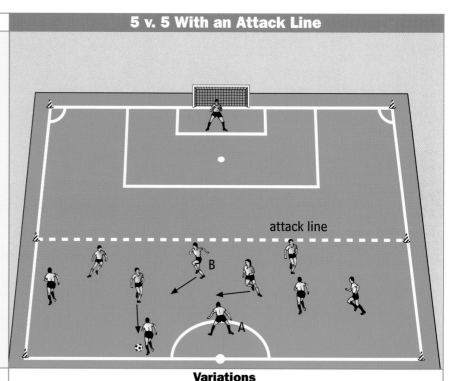

attack line

B

A

Focus On:
- Moving with the ball
- Defending as a team

Tips for Coaches
- Mark the attack line clearly.

Tips for Players
- Move as a unit with the ball.
- Form a compact unit and prevent attackers from breaking through.
- Work actively against the player with the ball. Watch the other players and cover the field so that dribbling lanes and deep passing lanes are blocked.

Variations

Level I	Level II	Level III
• A neutral player helps whichever team has the ball. • Same sequence, but as 4 v. 4. • Attackers who break through must play 1 v. 1 against the goalkeeper. • Set up four small goals (two meters wide) on the attack line at 10-meter intervals. Attackers dribble through them.	• If B successfully counter-attacks on the centerline, teams switch roles and directions. • Attackers who get across the attack line must play 1 v. 1 against a defender. • When an attacker dribbles across the attack line, all the defenders follow. • 4 v. 4 on a shorter attack line.	• An extra defender in front of the goal to attack any attacker who dribbles across the attack line. This defender tries to win the ball and then start a counter by passing to the sweeper. • As above, but with two extra defenders. • Same sequence, but as 3 v. 4 (or 4 v. 5): Attackers are outnumbered.

Setup/Sequence

Make a standard field slightly shorter by moving one of the goals up to the penalty area line.

Two teams play 6 v. 6, both using the same basic formation: flat four plus two forwards. Both teams play to score as quickly as possible. The outside defenders participate in attacks while the inside defenders only take part in the attack building phase. Attackers re-form the flat four immediately after scoring or winning the ball.

New attackers must complete five passes in a row before shooting, so that their opponents have enough time to re-form the flat four.

4 + 2 v. 2 + 4 on Two Goals

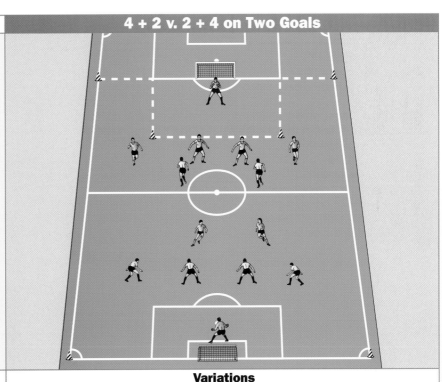

Focus On:

- Using a line defense

Tips for Coaches

- Mark the field boundaries clearly, to make it easier for players to orient themselves.

Tips for Players

- When attackers are moving outside, force them as far outside as possible.
- Use line defense to stop the forwards in the middle.
- Communicate and help each other.

Variations

Level I	Level II	Level III
• Make the field smaller; both teams use the same basic formation: flat four plus one forward. • Instead of the goal with goalkeeper, set up three small goals (two meters wide) on each endline of the field.	• Both teams use the same basic formation: flat four plus three forwards. • Shorten the field to about 65 meters. • On defense, forwards are not allowed to cross the centerline.	• If the defenders win the ball, they can attack the opposition's goal. The new defenders should try to keep them from building an effective attack, and also use positional play to prevent direct attacks on the goal, until they've had . time to get back into the basic formation.

Setup/Sequence

Two teams play 8 v. 8 on a standard field; B has a goalkeeper as well.

Team A has two forwards, five midfielders, and one "attack builder" in the backfield.

Team B (the defenders) has two groups of four positioned in front of three small goals (two meters wide) placed at 10-meter intervals along a line 15 meters behind the centerline.

A attacks eight to 10 times in a row. Attackers are not allowed to shoot at the goal with goalkeeper until they've dribbled through one of the small goals. If B wins the ball, they have to pass back to the "attack builder" in the backfield (= one "goal").

8 v. 8 on One Goal

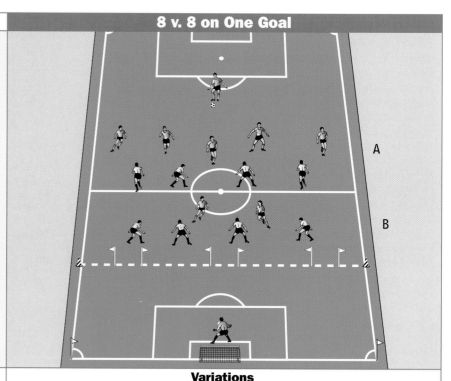

Focus On:

- Moving as a unit to follow the ball and closing down space
- Working closely together as a team and covering each other

Tips for Coaches

- Have the field ready (goals set up, lines marked) before practice starts.

Tips for Players

- Try to force attackers outside.
- Midfielders and defenders have to work together as a single unit.

Variations

Level I	Level II	Level III
• After dribbling through one of the small goals, attackers may shoot without interference at the goal with goalkeeper.	• Every five attacks, change the distance between the large goal and the line of small goals, so that the defenders have to move their line accordingly. • No small goals: Defenders have to try to keep attackers from dribbling across a marked line 35 meters in front of the goal.	• Team A has three forwards, four midfielders and one "attack builder" in the backfield. • Team B has a flat four behind two (or three) midfielders.

Setup/Sequence

Two teams play 8 v. 8 on two goals in a field that is 75 meters long and as wide as the penalty area. Players are assigned to three marked zones: 4 v. 4 in the center zone and 2 v. 2 in each attack zone. Each game begins with a 4 v. 4 in the center zone. Attackers try to pass to a teammate in the attack zone. One player from the center zone may join the attack in the attack zone (3 v. 2). If the three attackers in the attack zone lose the ball, they play 3 v. 2 to win the ball back and score. If the two defenders are able to dribble into the center zone, a new 4 v. 4 begins there, with the new attackers trying to pass into their attack zone, etc.

Pressing: 2 v. 2 / 4 v. 4

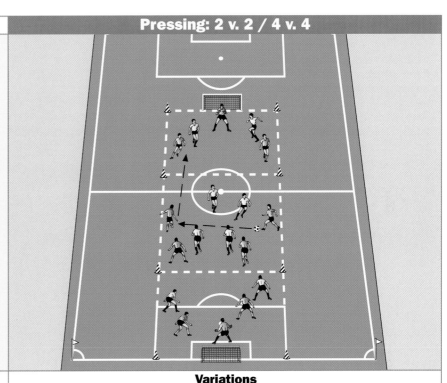

Focus On:

• Using decisive attack pressing to win the ball back quickly
• Playing an aggressive 1 v. 1 game

Tips for Coaches

• Mark each zone clearly.

Tips for Players

• If you lose the ball, try to outnumber and attack your opponents as quickly as possible in order to improve your chances of winning the ball back.
• Don't be too quick to shoot after you've won the ball.

Variations

Level I	Level II	Level III
• After a shot, the new attackers cannot start their attack on the opposite goal until one of the three forwards in the attack zone has fallen back into the center zone and restored the 4 v. 4 there.	• All players must stay in their own zones, but the two forwards in the attack zone should still try hard to win the ball back in 2 v. 2 play if they lose it. • If the three forwards lose their ball in the attack zone and then win it back, they're limited to two touches.	• If the three forwards lose their ball in the attack zone and then win it back, they must complete their attack within the next five touches. • 10 v. 10 in a larger field: 4 v. 4 in the center zone and 3 v. 3 in each attack zone.

Setup/Sequence

Pressing: 6 v. 4 on One Goal and Two Counterlines

Mark out two 20-meter-long counter-lines, one on each side of the field, 45 meters in front of a goal with goalkeeper. Two teams play 4 v. 6. The team of four (Team A) defends the large goal and attacks on the countergoals (dribbling across a counterline counts as a goal). They have unlimited touches.

The team of six (Team B) uses pressing to try to win the ball and then quickly attack on the large goal. They are limited to three touches.

Playing time is seven minutes.

Variations

Focus On:
- Using decisive attack pressing to win the ball back quickly
- Playing an aggressive 1 v. 1 game

Tips for Coaches
- Make sure the teams switch roles and all players have sufficient rest periods.

Tips for Players
- If you lose the ball, the player closest to it immediately puts on the pressure.
- All other players move toward the ball.

Level I
- Team B has unlimited touches on attacks.
- Any attacker from Team A who dribbles across a counterline can then shoot without interference at a goal with goalkeeper (distance shot). The goal should be about 20 meters away from the lines.

Level II
- Team B is limited to two touches in a row.
- Same sequence, but as 6 v. 5.
- 5 v. 5 with unlimited touches: Team B should still use attack pressing whenever appropriate, in spite of the equal numbers.

Level III
- Place one small goal on each sideline of a field half and three small goals on the centerline. 6 v. 4: The team of four defends the large goal with goalkeeper and can counter on any small goal. The team of six is limited to one touch outside the penalty area, three touches inside.

Setup/Sequence

Two teams play 7 v. 7 on two standard goals with goalkeepers in a field half. Divide the field laterally into three zones. Attackers have unlimited touches in their own attack zone but only two in the center zone and the opposite attack zone. All attackers must move up at least as far as the center zone before they can score.

7 v. 7 With Three Zones

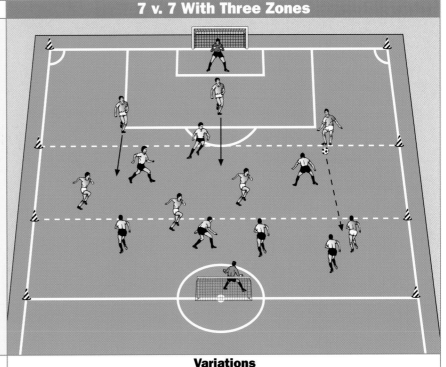

Focus On:
- Defending as a compact unit
- Quickly switching to defense and disrupting the opposition's attack building

Tips for Coaches
- Mark the zones and field boundaries clearly.

Tips for Players
- If you lose the ball in the opposition's attack zone, put pressure on them immediately.
- If you win the ball, move forward as far as possible.

Variations

Level I	Level II	Level III
• Same sequence, but attackers have unlimited touches in all three zones. • A neutral player helps whichever team has the ball.	• If the ball goes out on the side, instead of a throw-in from the goalkeeper, the attacking team throws it in and away from the goal, so that they often have to rebuild their attack from the rear. • Attackers can only score on direct shots.	• Attackers can only score on direct shots after back passes. • The offsides rule applies: The lines dividing the zones are also the offsides lines.

Setup/Sequence

Mark out a 35-meter-wide field centered on the centerline and divided into a 15-meter-wide center zone and two 10-meter wide endzones. Set up two small goals (two meters wide) on each endline.

Two teams play 6 v. 6 in this field, with no special restrictions.

Assign positional roles for both teams:

Team A: Two markers and four mid-fielders.

Team B: Two forwards and four mid-fielders.

Game on Two Small Goals

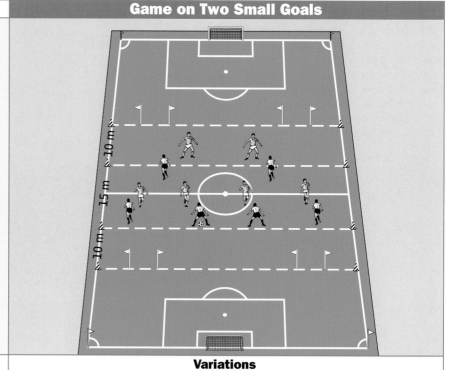

Focus On:

- Creating a compact presence in the midfield
- Switching quickly from attack to defense and vice versa
- Cooperation between midfielders and defenders
- "Handing off" attackers to fellow defenders when they change places

Tips for Players

- Move as a unit with the ball.
- When attackers change positions, "trade" them with your teammates.

Variations

Level I	Level II	Level III
• Enlarge the field and the goals. • A neutral player helps whichever team has the ball.	• Attackers can only score on shots from within the endzone in front of the opposition's goal. • Attackers are limited to two touches in a row. • 7 v. 7 (with five midfielders).	• Attackers can only score on direct shots from within the endzone in front of the opposition's goal. • Attackers must pass and shoot directly.

Setup/Sequence	Game With Three Defense Zones

Divide a 70-meter-long field laterally into three zones (30, 10 and 30 meters deep).

Two teams play 8 v. 8 on two goals with goalkeepers.

Assign players to both teams according to positional roles: two defenders, four midfielders and two forwards.

Shots do not count unless there are no attackers left in the 30-meter zone in front of their own goal.

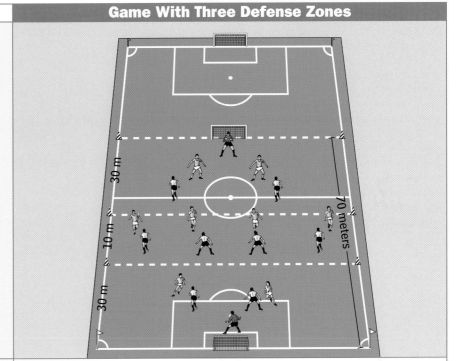

Variations

Focus On:
- Compact team presence
- Ball-oriented defense

Tips for Coaches
- Make sure the zones are clearly marked.

Tips for Players
- Always try to anticipate what the opposition is going to do.
- If you win the ball, move forward as far as possible, so that you clear your defense zone.

Level I	Level II	Level III
• Lengthen the field to 80 meters. • A neutral player helps whichever team has the ball.	• Midfielders are limited to two touches. All other players have unlimited touches. • Attackers can only score on direct shots.	• Attackers can only score on direct shots after back passes. • Add the offsides rule. • Same sequence, but as 9 v. 9: Add one midfielder to each team.

Setup/Sequence	Sweeper Training

Two teams play 6 v. 6 in a 50-meter-wide zone in the center of a normal field.
A seventh player (sweeper) from each group defends two small goals on the penalty zone line.
The player that has the ball tries to pass out of the center zone to a teammate just as that teammate runs into the attack zone. Only long passes on the ground or in the air are allowed. The sweeper is the only defender allowed to be in the attack zone. If the defenders win the ball, the sweeper stays in the rear and distributes the ball.

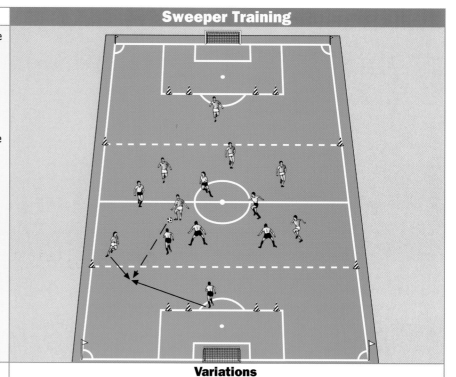

Variations

Focus On:
- Creating a compact presence in the midfield
- The sweeper's role: 1. Anticipating situations and intercepting passes, 2. Covering teammates' backs

Tips for Coaches
- Divide the field into the same zones as in a normal field to help the sweepers orient themselves.

Tips for Players
- For the sweeper: Move with the ball and coach your teammates.

Level I	Level II	Level III
• Attackers are allowed to dribble into the attack zones. • One extra attacker is allowed to join the pass receiver in the attack zone, creating a 2 v. 1 situation. • 5 v. 5 in the center zone. • A neutral player in the center zone helps whichever team has the ball.	• Attackers are limited to two touches in a row in the center zone. • 7 v. 7 in the center zone.	• Attackers must pass directly in the center zone. • Attackers must complete a wall pass across the attack zone line.

Setup/Sequence

Two teams play 8 v. 6 on two goals. Team A (eight players) defends a goal on the penalty area line. A 30-meter-wide "pressing zone" is centered on the centerline. Team A moves into its basic formation (five midfielders, one sweeper and two forwards) and attacks.

If Team B (six players) wins the ball, A mounts a decisive attack in the pressing zone to win it back. B attempts to maintain possession, dribble into the attack zone in front of A's goal and score. If they succeed in dribbling out of the pressing zone, A can no longer attack them.

Pressing: 8 v. 6 on Two Goals

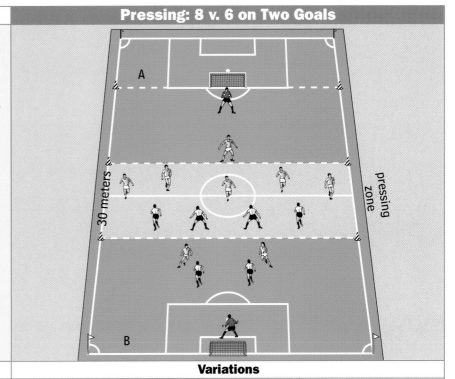

Focus On:

- Attacking decisively in the pressing zone
- Pressing on a predetermined signal

Tips for Coaches

- Have the field ready (goals set up, lines marked) before practice starts – this saves practice time.

Tips for Players

- Learn to recognize good pressing situations.
- Move in toward the ball from the far side.

Variations

Level I	Level II	Level III
• Only Team A attacks on a goal with goalkeeper; Team B only has to dribble across the attack zone line.	• Same sequence, but with 8 v. 7. • Team A is limited to two touches in a row. • If Team A loses the ball, they can start attacking in B's defense zone, depending on the situation (attack pressing).	• Same sequence, but with 8 v. 8. • A direct shot after a back pass counts double.

Setup/Sequence

Two teams play 7 v. 7 in three-quarters of a field, divided laterally into three zones (20, 30 and 20 meters wide). Players are assigned as follows: 5 v. 5 in the center zone and 2 v. 2 in one attack zone. The other attack zone remains open. Players are not allowed to leave their assigned zones.

Team A's midfielders try to pass to their forwards in the attack zone, who then play 2 v. 2 to score.

Any player from Team B who wins the ball tries to dribble across the opposite attack zone line and then shoot at the goal without interference.

5 v. 5 / 2 v. 2 on Two Goals

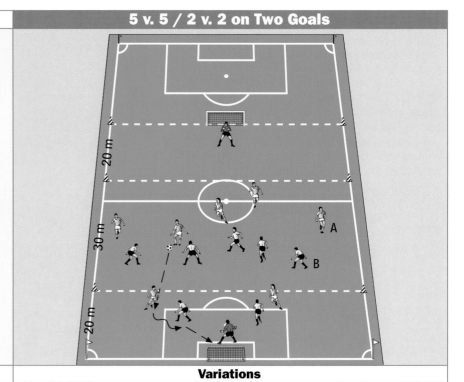

Variations

Focus On:
- Coordinated action in the midfield
- Blocking passing lanes
- "Handing off" attackers to fellow defenders when they change places

Tips for Players
- When attackers change positions, "trade" them with your teammates.
- Attack opponents aggressively to keep them from completing long-range passes to the forwards accurately.

Level I
- After passing to the forward, one midfielder from A is allowed to enter the attack zone, creating a 3 v. 2 situation.
- A neutral player in the center zone helps whichever team has the ball.

Level II
- The forward from A who receives the ball can only score on a solo run.
- A's two forwards must complete their attack within five touches after receiving the ball.

Level III
- A long shot by a midfielder after a back pass from a forward counts double.
- A shot after a wall pass between the two forwards counts double.
- Team B also has a sweeper in front of their goal.

Setup/Sequence

Team A has ten players: three defenders, five midfielders and two forwards.
Team B has nine: two defenders, five midfielders and two forwards.
Team A's objective is to move the defensive line as far toward the center-line as possible and defend actively.
You can also add the offsides rule.

9 v. 10 on Two Goals

Variations

Focus On:
- Attacking the opposition early
- On counterattacks, switching quickly to defense

Tips for Coaches
- Make sure the teams switch roles and all players have sufficient rest periods.

Tips for Players
- Mount a decisive attack while the opposition is still building.
- Move forward as a unit, two defenders can attack the player with the ball.

Level I	Level II	Level III
Only Team A attacks on a goal with goalkeeper; Team B only has to dribble across a marked line about 30 meters behind the center-line.	Team A is limited to three touches in a row. Same sequence, but with 10 v. 11.	Attackers can only score on direct shots set up by a teammate. If attackers can score within the first five touches after winning the ball in the attack zone, they score two points.

Exercise 1

Mark out a 40-meter long line 30 meters in front of a goal with goalkeeper. Four attackers (Group A) play against three defenders (Group B) to score on the line. Any attacker who succeeds in dribbling across the line (= "goal") can play 1 v. 1 against the goalkeeper to try for another goal. If the defenders win the ball, they try to pass to their two forwards in the other half, who then play 2 v. 2 to score.

3 v. 4 With Counterattack

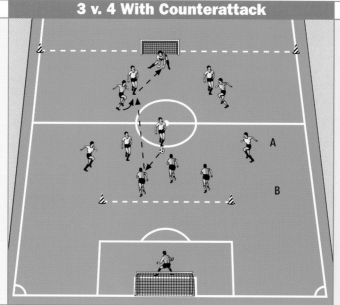

Variations

- 4 v. 4 on the line.
- Put three attackers and three defenders in the other half.
- Any attacker who dribbles across the line can score again by shooting from outside the penalty zone.

Exercise 2

Set up three goals 30 meters in front of the endline. Make the middle goal wider. Place two more goals on the centerline, 25 meters apart. Play starts with a 5 v. 4 on the three goals: The five attackers try to dribble through one of them. If the defenders win the ball, they try to pass through one of the centerline goals to one of the forwards, who then play 2 v. 2 to score.

4 v. 5 With Counterattack

Variations

- 4 v. 3 on the three goals.
- Put three attackers and three defenders in the other half.

Exercise 3

Two teams play in a field half, between a goal with goalkeeper and two counterlines. Group A (attackers): six players. Group B (defenders): flat four + midfielder. A attacks on the goal. Dribbling into the penalty area or passing to a teammate already in it = "goal." Attackers can then shoot to score an additional point. B counterattacks the goals behind the centerline.

5 v. 6 on One Goal and Two Counterlines

Variations

• Instead of counterattacking, Group B plays to maintain possession:
10 passes in a row = "goal."

Exercise 4

Mark out three 20 x 20-meter fields. Each has three attackers. The defense consists of four defenders and two midfielders, distributed across the entire width of the field. Attackers try to dribble across their field's endline. If they can't do that, they can pass to their teammates in the next field. Defenders orient themselves toward the ball, so that at least two defenders and one midfielder are on the ball.

3 v. 2 + 2 Midfielders

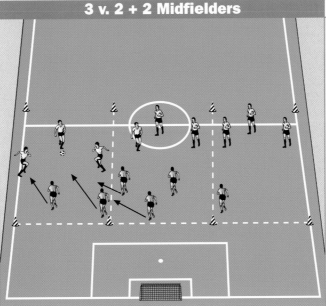

Variations

• After dribbling across the endline, attackers are allowed to shoot at the goal from outside the penalty area.
• If the defenders and midfielders win the ball, they counterattack on the opposite endline.

CHAPTER 6

CONDITION TRAINING

Condition Training: The Basics

Condition Training for All Age Levels

- "Condition" is the sum of all physical factors affecting performance. It can be broken down into separate elements: endurance, speed, power/mobility and coordination. The more you train these elements, the more you can optimize your performance. Today, soccer-specific condition training must be play-oriented. Practice should be primarily devoted to training games ranging from 1 v. 1 to 10 v. 10. The coach's job is to vary the challenges and exertion levels in these games so as to focus on specific aspects of condition.

Training games should be the main method of improving condition, particularly in youth soccer, but also at the low to middle amateur adult levels.

- So at the lower levels, practice should center on soccer training games (varying in terms of rules, team and field sizes, and playing times). This is a perfect way to combine condition training with technique/tactics training.

- Isolating the individual elements of condition is really only worthwhile if you practice every day. However, if you still want to train a specific element (without the ball), make sure that the exercises are play-oriented and motivational.

- Ultimately, any endurance, speed, power or mobility training exercise that does not involve the ball has to be judged in terms of how well it reflects the actual demands of the game.

By combining a wide variety of running, jumping and technique exercises, you can still build soccer-oriented practice sessions. This method has proven very effective for 14- to 18-year-olds.

Organization of Exercises

- For all these reasons, our condition training section consists of interesting soccer-specific games and exercises.

- To achieve the desired results, they must be executed according to certain principles.

- Once again, most of the exercises are assigned to specific training levels (see the overview on page 73), so that it's easy to see whether you should consider a given exercise for your team.

- However: Most of the exercises can be adapted for any team, with simple variations that make them easier or more demanding.

Illustration 1

Improving Condition by Playing Soccer

Conditioning Exercises

Complete

Endurance	Speed	Power/Mobility	Coordination
• Interesting running exercises • Circular courses plus running-related exercises • Circular courses plus technical exercises • Running/game combinations	• Running training • Exercises for takeoff power • Sprinting exercises • Soccer-specific speed exercises	• Mobility exercises (solo) • Mobility exercises (in pairs) • Strengthening exercises (solo) • Strengthening exercises (in pairs)	Exercises to improve... • Running coordination • Jumping coordination • Coordinated ball handling • Technical coordination

Endurance Training

Endurance in Soccer

Soccer is (and always will be) a running game. In 1960, studies showed that the world's best soccer players ran more than four kilometers per game. That figure was considered exceptional. Today, even upper-level amateurs run more than 10 kilometers per game, and the top professionals sometimes run more than 14!

What's more, the types of activity soccer requires can be unpredictable and varied. Every player has to be constantly moving, paying close attention to the game, ready to go into action with the ball at any moment. Players have to be able to be active for 90 minutes – changing position, moving up from the backfield, running into open spaces and putting up determined resistance to counterattacks. It requires endurance. And it means that players have to be able to postpone exhaustion (which could cause their intensity and their performance to suffer) as long as possible.

Soccer players face a wide variety of demands, in terms of running. While they spend most of the game jogging, periodically they also have to be able to execute plays at full speed, sometimes in combination with demanding techniques and tactics (shooting, solo runs, attacking opponents, for instance).

This means that endurance has a significantly different meaning for soccer players than it does for, say, middle- or long-distance runners. However, it still entails a certain basic running ability (basic endurance). Basic endurance ensures that players will be able to handle and recover from the demands of soccer (specialized endurance). Without well-developed basic endurance, high-level soccer-specific condition training would be impossible.

When the ball is involved, even endurance training can be fun!

Basic Endurance

Well-developed basic endurance is the only way to keep up with the pace of modern soccer:
- Players with good endurance can participate in the game more regularly, more intensively and for longer periods of time. Their performance stays at a high level, even toward the end of the game. They're capable of exhausting their performance reserves completely.
- Players with good endurance take less time to recover from intense plays. They recover faster after practices and matches as well. This is especially important at times when players have less rest than usual (training camp, weeks with two matches).
- Players with good endurance get hurt less often. Because they're always "fresh," at the end of the game they're still able to recognize dangerous situations in time and "maneuver" themselves out of the way.
- Players with good endurance are more stable, mentally. They're better able to deal with stress and losing the game, and their periods of low motivation pass more quickly.
- Players with good endurance can handle more responsibility too. They stay disciplined throughout the game, they don't deviate from the tactical plan (even at the end, when things get hectic), and they stay "wide awake" up until the last minute. They respond correctly in even the most intense game situations – situations that can mean the difference between victory and defeat.

Illustration 2

How to Train Endurance

Basic Endurance	**Endurance in Soccer**	Specialized Endurance

Running Exercises	**Endurance Parcourse**	**Specialized Exercises**	**Running/Game Combinations**
• Cross-country runs • Orienteering • Long-distance runs with occasional variations in: – running style – direction – pace	• Circular courses involving a variety of running styles and exercises (plus occasional changes in physical intensity) • Circular courses with simple technical exercises (plus occasional changes in physical intensity)	• Exercises on goals with goalkeepers (from 1 v. 1 to 8 v. 8), with appropriate playing times • Open-field exercises focusing on combination play and maintaining possession • Exercises on small goals (1 v. 1 to 8 v. 8), with appropriate playing times	• With two groups: Endurance game A vs. B, followed by endurance run for both • With three groups: Endurance game A vs. B while C runs (switch roles afterwards) • With four groups: Endurance game A vs. B while C and D run (switch roles afterwards)

- The lower the ability level, the less practice time you can afford to spend on separate endurance training sessions.

- In endurance training, physical workloads should be comprehensive but not necessarily intense.

- Endurance training has to be interesting – no running laps!

- Encourage players to do extra endurance runs on their own at home.

Specialized Endurance

Good basic endurance is the foundation of good performance on the soccer field, but basic endurance alone is not enough to meet all the demands of the game.

Besides basic endurance, players also need a specialized type of endurance that accounts for a factor unique to soccer: constant changes of intensity.

Specialized endurance allows players to
• change speed easily throughout the entire game.
• execute the extremely intense movements that are typical in soccer (explosive sprints and jumps, changes of direction, high-speed dribbling, powerful shots and headers) with little down time in between, at high speed and a high level of quality.

At the lower levels, endurance training should be combined with technical-tactical exercises.

Training Guidelines

For soccer players, basic endurance influences specialized endurance in many ways. Basic endurance ensures that players will be able to handle the exertion and recover. Without basic endurance, it's impossible to develop solid soccer-specific endurance.

In spite of the connections between them, players have to train both types of endurance separately, with special training methods and exercises for each.

However, there are a few basic principles that apply to all types of endurance training:
• Although endurance influences performance, it's just one of the many elements that make up a soccer player's performance profile. After all, long-distance runners are not necessarily good soccer players. Overdo endurance training, and you can't help but neglect other, more important areas such as technique and tactics, especially at the lower and middle amateur levels, where practice time is severely limited.
• Basically: The fewer practice sessions you have in a week, the less time you can spare for separate endurance training sessions.
• Low- and mid-level amateurs seldom manage more than two or three practice sessions per week, but they can combine endurance training with technical-tactical exercises. An interesting and comprehensive warm-up program can also help improve endurance. And finally, the cool-down run at the end of each session can boost endurance as well.
• When practice sessions are fairly frequent, you can add specialized endurance exercises — but avoid running laps at all costs! Endurance parcourses, exercises combining running and playing soccer, etc. are far more interesting, motivational, and efficient.
• At higher levels, where endurance training is separate and systematic, the principle of **regularity** is important. For example, it doesn't accomplish much to "force" endurance training during the pre-season, then suddenly quit when the season begins. If you want reliable results, you have to plan endurance training exercises throughout the season, even during finals.
• How comprehensive should your team's endurance training be, and how intense? That depends on their ranking, motivation, objectives and performance level.
• In normal youth soccer, endurance training should consist exclusively of training games, and perhaps an occasional endurance parcourse with the ball. Long-distance (cross-country) runs and endurance parcourses without the ball are only necessary at the advanced youth level.

Illustration 3

Endurance Training by Level

Level I

Endurance is:

- At the lower amateur levels, one of the most important benefits of good endurance is injury prevention. Players with good endurance get hurt less often, but unprepared players are practically "programmed" for injuries, especially at the end of the game.
- Free-time athletics produce a level of fitness that also benefits soccer performance.

Training Suggestions

- If practice time is limited, never sacrifice technique or tactics to work on endurance.
- Instead, integrate endurance training into technical-tactical games and exercises.
- Comprehensive, interesting warm-up programs with the ball also improve endurance.
- Running to improve basic endurance should take place at home on an individual basis.
- Match play improves endurance too!

Level II

Endurance is:

- Optimal soccer-specific endurance enables players to maintain high speed and reliable accuracy throughout an entire match.
- It also allows them to execute brief high-intensity moves (explosive sprints, high-speed dribbling, etc.) more easily during play and to recover more quickly afterwards.

Training Suggestions

- Occasionally supplement play-oriented condition training with specialized (but always interesting and soccer-specific) endurance exercises.
- Encourage players to improve their endurance by running on their own. This requires players who are mature, reasonable, responsible and cooperative.
- Regular cool-down runs after each session boost endurance too.

Level III

Endurance is:

- Basic endurance is linked to the immune system, which has a strong influence on a player's regeneration abilities.
- The continuous stress of practice and match play at the higher levels makes good basic endurance a necessary prerequisite for quick regeneration.

Training Suggestions

- Schedule special endurance maintenance exercises regularly throughout the season.
- For effective endurance training, form groups of players with comparable running skills, or else create individual running programs.
- Regeneration runs after practice and match play improve endurance.
- Review the efficiency of your endurance training on a regular basis.

Illustration 4

Exertion Levels for Standard Exercises

6 v. 6

Basic Exercises

6 v. 6

- between a large goal with goal-keeper and a counterline
- on two large goals with goal-keepers
- on two (or three) small goals per team
- from passer to passer
- on goal lines

Ideal Workload

- two to three repetitions with a playing time of six to seven minutes
- a five-minute active break before each new round

Training Objectives

- quick but safe attack building
- wide-ranging combination plays
- wing and endline play
- moving to the ball
- shifting quickly to attack/defense, game action speed
- mutual coaching and cooperation

5 v. 5

Basic Exercises

5 v. 5

- between a large goal with goal-keeper and a counterline
- on two large goals with goal-keepers
- on two (or three) small goals per team
- from passer to passer
- on goal lines

Ideal Workload

- three to four repetitions with a playing time of four to five minutes
- a three-minute active break before each new round

Training Objectives

- flexible use of group attack tactics in combination play (e.g. wall passes)
- wide-ranging combination plays
- moving to the ball
- shifting quickly to attack/defense, game action speed
- strength of will, concentration

4 v. 4

Basic Exercises

4 v. 4

- on one large goal with goal-keeper
- on one small goal
- on two large goals with goal-keepers
- on two small goals
- on two small goals per team
- on goal lines

Ideal Workload

- three to four repetitions with a playing time of two to three minutes
- a three-minute active break before each new round

Training Objectives

- flexible use of group attack tactics in combination play (e.g. wall passes)
- moving to the ball
- dynamic 1 v. 1 play
- shifting quickly to attack/defense, game action speed
- strength of will, concentration

3 v. 3

Basic Exercises

3 v. 3

– on one large goal with goal-keeper
– on one small goal
– on two large goals with goal-keepers
– on two small goals
– on goal lines

Ideal Workload

- three to four repetitions with a playing time of one minute to 90 seconds
- a three-minute active break before each new round

Training Objectives

- flexible use of group attack tactics in combination play (e.g. wall passes)
- moving to the ball
- dynamic 1 v. 1 play
- shifting quickly to attack/ defense, game action speed
- strength of will, concentration

2 v. 2

Basic Exercises

2 v. 2

– on one large goal with goal-keeper
– on one small goal
– on two large goals with goal-keepers
– on two small goals
– on goal lines

Ideal Workload

- five to six repetitions with a playing time of 30 seconds to one minute
- a three- to four-minute active break before each new round

Training Objectives

- quick energy supply for short, intensive exertions
- extremely high demands on concentration
- 1 v. 1 play and determination
- flexible use of group attack tactics in combination play (e.g. wall passes)

1 v. 1

Basic Exercises

1 v. 1

– on one large goal with goal-keeper
– on one small goal
– on two large goals with goal-keepers
– on two small goals
– on goal lines

Ideal Workload

- six to eight repetitions with a playing time of no more than 15 seconds
- longer 1 v. 1's (more than 15 seconds) should be interrupted

Training Objectives

- quick energy supply for short, intensive exertions
- 1 v. 1 play
- improving game action speed
- game action speed, concentration and determination

Special Endurance Training Games

Since training games are supposed to be the main focus of practice anyway, especially at the lower levels, it makes sense to use them for condition training as well: You can train condition in connection with technique and tactics. However, for best results, exertion levels have to be appropriate (see the recommended playing times and rest periods on pages 223-224). Another option is special soccer-specific endurance training games that use relatively large fields to achieve the necessary amount of running.

Endurance Game 1

Goal in the Middle

7 v. 7 on a small goal (marked with poles) with goalkeeper in the middle of the field. The two teams play between the two penalty areas, both trying to score on the goal. Attackers can score from either side, but shots must be no higher than the tops of the poles. If defenders win the ball, they have to dribble across one of the marked lines (each about 15 meters long) in the corners of the field before attacking on the goal. The attackers keep the ball if they score or the goalkeeper stops the shot. However, they also have to dribble across one of the corner lines before their next attack,

Playing Time

Two or three repetitions of six to seven minutes each, with five-minute active rest periods in between.

Variations

• Play without the goalkeeper, making the goal smaller instead. Players who run through the goal lose the ball and/or points for their team.
• Set up two portable goals with goalkeepers back to back on the centerline. Attackers can attack on either goal.
• One team attacks only on the corner lines and has to dribble across them (= one point). The other team attacks only on the goal.

More Endurance Games

Passing Through Small Goals

6 v. 6 in a field half: Five three-meter-wide goals are randomly distributed throughout the field. Attackers score by passing through the goals to their teammates.

Passing Into Goal Zones

6 v. 6 in a field half, with two marked goal zones on each endline.

Attackers play from goal zone to goal zone: The player with the ball tries to pass to a teammate just as that player moves into the goal zone (= "goal").

Shooting on Four Goals

6 v. 6 in a field half on four small goals (five meters wide) arranged in a square, with two goalkeepers. Attackers can attack on any of the goals. Shots must be no higher than the tops of the poles. Both goalkeepers guard whichever goal is currently under attack.

Endurance Game 2

Volley Goals

Two teams play 7 v. 7 (or 6 v. 6) in a field half on two goals with goalkeepers. The centerline is marked.

Both teams try to score, on either goal; however, they can only score on headers and volleys.

After scoring or winning the ball, attackers must first cross the centerline before starting a new attack on the goals.

Playing Time

Two or three repetitions of six to seven minutes each, with five-minute active rest periods in between.

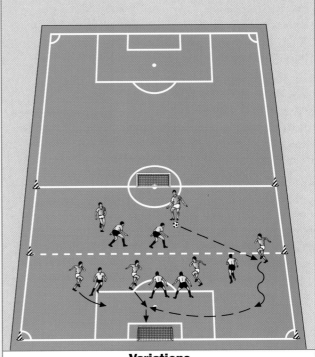

Variations

- The coach (or an extra player) acts as a "neutral" player who helps whichever team has the ball.
- Two neutral players help the team with the ball.
- For more advanced players: Make the field smaller.
- Attackers are limited to three touches in a row.
- Same sequence, but with 5 v. 5 inside a field twice the size of the penalty area.

Combining Games With Running

This type of setup, combining pure running exercises with training games, is effective, motivational endurance training.

The pace of the games is quite high at times, but the laps that follow allow players to regenerate, and also improve their endurance.

Another advantage of this setup is its flexibility. It's easy to organize good combinations of running and games, regardless of practice field, group size or ground conditions.

Combination 1

Setup

With four equally matched teams: Teams A and B play on two goals with goalkeepers in one half of the field, while C and D run an endurance course in the other half. The teams switch roles after each set of laps (e.g. five) or after a set time period (e.g. ten minutes).

Groups A/B

5 v. 5 with unlimited touches: Attackers focus on combination play and shooting.

Groups C/D

- Section 1: easy run
- Section 2: sideways run through a course of staggered cones
- Section 3: easy run, stopping periodically and turning all the way around three times
- Section 4: alternating between knee lifts and fast knee lifts

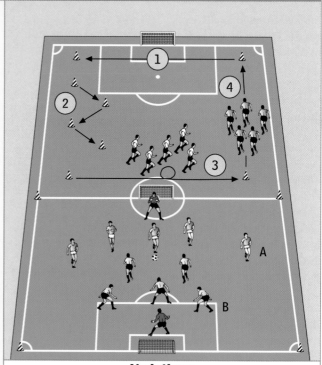

Variations

Groups A/B

5 v. 5 on both goals: Attackers are limited to two touches in a row.

Groups C/D (Each Player Has a Ball)

- Section 1: various forms of dribbling
- Section 2: dribbling through a narrow slalom course
- Section 3: dribbling with three different fakes
- Section 4: juggling the ball while moving forward

Combination 3
- Groups A and B: 5 v. 5 (unlimited touches) to maintain possession in one field half.
- Groups C and D: endurance parcourse with the ball (five laps).

Combination 4
- Groups A and B: 5 v. 5 on two goals placed side by side.
- Groups C and D: endurance parcourse without the ball (five laps).

Combination 5
- Groups A and B: 5 v. 5 to dribble across the opposition's endline.
- Groups C and D: cross-country runs outside the practice field.

Combination 6
- Two teams of seven play on three small goals each on the penalty area sidelines. Two players from one team run three laps around the outside of the field, creating a 7 v. 5 situation; then two players from the other team run. The team of seven tries to score as many goals as possible.

Combination 2

Setup
Two teams of equal size (seven to 10 players) play on two goals with goalkeepers on the endlines. Adjust the field size to fit the team sizes (from 60 x 50 to 70 x 60 meters). To make practice more efficient, have extra balls ready at both goals.

Sequence
Both teams have unlimited touches. At any given time, two players from each team are running four to six laps around the field at a moderate pace. Extra exercises:
- running through a slalom course
- jumping over hurdles
- using a given running form (e.g. knee lifts) on a given stretch

After each set of laps, at the earliest break in the game, the runners switch roles with their teammates.

Variations

Variations on the Game
- Alternating 7 v. 5 on two goals: First two players from one team run around the field, then two players from the other, so that there is always a 7 v. 5 situation on the field. The attackers' try to outplay their opponents and use their advantage.
- Attackers have limited touches.

Variations on Running Exercises (With Ball)
- Various forms of dribbling
- Dribbling through various slalom courses
- Dribbling with fakes
- Alternating between dribbling and juggling

Endurance Parcourse With Ball

Endurance parcourses that involve the ball make for interesting endurance training, for a number of reasons.

First, exercises with the ball distract players from the exertion of running, and second, they improve technical skills at the same time. Endurance parcourses with the ball can also be structured as interval training: for example, 4 x 3 laps with gymnastic exercises (with or without the ball) in between.

Parcourse 1

Sequence

All players start out dribbling in a "waiting zone" in one corner of the field. One after another, they dribble out of the zone and through a parcourse with the ball. Each section of the parcourse involves a different technique exercise.

- **Section 1:**
Dribble through a slalom course of cones.
- **Section 2:**
Pass to the coach, jump over three hurdles in a row, receive the ball from the coach and continue dribbling.
- **Section 3:**
Kick a gentle pass through a small goal from 10 meters away and catch up with the ball.
- **Section 4:**
Fast dribbling for 40 meters.
- **Section 5:**
Kick a gentle pass in the air for the goalkeeper to catch, then receive and control the ball and dribble back into the waiting zone.

Variations

- **Section 1:**
"Fast footwork" through the slalom course.
- **Section 2:**
Pass to the coach, do squat jumps over the hurdles, receive the ball and continue dribbling.
- **Section 3:**
Figure-eight dribbling around the two poles that mark the goal.

- **Section 4:**
Dribbling with extra tasks such as fakes.
- **Section 5:**
Well-aimed shot at the goal with goalkeeper.
Afterwards, continue dribbling in the waiting zone until the next turn.

More Parcourse Stations

- Wall passes with the coach.
- Slalom dribbling.
- Restricted dribbling, e.g. only with the right or left foot, only with the outside of the foot, etc.
- Dribbling with a fake (body fake with lunge step, step-over, shooting fake) in front of a pole.
- Juggling while moving quickly forward.
- Bouncing the ball while executing other movements (e.g. skipping, running backwards or sideways, changing hands).
- Skipping while throwing the ball up and catching it.
- Running backwards while holding the ball overhead with outstretched arms
- Holding the ball behind the back and kicking it with the heels.
- Jogging/skipping while passing the ball around the hips.
- Throwing the ball up and catching it while running.

Parcourse 2

Sequence

Players form pairs and distribute themselves equally among the four corners of the field. Each pair has a ball and must run all the way around the field, performing a different exercise on each side. Partners switch roles and positions each turn.

- **Side 1:**
Square passes (direct) into each other's paths from a distance of three to four meters.
- **Side 2:**
Standing three to four meters apart, A moves forward and B moves backwards. A passes to B, and B bounces the ball directly back to A.
- **Side 3:**
Square passes (with one touch allowed for ball control) into each other's paths from a distance of three to four meters.
- **Side 4:**
A moves forwards, B backwards. A throws high balls to B, who heads them back while moving backwards.

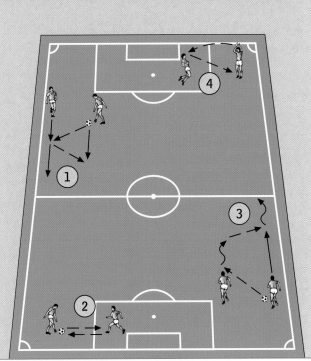

Variations

- **Side 1:**
Free combinations with position changes.

- **Side 2:**
A throws low balls to B, who volleys them back.

- **Side 3:**
Combination play limited to two touches, with frequent position changes

- **Side 4:**
A throws low balls to B, who stops them in the air with the left thigh (or the chest) and kicks them back with the right instep for A to catch.

Endurance Parcourse Without Ball

Endurance parcourses are a practical, adaptable way to make endurance training interesting. The principle is simple: Players take turns running through a parcourse, performing various running forms and exercises. The pace should be moderate, but more intensive sections can be built in, depending on training objectives and players' condition. Endurance parcourses lend themselves to an interval training structure, e.g. 4 x 3 laps with gymnastic exercises in between.

Parcourse 1

Sequence

Groups in each corner of the field. At the coach's signal, they run the parcourse, performing a different exercise in each section:

- **Section 1:**
Five simulated headers while running (alternate takeoff legs).
- **Section 2:**
Two or three short sprints (3-5 meters).
- **Section 3:**
Zigzag run moving from cone to cone with small sideways steps.
- **Section 4:**
Run a 20-meter stretch four times in a row, using a different running form each time:
1. Right heel kicks
2. Backwards run
3. Left heel kicks
4. Backwards run
- **Section 5:**
60-meter run, gradually increase speed.
- **Section 6:**
Alternate between sideways galloping one round and moderate skipping with arm circles the next.

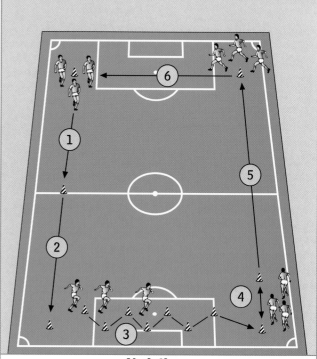

Variations

- **Section 1:**
Five squat jumps while running.
- **Section 2:**
Two simulated headers followed by short sprints.
- **Section 3:**
Slalom run.
- **Section 4:**
Run 20 meters four times, different running form each time:

1. Fast knee lifts
2. Backwards jog
3. Fast knee lifts
4. Backwards jog
- **Section 5:**
Start slow, speed up.
- **Section 6:**
Easy jogging with forwards arm circles one round, backwards circles the next.

More Parcourse Stations

- Various jumping exercises along the edge of the field.
- Sideways run along the goal line with five leaps in front of the goal.
- Forwards run through a straight or staggered slalom course of cones.
- Stair run (in a stadium).
- One- or two-legged jumps over a row of closely spaced poles.
- One- or two-legged jumps over a row of closely spaced ones.
- Leaping over pairs of cones.
- Fast, explosive knee lifts over a short distance.

Parcourse 2

Sequence

Same setup as Parcourse 1.
- **Section 1:**
Zigzag run from cone to cone, running first forwards, then backwards.
- **Section 2:**
Jump over four staggered hurdles.
- **Section 3:**
Six to eight balls are randomly distributed throughout the penalty zone. Players run from one ball to the next, taking short, quick steps and setting the sole of the foot briefly on each one.
- **Section 4:**
Alternate between easy knee lifts one round and heel kicks the next.
- **Section 5:**
60-meter run, starting slowly and gradually speeding up.

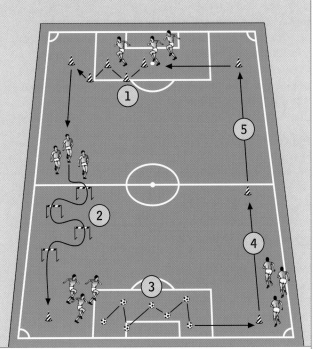

Variations

- **Section 1:**
Light-footed slalom run through the cones.

- **Section 2:**
Squat jumps over the four staggered hurdles.

- **Section 3:**
Players sit on each ball briefly.

- **Section 4:**
Alternate between easy skipping one round and sideways galloping the next.

- **Section 5:**
60-meter run, starting slowly and speeding up moderately.

Endurance Runs

The higher your level and the more often you practice, the more necessary special endurance exercises become. A solid foundation of basic endurance ensures that players will be able to handle the exertions of practice and match play.

In order to improve running endurance, players should run for relatively long periods of time (30 to 40 minutes in all) at a moderate pace (pulse: 140 to 160 beats per minute for youth players). But don't just run laps! Think of the attractive variations made possible by changing running paths, forms and speeds.

Running Patterns

Using The Field

General Information

Clearly, endurance runs have a positive effect on basic endurance. On the other hand, running laps is boring: definitely not a "soccer-friendly" way to fill this need. However, a few simple variations in the running paths are all it takes to make your endurance training program interesting.

Levels I

- Running programs should only be used occasionally.
- Include technique exercises at various points along the parcourse.

Levels II

- Vary the running forms as well as the paths.
- Players should dribble on some sections of the parcourse.

Levels III

- Running programs should be a regular part of practice.
- They're especially good for regeneration.

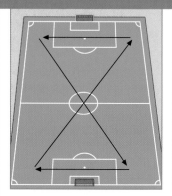
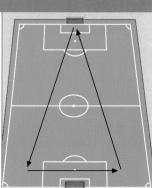
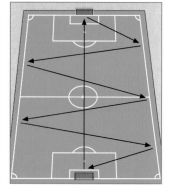
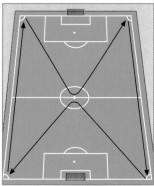
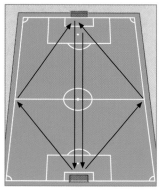
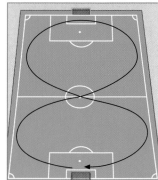

Exercise 1

Set up a square course, 50 meters on a side. Players run around it, alternating between two speeds: first one side at a fast pace, then the next at an easy jog.

Levels II/III

Square Run

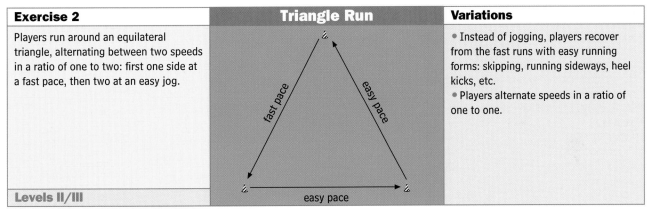

Variations

- Instead of jogging, players recover from the fast runs with easy running forms: skipping, running sideways, heel kicks, etc.
- Include easy running exercises on one side, such as a slalom course.

Exercise 2

Players run around an equilateral triangle, alternating between two speeds in a ratio of one to two: first one side at a fast pace, then two at an easy jog.

Levels II/III

Triangle Run

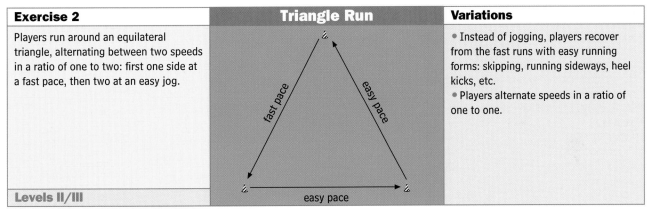

Variations

- Instead of jogging, players recover from the fast runs with easy running forms: skipping, running sideways, heel kicks, etc.
- Players alternate speeds in a ratio of one to one.

Exercise 3

Players run a series of "endurance runs" at a moderate pace. After each individual run, they jog twice that distance. Endurance run distances: 6 x 100 meters, 5 x 200, 4 x 300, 3 x 400, 1 x 500.

Level III

Pyramid Run

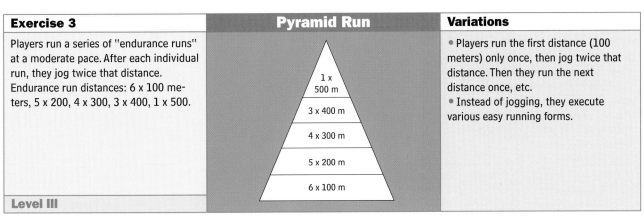

1 x 500 m

3 x 400 m

4 x 300 m

5 x 200 m

6 x 100 m

Variations

- Players run the first distance (100 meters) only once, then jog twice that distance. Then they run the next distance once, etc.
- Instead of jogging, they execute various easy running forms.

Exercise 4

Players run the following distances at a fast pace: 100, 200, 300, 400, 500, 600, 700 and 800 meters.
After each run, they jog twice that distance.

Level III

Multi-Stage Run

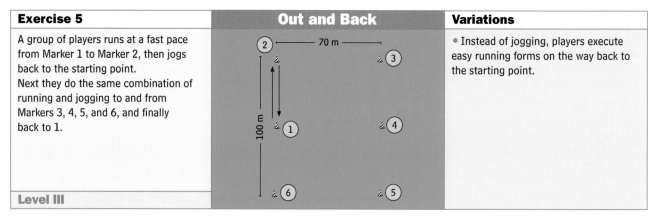

Variations

• Reverse the sequence of distances: 800, 700, 600, 500, 400, 300, 200 and 100 meters. Jogging breaks are as above.
• Instead of jogging, players execute easy running forms: skipping, running sideways, etc.

Exercise 5

A group of players runs at a fast pace from Marker 1 to Marker 2, then jogs back to the starting point.
Next they do the same combination of running and jogging to and from Markers 3, 4, 5, and 6, and finally back to 1.

Level III

Out and Back

Variations

• Instead of jogging, players execute easy running forms on the way back to the starting point.

Exercise 6

A pair of players starts at the centerline and jogs to one corner of the field. Then Player A speeds up and runs along the edge of the field to the opposite corner, while B jogs there on the diagonal, at a relatively easy pace. Both jog back to the starting point together, where they switch roles.

Level III

Diagonal Run

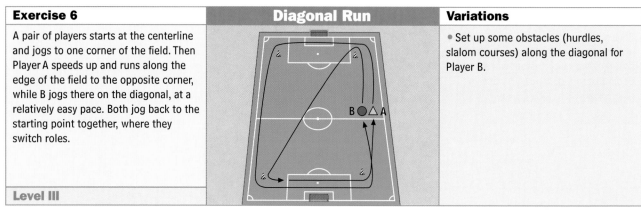

Variations

• Set up some obstacles (hurdles, slalom courses) along the diagonal for Player B.

Running Games

General Information

A "running game" combines a variety of running distances, paces and forms with other exercises (such as jumping). You can vary the exertion levels considerably and focus on different concepts, depending on your objective (e.g. running games for re-generation, speed training, or specialized endurance).

Level I

• Encourage players to work more on endurance on their own at home.
• To help them, write down running programs and pass them out.

Level II

• Combine running games with specialized endurance training exercises in your practice sessions.
• Once again, encourage players to run on their own.

Level III

• Make an interesting regeneration program out of running games with low exertion levels and easy exercises.
• To maintain specialized endurance, include running games with match-character pace and exertion levels on a regular basis.

Game 1

• Warm-up (five to eight minutes): easy jog with gymnastic exercises.
• Aerobic endurance run (ten minutes).
• Gymnastic exercises: stretching and limbering exercises (10 minutes).
• Easy jog, speeding up three or four times to run 20 to 40 meters (300-meter jogs in between runs).
• Five 20-meter sprints, each followed by a 300-meter jog.
• Jogging (five minutes).
• Five leaping runs of 30 meters each, each followed by a 300-meter jog.
• Slow run (10 minutes).

Game 2

• 1000-meter warm-up run at a slow pace.
• 1500 meters, changing pace slightly (500 meters at an easy pace, 500 slightly faster, 500 easy). Don't get out of breath!
• Gymnastic exercises (ten minutes).
• 500-meter jog, 1000-meter "fast endur-ance run," 500-meter jog.
• Gymnastic exercises (ten minutes).
• 500-meter jog, 1000-meter "fast endur-ance run," 500-meter jog.
• Cool-down run (ten minutes).

Game 3

• Warm-up run (10 minutes).
• Gymnastic exercises (five minutes).
• Easy run including skipping, running backwards and running sideways (five minutes).
• Three to five stretches of 60 to 80 meters each, starting slowly and gradually speeding up, each followed by a 200-meter jog.
• Easy run (two minutes).
• Functional gymnastic exercises (five minutes).
• Three 60-meter coordination runs (heel kicks, leaping, knee lifts), starting slowly and speeding up, each followed by a 200-meter jog.
• Cool-down run (10 minutes).

Game 4

• Warm-up run (10 minutes).
• Stretching (five minutes).
• Hard run (five minutes).
• Easy running forms (three minutes).
• Two 60-meter runs, gradually speeding up, each followed by a 200-meter jog.
• Skipping, jogging afterwards.
• Five two-legged squat jumps from a standing position, followed by jogging.
• One-legged jumps (six with the right leg and six with the left) followed by short sprints, then jogging.
• "Fast endurance run" (five minutes).
• Cool-down run (eight minutes).

Speed

Speed in Soccer

In today's soccer, speed is an essential part of performance.

What exactly is "speed," for a soccer player? A look at the game reveals that a "fast" player has to be able to do more than just run fast. In soccer, the requirements for speed are much more comprehensive. High-speed dribbling followed by a shot, defensive tackling at a full run, fakes with sudden changes of speed, quick sprints to get clear of tight situations and show for passes‐these are just a few examples. The success or failure of almost every play depends on high-speed performance.

A soccer player's speed is more than just sprinting or basic speed; it also includes fast ball handling (action speed), fast moves (game action speed), quick stops and starts (irregular speed), and quick comprehension of situations (e.g. anticipation speed). An effective training program has to take all of these factors into account.

Speed: The Basics

So the nature of speed in soccer is exceptionally complex. Even the sprinters miss opportunities – if they assess a situation incorrectly or too late, or if they're unable to execute techniques at top speed.

Therefore, when we talk about speed in the context of soccer, we're always talking about two components: cognitive (mental) and motor (coordinative and conditional).

Sprinting speed (one of the facets of soccer-specific speed) is a valuable asset, especially 1 v. 1.

Coordinative and Conditional Components

• The fact that a given player is able to sprint 20 or 30 meters reasonably quickly does not necessarily mean that that same player can combine those short sprints with sudden stops and changes of direction, fluidly and without slowing down significantly. The reason is usually a lack of coordination. Coordination is essential to playing

Illustration 5

Speed and How to Train It

Motor Components	**Speed in Soccer**	Cognitive Components

Action and Sprinting Speed	Game Action Speed	Running Coordination	Takeoff Power
• Sprints to the ball and quick, precise follow-ups (shots, 1 v. 1's, etc.) • Sprints from various starting positions • Sprints at various starting signals • Sprints with changes of direction • Sprints combined with other exercises	• Exercises in tight spaces, focusing on continuous readjustment to new situations • Exercises focusing on switching quickly from attack to defense and back • Exercises focusing on quick, versatile, flexible use of individual and group tactics	• "The ABC's of Running:" basic running technique as the basis of running speed • Running exercises with cones and/or poles • Running exercises followed by short sprints • Running exercises followed by shots • Running exercises followed by technique exercises	• For low- and mid-level amateurs: takeoff power training to improve speed: 1. Various jumping combinations 2. Jumping exercises with partners and obstacles • For upper-level players only: maximum power training /muscle-building to improve speed

- Speed and takeoff power training should be a part of every practice session, regardless of ability level.

- Make speed training complex (with variations in training methods, contents and equipment).

- For lower-level players, create complex exercises that integrate the various components of speed.

- Speed exercises should always be evaluated in terms of how well they reflect the actual demands of the game.

soccer, and soccer-specific exercises are the best way to train it.

• Next to coordination, the most important factor in sprinting speed is takeoff power. That's why speed training should also regularly include exercises to improve takeoff power.

Cognitive Components

The speed of plays in tight spaces is continually increasing. Players have less and less time to adjust to new game situations, orient themselves and respond quickly and appropriately.

Therefore, you should also offer exercises that develop certain cognitive components of speed:

• Players must be able to comprehend game situations as quickly as possible and notice changes instantly.

• Players must be able to "read" the game in order to anticipate upcoming developments.

• Players must make decisions and react to changes within moments.

More advanced players possess these abilities: They comprehend situations at a glance and almost never lose sight of the big picture. They're able to perceive the intentions of their teammates and opponents ahead of time (anticipation) and can adjust their own actions accordingly in an instant. The result: The players with "game intelligence" are often the ones who reach the ball that one deciding step ahead of everyone else.

A close look at how players deal with game situations that require high speed reveals that the cognitive components of high-speed performance in soccer are just as complex as the physical. Choose your speed training methods and exercises accordingly!

Step-by-Step Speed Training

• Speed is a complex quality; it can only be improved with a well-balanced and appropriate mixture of exercises that take all the different components of speed into account.

• Soccer players have to develop lots of abilities, especially mental abilities. Speed training should reflect this concept of speed: Up-to-date, soccer-specific speed training should train both motor and cognitive components, both in isolation and in combination.

• However, at the same time, it's also true that at the lower levels, where practice sessions are not as frequent, isolating the individual components of speed (e.g. running coordination, sprinting speed) is possible only occasionally. On those rare occasions when this does happen, the coach must be sure that the exercises in question are both play-oriented and motivational. For lower-level players, speed training should consist primarily of complex exercises and training games designed to emphasize specific aspects of speed.

• All speed exercises, both simple and complex, should always be evaluated in terms of how well they reflect the actual demands of the game.

With the addition of simple supplementary tasks, you can change many "traditional" sprinting exercises and training games so that they focus more precisely on specific components of speed. This insures that speed training will be both attractive and demanding in terms of coordination.

• Finally, a few important rules to keep in mind any time you're planning and organizing a speed training session:

1. Before speed training, players have to have a comprehensive, focused and intensive warm-up session.

2. Efficient speed training is only possible when players are highly motivated and in good physical condition.

3. Make sure that breaks are long enough and properly spaced, so that players get the optimal amount of rest: i.e, short, intensive periods of exertion with one- to two-minute breaks after each one.

4. Adjust the demands and contents of your speed training program to fit your players' level. Exercises should be soccer-specific whenever possible.

Illustration 6

Speed Training by Level

Level I

Speed is:

- For soccer players, speed is primarily measured by how well they can execute a given task quickly and with technical/tactical precision.
- This is the main focus of speed training at lower levels (where practice time is limited). By playing as much as possible, players improve their speed by improving their overall ability.

Consequences

- When practice time is limited, speed training (e.g. isolated sprinting exercises) should never be allowed to take time away from technical/tactical and other more play-oriented aspects of the game.
- Instead, work on speed "alongside" tactics and technique, with speed-oriented games and exercises.
- Every practice session should make demands on players' speed.
- The occasional specialized speed training exercise should always be soccer-oriented.

Level II

Speed is:

- On one hand, the main performance criteria for mid-level players are: how well they deal with game situations and how precisely they handle the ball, in spite of time and opposition pressure.
- However, the conditional factors of basic speed and sprinting speed become more important as we move to higher levels.

Consequences

- Supplement integrated speed training games with specialized exercises that are also soccer-oriented and motivational.
- Make "traditional" sprinting exercises more interesting and (especially) more soccer-oriented by adding coordinative and/or technical challenges.
- Games and exercises for game action speed training should become systematically more challenging (e.g. by increasing opposition pressure).

Level III

Speed is:

- To optimize all aspects of speed at the higher levels (where you finally have enough practice time), isolate individual components such as running coordination and sprinting speed.
- In top-level soccer, it's virtually impossible to compensate for shortcomings in any aspect of speed.

Consequences

- Special speed-oriented strength training (e.g. muscle building) is essential for soccer-specific speed and should be a regular part of practice.
- Never schedule speed training the day after a match.
- When you have two practice sessions in one day, never schedule intensive speed training for the second session.
- Players should execute all technical/tactical exercises at high speed without sacrificing precision.

Action Speed

With a few simple changes, most traditionally structured sprinting exercises can be made significantly more motivational and, more importantly, more like actual play. In these exercises, first of all, players start sprinting on typical visual signals (e.g. a moving opponent or ball); second, every sprint to the ball is followed by a fast, accurate follow-up action (e.g. a well-aimed shot), just like in actual play. When speed training is play-oriented like this, it's both efficient and attractive at the same time, which is why it should be a regular part of practice, especially at the lower levels of play.

Basic Exercises

Sprints to the Ball

Sprints to the Ball
- Running distances should be based on actual play: Sprints should be short, no more than ten to 20 meters.
- Players should warm up intensively before these speed exercises. Technique exercises are perfect for this.
- Proper exertion levels are also important: Always schedule breaks of a minute or more between high-intensity plays.
- Each player should also get a longer active rest period after four or five plays, consisting of simple but interesting shooting exercises.
- Although the main focus may be on speed, every exercise should be a technical challenge for most players as well.

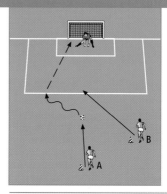

Sprinting and Shooting
Place a ball 20 meters in front of a goal with goalkeeper. A and B start from different positions. simultaneously. Whomever reaches the ball first shoots. The other player attempts to block the shot.

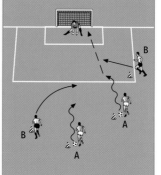

Interfering With a Dribbler
A (with ball) and B run to a goal with goalkeeper from different positions. A's first touch is B's starting signal. A tries to score, while B follows at top speed and tries to stop the shot and win the ball. Afterwards, both players switch roles.

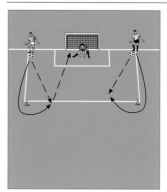

Race to Shoot
At the coach's signal, each player passes a ball from the rear corner of the penalty area in front of the goal, then sprints around a marker on the front penalty area corner. First to touch a ball shoots. The other one has to dribble around the cone once before shooting.

Exercise 1	**Sprint to Pass From Coach**	Variations

The coach stands between two players and suddenly passes toward the goal. Whichever player reaches the ball first is allowed to shoot.

Level II

- The two players start from various positions (lying on their backs or stomachs, squatting, kneeling, sitting with legs outstretched).
- The coach bounces the ball so that the first attacker has to control it before shooting.

Exercise 2	**Out and Back to the Ball**	Variations

Two players run around two markers and back to the ball, placed directly in front of the goal with goalkeeper.
B starts moving as soon as A does, and tries to stop A's shot.
Players switch roles afterwards.

Level II

- The two players start from various positions (lying on their backs or stomachs, squatting, kneeling, sitting with legs outstretched).
- Either player can shoot.
- Players have to get past obstacles on the way to the ball, e.g. a hurdle or a short slalom course.

Exercise 3	**Reverse to the Ball**	Variations

Two players stand side by side on a line, then run backwards away from the ball. As soon as A starts moving forward toward the ball, the race begins, ending in a 1 v. 1 to shoot at the goal with goalkeeper.

Levels I/II

- A has to execute various movements while running backwards (e.g. squatting, simulated header), and B has to imitate them immediately.
- Same sequence on a small goal.

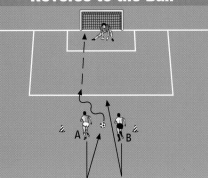

Exercise 4	**Reverse to the Ball**	**Variations**
A places a ball on the penalty zone line and jogs three meters to B. As soon as A turns around, both start racing toward the ball. Whichever one reaches it first is allowed to shoot, while the other tries to interfere.	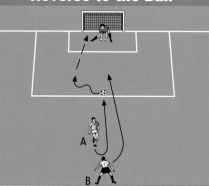	• Mark a line between B and the ball. B is allowed to start as soon as A crosses this line. • A starts out jogging backwards away from the ball. As soon as A "switches over" and starts sprinting toward the ball, B moves to try to stop A's shot.
Levels I/II		

Exercise 5	**Racing by Numbers**	**Variations**
Two groups of players stand next to a goal with goalkeeper, one on either side. The players in each group are numbered in sequence. The coach calls out a number and passes the ball toward the goal at the same time. The two players who have that number immediately start for the ball. Whichever one reaches it first tries to shoot, while the other one defends.		• Players start from various positions (lying on their stomachs, squatting, in push-up position, sitting with legs crossed). • The coach kicks high balls toward the goal. • Team competition: Which team can score more goals in ten rounds?
Levels II/III		

Exercise 6	**Juggling Start**	**Variations**
Players stand in pairs behind a starting line about 30 meters in front of a goal with goalkeeper. A third player (or the coach) stands just outside the penalty zone, juggling. As soon as the ball falls to the ground, the other two players start moving. Whichever one reaches the ball first tries to shoot, while the other tries to stop the shot.	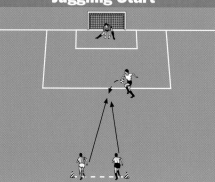	• 1 v. 1 to shoot; both players are allowed to shoot. Or, A is always the shooter and B tries to stop the shot. • Two players juggle one ball between them on the penalty zone line. • One player juggles at each corner of the penalty zone. As soon as one of the balls falls, the other two players start. • Players start from various positions.
Level II		

Exercise 7

B kicks a short pass between A's legs (A is standing with legs apart, facing the goal) and runs after the ball. A starts too, as soon as the ball comes into view, and tries to stop B's shot.

Levels I/II

Tunnel Pass

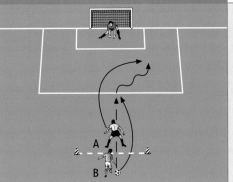

Variations

- 1 v. 1 to shoot; **both** players are allowed to shoot.
- A stands with legs apart, facing away from the goal (i.e. facing B).

Exercise 8

Players in Pair A stand 25 meters in front of a goal with goalkeeper, passing a ball back and forth . Other pairs stand behind waiting. After they've passed back and forth a few times, one of them passes toward the goal. This is the signal for the next pair in line to race to the ball.

Level II

Passing to Start

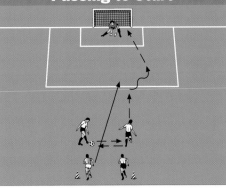

Variations

- The players in Pair A juggle the ball between them until one volleys toward the goal (starting signal). Whichever player reaches the ball first plays 1 v. 1 to score.
- One player in Pair A throws the ball to the other, who either heads it back or toward the goal; toward the goal is the starting signal for the next pair.

Exercise 9

Two players facing each other behind two lines 20 meters apart. The coach passes a ball into the field from one endline. Both players play 1 v. 1 for an opportunity to dribble across the opposite endline (one point).
The other pairs wait behind the first pair.

Levels I/II

1 v. 1 After Pass From Coach

Variations

- Same sequence, but with two small goals or two large goals with goal-keepers.
- As a starting signal, the coach throws a high ball into the field.
- Players start the race to the ball from various positions.
- Any defender who wins the ball has a chance to counterattack.

Sprinting Speed

Speed training should include more than just sprinting exercises, because sprinting is just one of the many complex speed-related requirements in soccer.

However, in the context of a comprehensive speed training program, exercises specifically designed to improve basic speed and sprinting speed are entirely appropriate.

They should be a more or less regular part of speed training, depending on your players' ability level and frequency of practice.

Supplementary Exercises

Sprinting Courses

General Information

- Sprinting exercises can be made more motivational by adding simple tasks and plays typical of the game.
- Running distances should be based on actual play: Sprints should be short, no longer than 20 meters.
- For optimal effectiveness, sprinting exercises must be run at full speed in order to activate the muscles in question.
- Effective training is impossible when players are tired or unmotivated and going through the motions.
- An intensive warm-up program is mandatory before each speed training session.
- Higher-level players need individualized speed training to fit their positions and individual abilities.

Variation 1
Sprint to a cone (from various starting positions).

Variation 2
Sprint through a staggered row of cones.

Variation 3
Sprint through a straight row of cones.

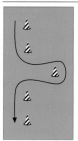

Variation 4
Sprint through a parcourse with one cone set off to the side.

Variation 5
Sprint through a parcourse with two cones set off to the side.

Variation 6
Sprint through a straight parcourse and circle around one cone.

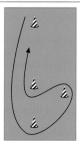

Variation 7
Sprint through a straight parcourse with the last cone set off to the side.

Variation 8
Sprint to Cone 1, back to the starting position and then to Cone 2.

Exercise 1	Reverse Sprint	Variations
Players line up and start jogging away from the goal line. At a signal, they turn around instantly and sprint back to the goal line. Which player will cross it first?		• Before sprinting back, players have to perform an extra task (e.g. turning around once, simulated header). • As a starting signal, the coach drops a ball (visual signal).

Levels I/II/III

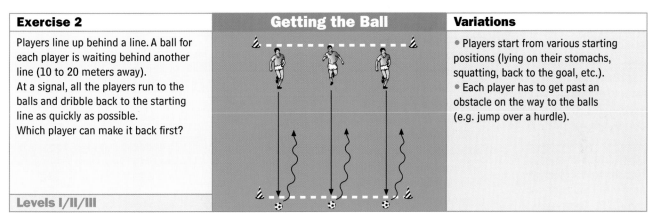

Exercise 2	Getting the Ball	Variations
Players line up behind a line. A ball for each player is waiting behind another line (10 to 20 meters away). At a signal, all the players run to the balls and dribble back to the starting line as quickly as possible. Which player can make it back first?		• Players start from various starting positions (lying on their stomachs, squatting, back to the goal, etc.). • Each player has to get past an obstacle on the way to the balls (e.g. jump over a hurdle).

Levels I/II/III

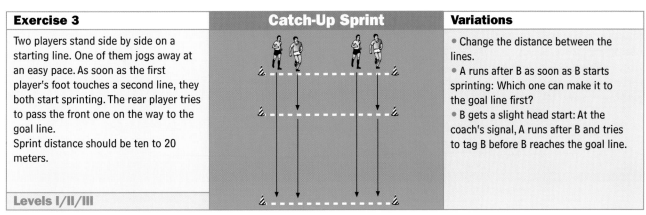

Exercise 3	Catch-Up Sprint	Variations
Two players stand side by side on a starting line. One of them jogs away at an easy pace. As soon as the first player's foot touches a second line, they both start sprinting. The rear player tries to pass the front one on the way to the goal line. Sprint distance should be ten to 20 meters.		• Change the distance between the lines. • A runs after B as soon as B starts sprinting: Which one can make it to the goal line first? • B gets a slight head start: At the coach's signal, A runs after B and tries to tag B before B reaches the goal line.

Levels I/II/III

Game Action Speed

"Game action speed" combines all the elements of soccer-specific speed into one concept. Optimal game action speed enables players to execute technical/tactical actions accurately and appropriately, at top speed and with maximum intensity.

This requires players to master all the coordinative, conditional and cognitive abilities that make up soccer-specific speed. All these components are intimately interconnected; all of them have to be trained together in order to achieve real improvements in game action speed. The best way to do this is to confront players with constantly changing game situations, which they have to resolve instantly and appropriately.

Basic Exercises

Exercises With Time, Opposition Pressure

General Information
- Try to structure exercises so that they repeatedly confront players with new game situations. This forces players to resolve each situation quickly, intelligently and appropriately.
- Don't overwork your players! However, most of the complex exercises designed to improve game action speed do require a broad spectrum of technical/tactical skills. The pace of play should always allow players to work out good tactical solutions.
- Make sure that exertion levels are well-balanced, alternating short, intensive exercises with long, active rest periods.

5 v. 3 on Two Goals
Two groups play 5 v. 3 on two goals with goalkeepers in a field twice the size of the penalty zone. The group of five is limited to two touches in a row, while the other group has unlimited touches.

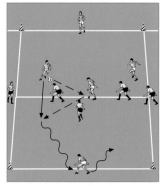

3 v. 3 on Goal Lines
Two teams play 3 v. 3: One plays on the two endlines; the other plays on the sidelines. Each team has another player behind each of its goal lines. Any attacker who dribbles across a goal line immediately trades places with the attacker waiting there. Change direction

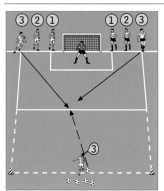

Expanding Groups
Players form two teams of three; the players on each team are numbered. The coach calls out a number and passes in front of the goal. The two identified playersgo to the ball. The coach calls out the other numbers so that the 1 v. 1 becomes a 2 v. 2 and ultimately a 3 v. 3.

Exercise 1

Two teams play 4 v. 4 in the penalty area on one goal with goalkeeper. Each team has an additional player waiting outside the penalty area to help secure the ball by receiving and passing.

Playing time: four to five minutes.

Levels II/III

4 v. 4 With Backfield Passer

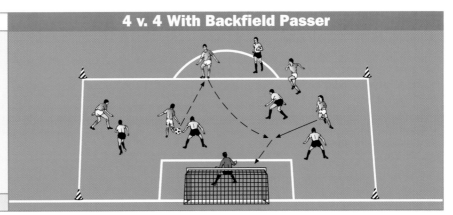

Exercise 2

Two teams play 4 v. 4 on two goals with goalkeepers. Each team has four additional players (passers), one on each side of each goal. Attackers must score on one touch from passers. When attackers score, they keep the ball and attack in the opposite direction.
Playing time: four minutes.

Level III

4 v. 4 With Passer

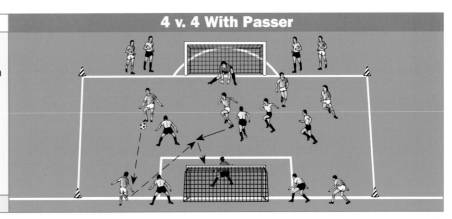

Exercise 3

Two teams play 4 v. 4 in the penalty area on two goals with goalkeepers. Each team has two additional players (wing players) in marked wing zones, one on either side of the penalty area. Headers set up by wing players count double (or triple).

Playing time: five minutes.

Level II

4 v. 4 With Wing Players

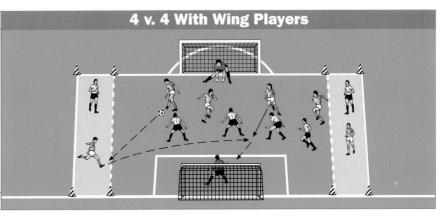

Exercise 4

Two teams play 6 v. 3 in the penalty area. The six defenders try to keep the ball away from the attackers as long as possible. They are limited to three touches in a row. If the attackers win the ball, their job is to shoot as quickly as possible.
Playing time: three minutes.

Levels II/III

6 v. 3 in the Penalty Zone

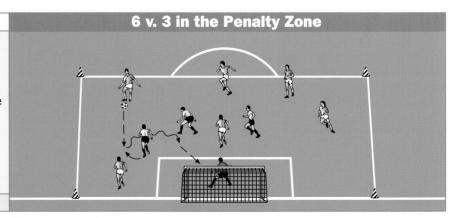

Exercise 5

Two teams play 6 v. 3 in the penalty zone on three goals. The team of six is limited to one touch (or two in a row) and attacks on the goal with goalkeeper. The other team has unlimited touches and attacks on two small goals on the penalty area line.
Playing time: three minutes.

Level III

6 v. 3 on Three Goals

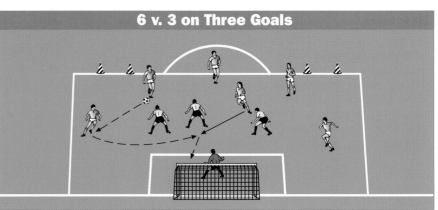

Exercise 6

Three (!) different teams of four play in a 20 x 20-meter square. Whichever team has the ball plays 4 v. 8 to keep it as long as possible. If they lose it, they switch roles with the team that won it. The "team" of eight must pass directly.
Playing time: five minutes.

Level III

4 v. 8 in a Field

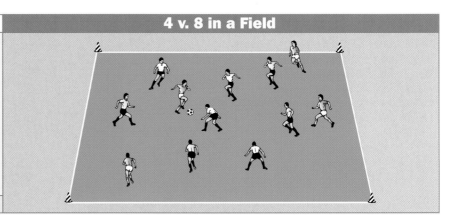

Exercise 7

Two teams play 6 v. 6 in a field between the penalty area and the centerline. One small goal on each side of this field. Team A defends Goals 1 and 2 and attacks on Goals 3 and 4; Team B does the opposite.
Encourage fast plays and quick attack/defense shifts.
Playing time: six minutes.

Level II

Diagonal Goals

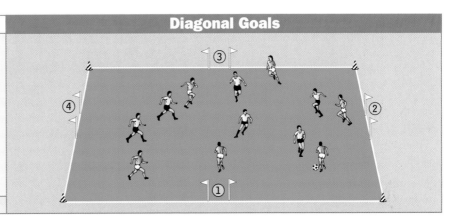

Exercise 8

Two teams play 7 v. 7 on two goals in a field half. The following rule applies: If one attacker has dribbled before passing, then the pass receiver has to pass directly. The next attacker then has unlimited touches, etc.
Playing time: seven minutes.

Levels II/III

Limited/Unlimited Touches

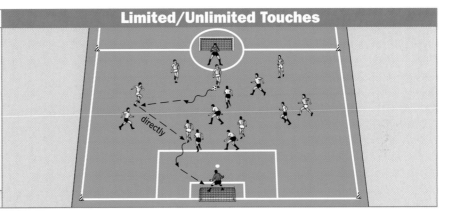

Exercise 9

Two teams play 9 v. 7 to maintain possession in a marked field (see illustration).
The players on the team of nine are limited to two touches in a row, while their opponents have unlimited touches. Defenders try to win the ball back as quickly as possible!
Playing time: seven minutes.

Levels II/III

7 v. 9 in a Field

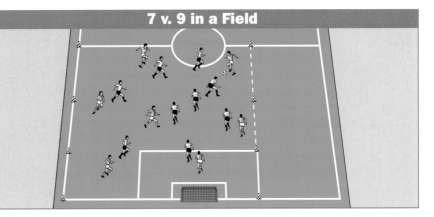

Running Coordination

Soccer players have to master an extremely wide variety of running movements: short- and long-distance running, with sudden changes in speed and direction, etc.

A flexible mastery of basic running skills (length and frequency of steps, rhythm and running technique) is the "coordinative basis" that defines a soccer player's running performance. Youth players, in particular, tend to have serious problems in this area⁻which makes systematic running training all the more important. Don't forget to make it fun too!

Supplementary Exercises

The ABC's of Running

- Our "ABC's of Running" is a collection of important exercises for systematic training in basic running technique.
- Try to use these exercises in your practice sessions as often as possible; for example, during warm-up.
- Coaches need to know basic characteristics of each exercise in order to be able to help players.
- Teach each basic element carefully and systematically.
- For motivational purposes, exercises can be combined with play-oriented follow-up actions (e.g. shooting).
- Players should be fresh for running training.
- Demand maximum effort and focus.
- Maximum distance should be 20 meters.

Skipping
- Extend the foot, knee and hip of takeoff leg completely.
- Set the foot down.

Leaping
- Swing the calf forward and land on the whole sole of the foot each time.

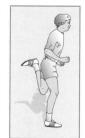

Heel Kicks
- Keep thigh perfectly vertical.
- Set foot down on toes; heel shouldn't touch down.

Ankle Work
- Practice "propulsion" by alternately flexing and extending the ankles.

Knee Lifts
- Lift thigh up quickly.
- Set foot down.
- Extend leg completely.

One-Legged Jumps
- From the ankle, with knee extended; don't stop between jumps.

Fast Knee Lifts
- Like knee lifts, but faste.
- Don't raise your knees as high.

High Kicks
- Swing calf forward at the end of each kick.
- Work the arms energetically.

Exercise 1

Place four to seven poles on the ground across the running path, evenly spaced (40 to 60 meters apart). Players run over the poles at top speed.

Levels II/III

Pole Runs

Variations

- Run over two poles forwards, then one pole backwards.
- The distances between poles vary; adjust the frequency of your steps accordingly.
- Take lots of tiny steps over the poles.
- Do lots of short two-legged jumps over the poles.
- Sprint a short distance (ten meters) after the last pole.

Exercise 2

Set up five or six cones in a zigzag pattern. Players run from cone to cone at top speed. Organize small competitions if possible, e.g. with two courses side by side.

Levels II/III

Cone Runs

Variations

- Run sideways, briefly touching each cone.
- Run forward, circling each cone.
- Run backwards as fast.
- Competition with follow-up play: Two players run toward a ball. The winner passes it to a third player, who shoots at a goal with goalkeeper (shot = one point, scoring shot = two).

Exercise 3

Players form groups of three. Two players are "turning points" and stand about five meters apart. The third player runs around them three to five times, then players switch roles. Organize competitions between groups.

Levels I/II

Turning Points

Variations

- Both "turning points" kneel on hands and knees; the runner has to jump over them.
- Same sequence, but the "turning points" squat on hands and knees, and the runner "leapfrogs" them.
- The "turning points" squat with both arms extended ; the runner has to jump over both arms (pausing between jumps).

Takeoff Power

In soccer, the most important form of power is takeoff power. That's because the game tends to be dominated by dynamic and even explosive movements like quick sprints, sudden changes of direction and explosive shots. However, takeoff power also has a strong influence on speed, which means that systematic takeoff power training is an ideal way to improve sprinting speed. One good way to do this is with jumping exercises. You can also create interesting, motivational takeoff power exercises with various obstacles, especially for indoor training in winter.

Supplementary Exercises

Obstacle Jumping Courses

General Information
• In addition to obstacle courses, you can also use the following types of jumps to improve takeoff power:
 – one-legged jumps (right/left)
 – two-legged jumps
 – running jumps
 – sideways/backwards jumps
• When using obstacles, always adapt the exercises to the age and ability level of your players (don't overwork the spine).
• Jumping in and out of tires is ideal for children and beginners, while older and more advanced players can use boxes and benches.
• Hurdles and tall boxes are primarily for the highest levels.
• Be sure to accompany these exercises with full-body strengthening and plenty of warm-up time.

Cones
• Run forwards
• Run sideways.
• Do knee lifts.
• Do fast knee lifts.
• Jump over the cones without extra steps in between.

Barriers
• Explosive squat jumps, grasping the bar.
• Explosive straddle jumps, grasping the bar.
• Explosive scissors jumps, grasping the bar.
• Front vaults.

Hurdles
• Running jumps over the hurdles (varying the number of steps).
• Jumps over hurdles, pausing after each one.
• Jumps over hurdles, pausing after each one.

Low Boxes
• Running jumps over the boxes (varying the number of steps).
• Two-legged jumps, pausing after each one.
• One-legged jumps.
• Sideways jumps.
• Fast knee lifts on top.

Exercise 1

Divide a space into two sections: Players hop on one leg to the first cone, wait a moment and then **sprint** across the goal line at the coach's signal.

Levels II/III

Takeoff Power/Speed

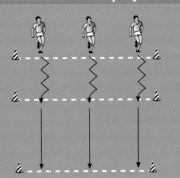

Variations

- Same sequence, but with running jumps to the first cone.
- Same sequence, but with two-legged jumps, pausing after each jump.
- Same sequence, but with explosive skipping.
- Easy run to the first cone, three explosive squat jumps and a race to the goal line at the coach's signal.

Exercise 2

Using cones, lay out three equally long line segments at right angles to each other.

Organize various running/jumping competitions between two groups: Explosive skipping on Section 1, sideways run on Section 2, short wait for a starting signal, then sprint on Section 3.

Levels II/III

Zigzag Course

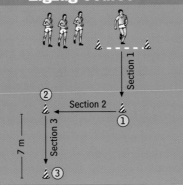

Variations

- Section 1: fast knee lifts; Section 2: sideways run; Section 3: sprint.
- Section 1: simulated header with a running start; Section 2: sideways run; starting signal; Section 3: sprint.
- Section 1: explosive skipping; Section 2: normal run; two squat jumps at Cone 2; starting signal; sprint.

Exercise 3

Player form groups of three: In each group, two players kneel, facing each other, reach out and link hands. The third player does a two-legged jump over their arms from a standing start. Players switch roles after ten jumps.

Levels I/II

Jumping With Partners

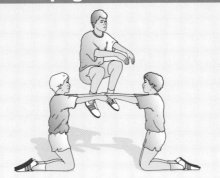

Variations

- The jumper takes a short running start, takes off from one leg, pulls the knee of that leg up to the chest and lands on the same leg. Then the jumper turns around and jumps again.
- The jumper does two-legged sideways jumps.
- The jumper takes a short running start and leaps over the arms.

Power and Mobility

Power in Soccer

Since playing styles in today's professional soccer are becoming more dynamic and athletic, "power" has become an important aspect of condition for soccer players. The importance of soccer-specific power training continues to increase.

But don't get the wrong idea: Soccer players are not bodybuilders! The object is not simply to achieve maximum power but to achieve a level of power that's optimally adapted to the demands of the game.

What are the special types of power that soccer players need?

Takeoff Power

A look at typical movement sequences in soccer makes it clear that the most important type of power in soccer is undoubtedly takeoff power. The game is dominated by dynamic, often explosive movements (abrupt stops and changes of direction, quick sprints and explosive shots) that all depend on plenty of takeoff power.

Reserve (Takeoff) Power

Good soccer players can't do without reserve (takeoff) power either. Ultimately, players have to be able to keep playing a dynamic game for the entire 90 minutes of a match, without lowering their level of performance. Explosive shots and well-timed saves can make the difference between victory and defeat, especially in the final minutes of the game.

The Importance of Full-Body Power

• For soccer players, muscular power has a direct influence on performance. For example, increased power speeds up movement (sprints, changes of direction). Technical precision and efficiency (e.g. powerful passes, dynamic headers) also depend on certain types of power.

• We also should not overlook the fact that all-around athletic development makes players tougher and more assertive, particularly in direct 1 v. 1 play against opponents.

• Besides the immediate positive effects that improving power has on performance, strength training also helps to protect players and prevent both injuries and long-term wear and tear due to the specialized demands of the game.

• In match play, player's bodies are subjected to extreme forces from both outside and

Optimal speed in movement – here, for example, sprinting speed – depends on a solid power base.

Illustration 7

The Elements of Power in Soccer

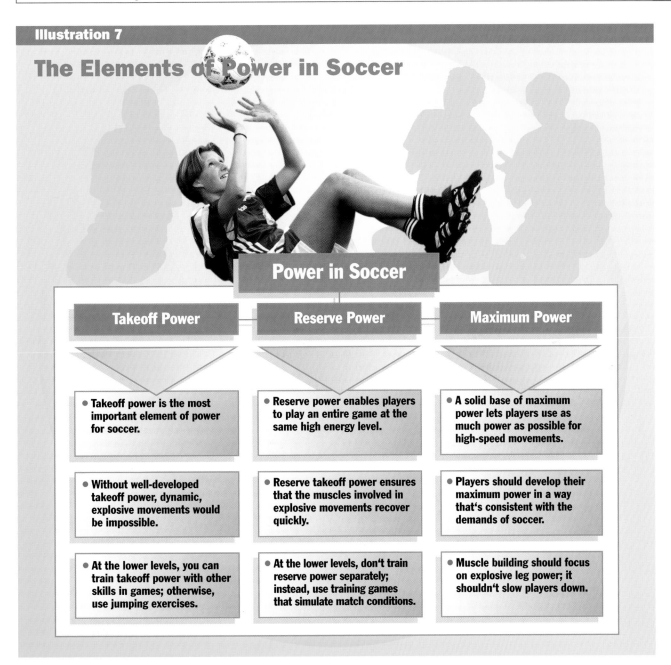

Power in Soccer

Takeoff Power	Reserve Power	Maximum Power
• Takeoff power is the most important element of power for soccer.	• Reserve power enables players to play an entire game at the same high energy level.	• A solid base of maximum power lets players use as much power as possible for high-speed movements.
• Without well-developed takeoff power, dynamic, explosive movements would be impossible.	• Reserve takeoff power ensures that the muscles involved in explosive movements recover quickly.	• Players should develop their maximum power in a way that's consistent with the demands of soccer.
• At the lower levels, you can train takeoff power with other skills in games; otherwise, use jumping exercises.	• At the lower levels, don't train reserve power separately; instead, use training games that simulate match conditions.	• Muscle building should focus on explosive leg power; it shouldn't slow players down.

inside. For example, if a movement is suddenly blocked by a collision with another player, the result may be twisted or hyperextended muscles. A well-developed musculature is the soccer player's "armor" and the best insurance against damage to bones, ligaments and joints.

• However, short-term injuries aren't the only problem soccer players face. Many players suffer from long-term problems that regularly force them to take time off from practice and competition.

Usually, these problems are caused by one-sided muscular demands connected with the typical movements of soccer.

The result is an imbalance between "soccer muscles" and the rest of the musculature, i.e. the posture muscles, which we rarely think about. Soccer players tend to have two definite weak points:

1. shoulder and upper body muscles
2. torso-stabilizing muscles, especially the stomach and back muscles.

These muscular imbalances and weaknesses are frequently the cause of poor performance and chronic complaints. A functional strength training program designed to even out muscular imbalances can help with these problems and has a lasting preventive effect as well.

Mobility in Soccer

Good mobility also influences player's performance in a number of ways.

Mobility and Condition

When mobility is well-developed, movements become more efficient and require less energy. This means that players don't get tired as quickly. Therefore, mobility indirectly improves endurance. It also has a positive effect on power and speed, since mobility training breaks down muscular "blockers."

Mobility and Technique

Well-developed mobility is what enables players to execute soccer techniques perfectly. For example, "stiff-hipped" players are rarely able to incorporate convincing upper-body movements into their fakes. If players are unable to extend their ankles sufficiently (preferably completely), then they won't be able to execute accurate in-step kicks. And good hip mobility is essential to executing a perfect turning kick.

Mobility and the Risk of Injury

Short sprints, abrupt changes of direction and explosive sprints and shots are typical movements in soccer. These extremely intense movements place extreme demands on muscles, which increase the risk of injury. Shortened muscles (and the ligaments connected to them) are more susceptible. So naturally, flexibility has a positive effect:

Fakes that truly fool opponents depend on two things: deceptive upper body movements and good mobility.

Illustration 8

Mandatory Program Before Practice and Match Play

Mobility Exercises

During Practice

- Include mobility training in every warm-up session, in the form of soccer-specific stretching exercises.

- Special mobility training sessions are only appropriate for upper-level players.

- Tailor your mobility training program to your players' individual "problem areas."

Before Matches

- Adjust the amount of stretching and structure of exercises to fit external conditions.

- Don't start stretching until you've activated the heart and circulatory system (warm-up run).

- Stretching before matches is to achieve optimal pre-game condition, not to improve mobility.

Youth Training

Mobility Training for Children and Young Adults

- Even the youngest players (6- to 10-year-olds) need to stabilize their mobility with the help of age-appropriate (i.e. versatile and play-oriented) exercises.
- Since children have such a pronounced need to be active, the majority of mobility exercises for youth players should be active and dynamic rather than passive and static.
- We can prepare children for the future demands of practice and match play by working carefully and comprehensively to build an age-appropriate (= "playful") gymnastic foundation, and also by consciously cultivating a positive attitude toward mobility training. Most importantly, youth mobility training counteracts muscular imbalances at the early stages.
- By age 14, youth players usually start to experience a growth spurt that causes mobility to deteriorate. That's why focused mobility training is indispensable at this age. However, be sure to avoid overworking the passive locomotor system (particularly the spine) by focusing on intensive passive stretching.

It helps the muscles involved handle the strain and avoid being injured.

A comprehensive, systematic mobility training program is an essential part of every practice session and pre-game workout.

Power and Mobility: Connections

For soccer players, power and mobility are intimately interconnected. Power and mobility can influence one another both positively and negatively.

Therefore, any focused strength training program must be accompanied by a coordinated mobility training program. Strengthening alone, over long periods of time, only leads to shortened muscles. If this shortness is not counteracted by mobility training, the musculature will remain shortened indefinitely. However, shortened muscles are not capable of exerting their maximum power (necessary for fast, high-power movements, for example). They're also more susceptible to injury.

Stretching tends to make the muscles and ligaments more flexible, but stretching must always be accompanied by focused strengthening exercises, to stabilize the musculature.

To repeat: Strength training must always be accompanied by a coordinated mobility training program and vice versa. And to supply the musculature with blood and energy, strength training should always be followed by endurance training.

Illustration 9

Power and Mobility by Level

Level I

Power: How and Why

- Even lower-level players need a certain minimum amount of power in order to be able to handle the challenges of the game (e.g. explosive shots, sprints, tough 1 v. 1 play).
- However, once again, the rule is: The less often you practice, the less time you have for isolated strength training. That's why we integrate strength training into games.

Mobility: How and Why

- At the lower levels, the main benefit of mobility training is injury prevention.
- Teach players about the positive effects of focused, dedicated stretching before practice sessions and matches.
- At the same time, stretching alone is not sufficient to prepare players for practice and match play.

Level II

Power: How and Why

- Play-oriented training, i.e. complex games and exercises, can only do so much to improve power and takeoff power.
- Therefore, you should regularly supplement these exercises with special programs to increase soccer-specific power: circle exercises, various jumping exercises and condition stretching.

Mobility: How and Why

- A player's individual level of mobility influences technical quality and precision. Increased technical demands require mobility to be better and more soccer-specific.
- Stretching before and after practice has to be more comprehensive and individualized.
- Encourage players to take the initiative for their own training.

Level III

Power: How and Why

- Today's high-speed soccer, with its high athletic demands, is impossible without well-developed power.
- Players at the higher youth and amateur levels need to improve their power on an individual basis, with a systematic program of specialized strengthening exercises.
- This type of specialized strength training is a long-term project.

Mobility: How and Why

- Warm-up stretching should be appropriate to practice conditions (e.g. weather), upcoming demands (training objectives) and each player's individual mental and physical characteristics (e.g. "problem muscles.")
- Muscle and joint tests form the basis for individualized mobility training.
- Encourage players to take the initiative for their own training.

Stretching Exercises

Almost every team does some stretching exercises before practice and match play, regardless of ability level. However, they often do them half-heartedly, and sometimes they do them wrong.

Stretching exercises should be chosen carefully to fit training objectives, practice situation, individual characteristics, etc. Pre-game stretching programs, for example, should be structured differently from stretching programs designed specifically to increase mobility.

Tips on Stretching

1. Holding the stretch gets the best results.

There are lots of different stretching exercises, each with its own advantages and disadvantages; however, the most appropriate method is the "held" stretch. As a result, all the stretching exercises described in this chapter are oriented toward that technique. The player eases into the optimal stretch (final position) and holds it for ten to 15 seconds. This technique is easy to learn and does not require any additional equipment.

2. Stretching alone is not a full warm-up.

Warm-up stretching should always come after ten to 15 minutes of running or technique exercises with the ball. This warms up the large muscle groups, activates the circulation and raises body temperature. Without this groundwork, muscles will not stretch to their optimal length.

3. Combine basic exercises with individually tailored stretching.

Typical soccer movement sequences lead to soccer-specific shortening of individual muscles. For example, after hundreds of shooting movements, the hip muscles and leg biceps tend to be shortened, as well as the calf muscles. A minimal stretching program with a few standard exercises will take care of this. Additional specialized stretching exercises (e.g. toning the shoulder muscles, for goalkeepers) must be adapted to each player's individual characteristics (e.g. old injuries).

4. Always adapt the stretching to the situation.

In addition to players' individual needs, a stretching program must also take into account a variety of external factors. For example, if the weather is wet and cold, or if ground conditions are unacceptable, then stretching exercises in the locker room can be a workable alternative.

Furthermore, certain types of training (e.g. shooting or speed training) require especially intensive preparation for the muscle groups involved.

5. Always remember the following basic principles of stretching:

- Feel your way gradually toward your own personal final position.
- Hold the final position for ten to 15 seconds. You should feel a mild pull.
- If players are having trouble achieving the end position, leave the exercise out.
- Don't swing, bounce or rock.
- Breathing should be regular and smooth; relax!
- Loosen up your muscles periodically.
- Always stretch both sides (right and left).

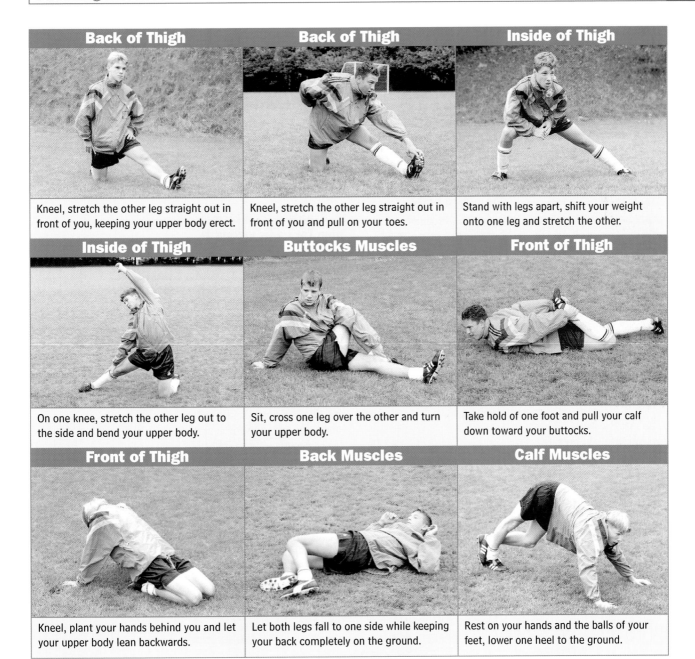

Back of Thigh

Kneel, stretch the other leg straight out in front of you, keeping your upper body erect.

Back of Thigh

Kneel, stretch the other leg straight out in front of you and pull on your toes.

Inside of Thigh

Stand with legs apart, shift your weight onto one leg and stretch the other.

Inside of Thigh

On one knee, stretch the other leg out to the side and bend your upper body.

Buttocks Muscles

Sit, cross one leg over the other and turn your upper body.

Front of Thigh

Take hold of one foot and pull your calf down toward your buttocks.

Front of Thigh

Kneel, plant your hands behind you and let your upper body lean backwards.

Back Muscles

Let both legs fall to one side while keeping your back completely on the ground.

Calf Muscles

Rest on your hands and the balls of your feet, lower one heel to the ground.

Strengthening Exercises

Athletic gymnastic exercises are often neglected. The result is mediocre performance, caused by a lack of power. Lots of teams are unable to turn their technical and tactical advantages into victory, because they don't have the athletic abilities needed to win key 1 v. 1's.

The only long-term remedy is a program of regularly scheduled exercises to increase basic power. These strengthening exercises are especially appropriate for the warm-up or cooldown phases of practice.

Also, you should always encourage players to practice gymnastic exercises on their own at home.

Tips on Strengthening

1. The main objective is to increase basic power, so each practice session should include exercises to strengthen the entire body.

Full-body strengthening improves all-around performance, corrects posture problems, and is the foundation for a more soccer-specific strength training.

The torso muscles absorb an enormous amount of strain from the rest of the body (mainly from the leg joints, in soccer). The more dynamic a players' movements are, the stronger the stomach and back muscles have to be.

The following rules apply to basic strength training:
• Avoid ineffective or damaging exercises (for example, curving the spine excessively) at all costs!
• A gymnastic program for full-body strengthening should focus primarily on the back and stomach muscles.
• Players should be able to execute every exercise perfectly. Adapt the level of difficulty to individual players' abilities as necessary.
• If you feel pain, stop the exercise.
• Breathing should not be forced.
• The more intensive the exertion is, the more intensive the regeneration should be.

2. Create a long-term plan for basic strength training.

Strengthening programs cannot create long-lasting benefits if they're only practiced sporadically. The only way to achieve positive results is to make strength training part of every practice session. It's also important to teach players about the function and value of strength training; for one thing, because it motivates them to do extra training on their own at home.

At-home strength training should focus on individual weak points revealed by strength tests. It may be possible to work together with a qualified local gym.

3. Make basic power training interesting.

Stomach and back muscles, in particular, should only be strengthened with static or slow-moving exercises. However, these exercises should not be monotonous or boring.

A standard exercise, for example, might be enriched with a variety of new exercises, and in many cases you can improve motivation by including the ball.

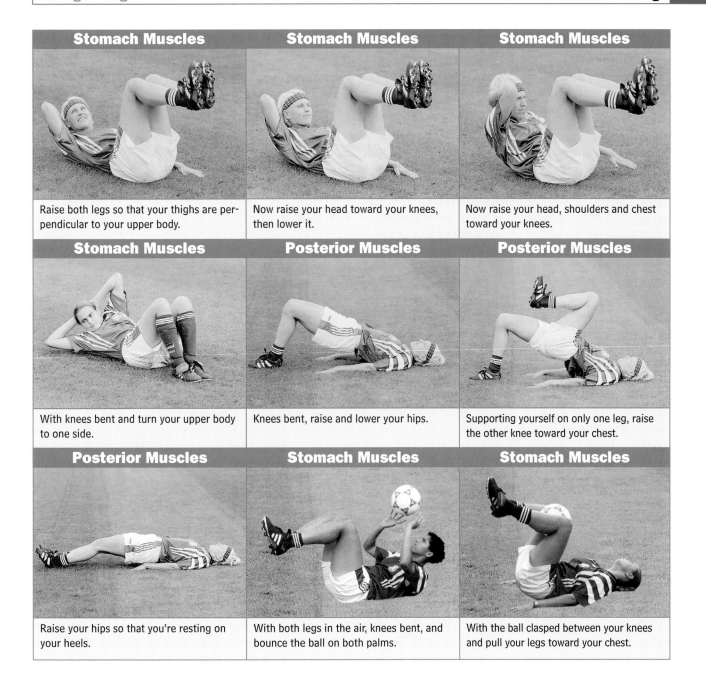

Stomach Muscles
Raise both legs so that your thighs are perpendicular to your upper body.

Stomach Muscles
Now raise your head toward your knees, then lower it.

Stomach Muscles
Now raise your head, shoulders and chest toward your knees.

Stomach Muscles
With knees bent and turn your upper body to one side.

Posterior Muscles
Knees bent, raise and lower your hips.

Posterior Muscles
Supporting yourself on only one leg, raise the other knee toward your chest.

Posterior Muscles
Raise your hips so that you're resting on your heels.

Stomach Muscles
With both legs in the air, knees bent, and bounce the ball on both palms.

Stomach Muscles
With the ball clasped between your knees and pull your legs toward your chest.

Stretching Exercises for Soccer Players

Every soccer-specific gymnastic exercise should contain elements that improve power, mobility and coordination. In order to make them more attractive, it's important to provide plenty of variety. Individual exercises with the ball and exercises with partners are ideal.

It All Depends on Stretching and Strengthening

Tip: Gymnastic exercises should be a regular part of practice. They should also always be consistent with the muscular demands of the game.

- Certain muscles are neglected due to the one-sided demands of the game and tend to be weak; **strengthen** these muscles.
- Other muscles support the muscles that are important for soccer performance; **strengthen** these too.
- Certain muscles are overworked by the demands of the game and tend to be shortened; **stretch** these muscles.
- The muscles that support the "performance muscles" should also be **stretched**.
- Every program of gymnastic exercises should include full-body strengthening exercises, particularly for the torso muscles.
- Along with strengthening exercises, you should always offer stretching exercises as well, in order to prevent muscle shortness. On the other hand, strengthening exercises are required to stabilize the mobility achieved by stretching.
- To avoid overexertion, alternate between different areas of the body.

Individual Exercises	Exercises With the Ball	Partner Exercises
Can be tailored to each player's personal needs.	The ball: an ideal tool for making exercises more attractive.	Partner exercises also serve to improve group dynamics.

Illustration 10

Functional Stretching Exercises for Soccer Players

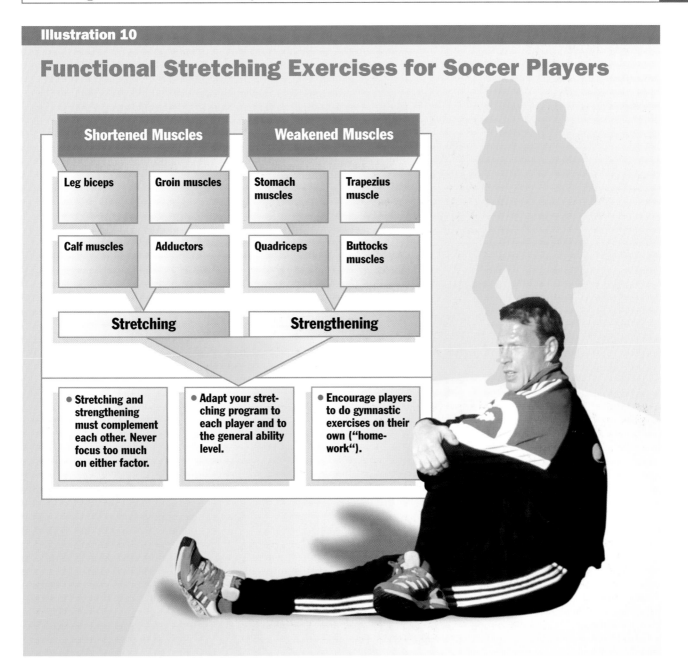

Shortened Muscles		Weakened Muscles	
Leg biceps	Groin muscles	Stomach muscles	Trapezius muscle
Calf muscles	Adductors	Quadriceps	Buttocks muscles
Stretching		**Strengthening**	

- Stretching and strengthening must complement each other. Never focus too much on either factor.

- Adapt your stretching program to each player and to the general ability level.

- Encourage players to do gymnastic exercises on their own ("homework").

Stretching Programs (Individual Exercises)

A

1. Extend one leg straight out to one side, bending from the waist.

2. Raise your head and rest your weight on your heels.

3. Clasp your hands around one knee, stretch the leg and pull it in toward your body.

B

1. Support yourself on one leg and extend the other out to the side.

2. Stretch your arms out in front of you and "roll up" your upper body.

3. Kneel on one knee, stretch the other leg out in front of you and grasp your toes.

C

1. Take a deep lunge step and shift your weight onto the front leg.

2. With your knees bent, raise your upper body toward your knees.

3. Lie on your stomach, take hold of one foot and pull your calf down.

D

1. Take a deep lunge step and shift your weight onto the front leg.

2. Take hold of one elbow with the other hand, pull it down and back.

3. Kneel on one knee and push your hips forward.

Stretching Programs (Individual Exercises)

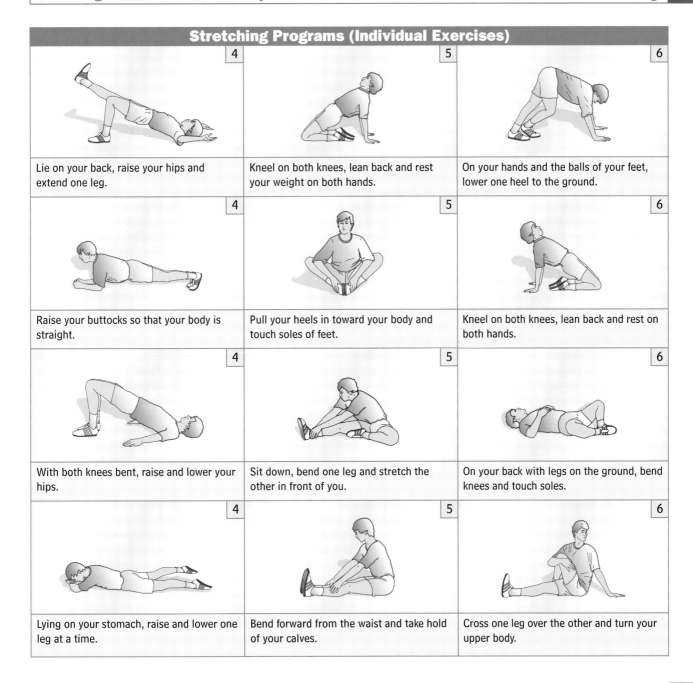

4 Lie on your back, raise your hips and extend one leg.

5 Kneel on both knees, lean back and rest your weight on both hands.

6 On your hands and the balls of your feet, lower one heel to the ground.

4 Raise your buttocks so that your body is straight.

5 Pull your heels in toward your body and touch soles of feet.

6 Kneel on both knees, lean back and rest on both hands.

4 With both knees bent, raise and lower your hips.

5 Sit down, bend one leg and stretch the other in front of you.

6 On your back with legs on the ground, bend knees and touch soles.

4 Lying on your stomach, raise and lower one leg at a time.

5 Bend forward from the waist and take hold of your calves.

6 Cross one leg over the other and turn your upper body.

Stretching Programs (Partner Exercises)

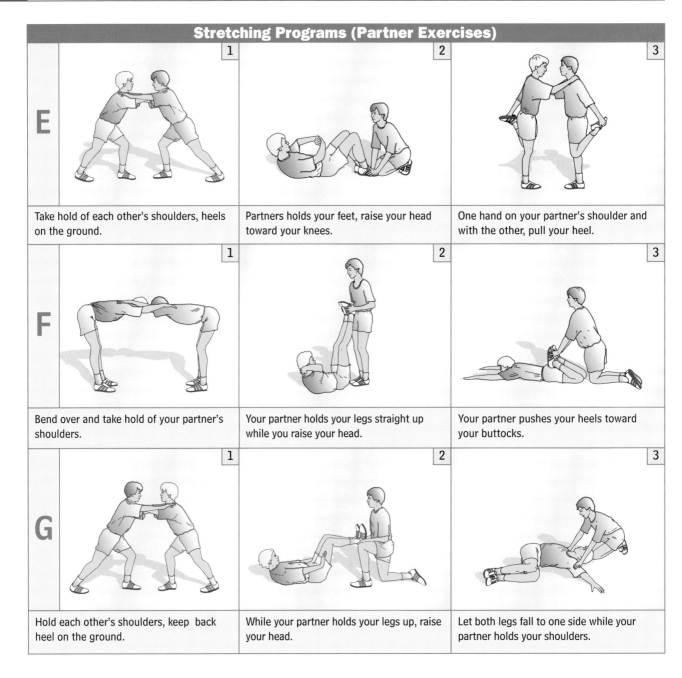

E

1 Take hold of each other's shoulders, heels on the ground.

2 Partners holds your feet, raise your head toward your knees.

3 One hand on your partner's shoulder and with the other, pull your heel.

F

1 Bend over and take hold of your partner's shoulders.

2 Your partner holds your legs straight up while you raise your head.

3 Your partner pushes your heels toward your buttocks.

G

1 Hold each other's shoulders, keep back heel on the ground.

2 While your partner holds your legs up, raise your head.

3 Let both legs fall to one side while your partner holds your shoulders.

Stretching Programs (Partner Exercises)

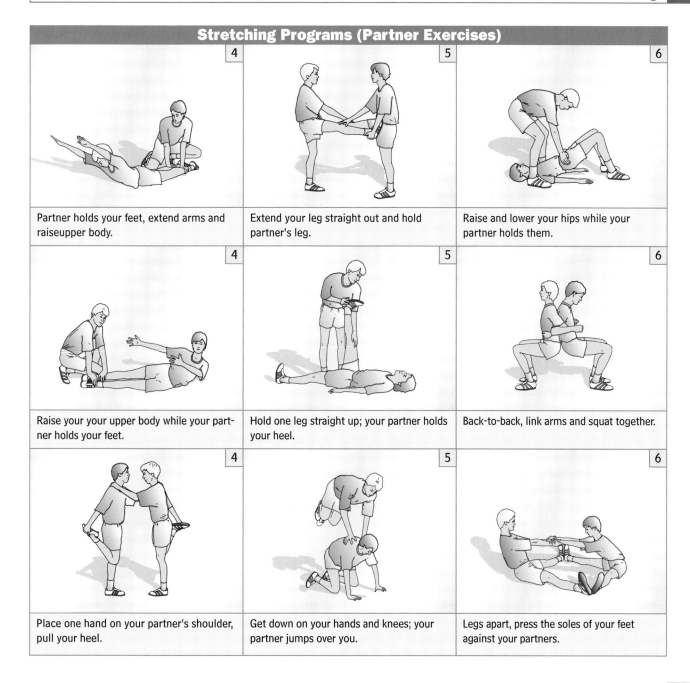

4 Partner holds your feet, extend arms and raiseupper body.

5 Extend your leg straight out and hold partner's leg.

6 Raise and lower your hips while your partner holds them.

4 Raise your your upper body while your partner holds your feet.

5 Hold one leg straight up; your partner holds your heel.

6 Back-to-back, link arms and squat together.

4 Place one hand on your partner's shoulder, pull your heel.

5 Get down on your hands and knees; your partner jumps over you.

6 Legs apart, press the soles of your feet against your partners.

CHAPTER 7

GOAL-KEEPER TRAINING

The Challenge of Goalkeeping

What Is Goalkeeping?

A great goalkeeper can be the backbone of the team. Sometimes the goalkeeper single-handedly decides the outcome of a match. On the other hand, a single mistake on the part of the keeper can instantly turn victory into defeat. In this context, the goalkeeper has a very important position on the team.

In order to develop effective methods and exercises for goalkeeper training, the first thing to consider is what a goalkeeper actually does. For goalkeepers, as for field players, performance breaks down into four areas:

- technique
- tactics
- condition
- psychology.

All of these areas influence each other in innumerable ways; a play-oriented goalkeeper training program must take all of these interconnections into account.

Each individual goalkeeper's strengths lie at various points along this spectrum: One may be agile and bold, while another is calm and reliable, with "nerves of steel." One may be famous for a good sense of the game, intelligent positional play and never making a wrong move; another has excellent reflexes and plays a mostly intuitive game. The best goalkeepers combine all of these qualities in one person, by and large. In top-level soccer, compensating for weaknesses in some areas with excellence in others is simply not an option. The top goalkeepers have to "do it all!"

Goalkeeper Technique

Well-developed technique prepares soccer players to handle even the most difficult game situations. This is just as true for goalkeepers as it is for fielders. As a goalkeeper, the more confident and comprehensive your command of technique is, the more effective you can be at blocking shots.

Goalkeeper technique training is not just a matter of repeating the same movement sequences over and over again; it's about making the exercises so varied and so similar to actual match play that goalkeepers learn how to use the right technique every time, in a situation that's constantly changing. In principle, a goalkeeper's movements should be as close as possible to the "ideal technique," but at the same time, they also have to be tailored to individual characteristics (= personal style).

Goalkeeper Tactics

Essentially, the goalkeeper's tactics can be divided into: positional play, coming off the line, and attack building.

Positional play is especially important in normal game situations and on set plays in which the ball is at rest (i.e. corner kicks and free kicks with a defensive wall). Coming off the line is important in 1 v. 1's against solo

The only way to stop hard, well-aimed penalty kicks is to anticipate and move to the "right" side.

Illustration 1

What Does a Goalkeeper Need?

Technique
- Catching balls on the ground and in the air
- Punching out high balls
- Jumping, diving and landing
- Winning the ball from a dribbling attacker
- Punting, throwing and passing the ball (distribution)

Condition
- Mobility/agility
- Speed (action and reaction speed)
- Basic endurance
- Jumping power
- Physical fitness

Tactics
- Positional play on shots from various positions and distances
- Positional play on crosses and passes in front of the goal
- Positional play on set plays
- "Directing" the defense
- Thinking and acting as the "first attacker"

Psychology
- Motivation and positive attitude
- Willingness to get involved
- Concentration
- Courage/willingness to take risks
- Assertiveness
- Self-confidence

attackers, crosses from the outside, and occasionally when the opposition plays a long pass to the front of the attack (i.e. into open space). Attack building is primarily a matter of getting your team's attack off to the best start possible.

Goalkeeper Condition

A look at the goalkeeper's "job description" makes it clear that goalkeepers need to be in excellent condition too.

Basic Endurance

Basic endurance insures that a goalkeeper will be able to play dynamically and at a high level of quality throughout an entire match. More than perhaps any other player, the goalkeeper needs to be able to play with maximum concentration, precision and speed, even in the final minutes.

Takeoff Power/Jumping Power

In general, proper positional play makes risky "flying saves" on the goal line unnecessary. However, goalkeepers will always face situations that require explosive jumps, such as intercepting crosses.

Mobility/Agility

The more agile the goalkeeper, the more flexible the goalkeeping! Goalkeepers have to be able to stop the ball in all kinds of situations, in all positions and in conjunction with all kinds of movements (while running forwards, backwards and sideways; while jumping; just after standing up; etc.).

Action/Reaction Speed

Almost all goalkeeper plays are fast, dynamic and explosive. In many situations, reflexes are the only solution. In short: Goalkeepers need to work on their speed too!

Physical Fitness

Comprehensive muscular development not only protects players from injuries, it's also indispensable for playing assertively in many situations: 1 v. 1's on the ground or in the air, for example. Moreover, being physically fit gives goalkeepers mental advantages as well: Physically strong goalkeepers tend to be mentally strong too, with lots of self-confidence and self-awareness.

Goalkeeper Psychology

For goalkeepers, performance is heavily influenced by psychological factors, much more so than for fielders. That's because when the goalkeeper makes a mistake, the results are serious and immediate – in other words, the opposition scores.

Therefore, goalkeepers have to deal with a lot more stress than fielders do. Fear of failure can have a negative effect on a goalkeeper's performance. Goalkeepers have to be able to free themselves from these negative influences.

Secure every ball; never give your opponents a second chance!

Illustration 2

The Goalkeeper's Job

1 v. 1 Play
- In various configurations
- With or without a teammate's help

Attack Building
- In various situations (after crosses, shots, back passes)
- On set plays (free kick, kick away from the goal)

Shots
- From various positions and distances
- On set plays (penalty kick, direct/indirect free kick)

Crosses
- High crosses in the air, medium- to long-distance
- Low crosses/crosses on the ground, short- to medium-distance

Organizing the Defense
- In various situations
- On set plays (corner kick, free kick)

Match Monitoring
- Regardless of which team has the ball

Low Shot to the Body | Low Shot to the Corner | High Shot to the Corner

On low shots that come directly to you or slightly off to one side:

● Try to get behind the ball. If you have time, use quick sideways steps.
● Stretch out your arms and hands to meet the ball as far away from the goal as possible. Open your hands and keep your elbows as close together as you can.
● Secure the ball **in front of** your body.

On hard, low shots to the corner, that you can't run to and catch with both hands:

● Take a quick preliminary step and then take off from the leg closer to the ball.
● Always keep your eye on the ball.
● Reach out with the hand that's closer to the ball and secure it against your body as quickly as possible.
● Land on the outside of your thigh first, then roll onto your hip, side and shoulder. Don't land on your stomach.
● Avoid unnecessary movements such as kicking your legs into the air or a spectacular roll after landing.

On medium to high shots to the corner, that you can't run to:

● Decide how many steps you'll be able to take before jumping. Make the last step a big one, aimed diagonally forward.
● Shift your center of gravity onto the takeoff leg and jump directly at the ball from this position.
● Secure the ball against your body as quickly as possible.
● On landing, keep your body flexed. Land on the outside of your upper arm first.

High Shot to the Body	Cross From the Outside	1 v. 1

On shots that come (relatively) directly to you, between hip and chest level:

● Try to get your entire body behind the ball.
● Stretch out your arms and hands as far as possible to meet the ball.
● Keep your elbows as close together as you can.
● Make the initial contact with the ball with your arms, then bring your upper body down over it and your hands around it.
● Stay loose!

On crosses from the outside:

● Take the most direct route possible to the ball. Sideways movements cost valuable time.
● Always take off with the leg closer to the ball. In other words, on a cross from the left, take off with the left leg, and with the right on a ball from the right.
● This makes it easier to use the other leg as a shield against approaching attackers. It also makes your landing more stable.
● Catch the ball at the highest point possible, overhead or in front of you, and secure it against your body immediately.
● If you can't catch the ball safely, try a one-handed punch to get it as far away to the side as possible.

When a solo attacker is dribbling toward you:

● Meet the attacker as far away from the goal as possible, but be sure to stop in time. Hold your hands out to the sides (fingers spread, palms toward your opponent) in order to make yourself seem as "wide" as possible.
● Wait and let your opponent take the initiative, but react quickly!
● Watch the attacker carefully and try to slow things down (this gives your teammates time to catch up). You should watch not only the ball, but the attacker's moves and fakes as well.
● Wait until the attacker lets the ball get too far away, and then attack quickly and decisively.

Goalkeeper Training: Guidelines

How to Train Goalkeepers

Because the goalkeeper plays such a special role, goalkeeper training has to be planned and conducted with special care. That's not always easy, especially for coaches who don't have any goalkeeping experience themselves. The only solution is to immerse yourself completely in the objectives, methods and content of goalkeeper training. You can also turn to the experts in your league for help (e.g. goalkeepers from the adult or senior teams). Ideally, they'll be able to help not just with goalkeeper exercises, but with tactical advice (e.g. on positional play) and suggestions for teaching basic goalkeeper techniques as well.

A command of basic technique is indispensable.

Game analyses show that on average, goalkeepers have to deal with fewer than ten explosive plays in the course of a match. That may not seem like a lot, but don't be deceived: These situations place extreme demands on goalkeepers, requiring them to (re)act correctly and with perfect technique in order to protect the goal. The wrong choice can negate the best intentions, and often a small technical defect makes all the difference between a successful goalkeeper play and an unsuccessful one.

What this means is that the primary objective of goalkeeper training, regardless of age and ability level, must be: to learn, improve and internalize all necessary goalkeeper techniques.

Naturally, goalkeeper training requires different contents and methods at different age and ability levels, but some general rules are:

• In developing a goalkeeper training program, never forget that exercises and training games must have an direct relation to the actual demands of the game.
• Always work to create connections between technique training and play-oriented tactics training (especially important for optimizing positional play).

Exertion levels in practice sessions should simulate match play.

Match conditions should also be your orientation point for the exertion levels your goalkeepers encounter in practice.

Experience has shown that goalkeepers are frequently overworked during practice. But the real demands of the game, for goalkeepers, are easy to describe: They have to be able to execute a few fundamental plays, as dynamically and explosively as possible – and goalkeeper training should prepare them for that.

1 v. 1's against solo attackers are the most difficult situations goalkeepers have to face.

Illustration 3

How to Structure Goalkeeper Training

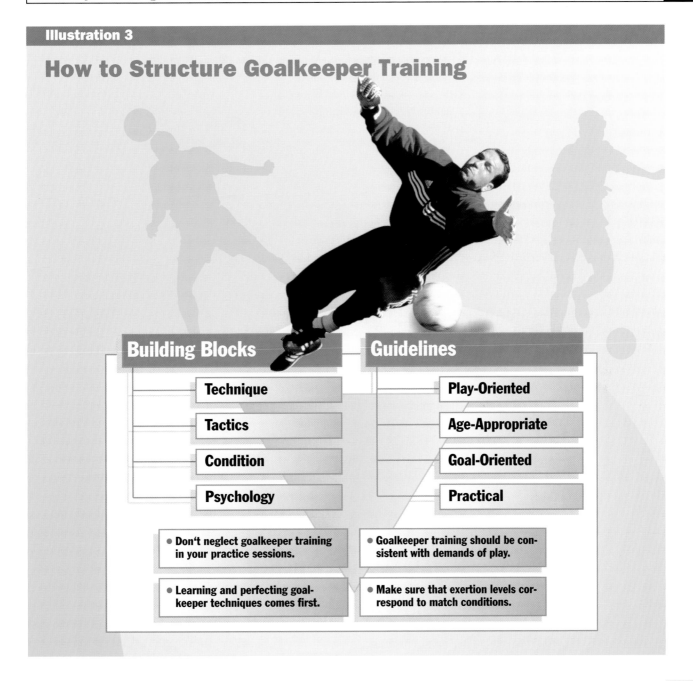

Building Blocks

- Technique
- Tactics
- Condition
- Psychology

- Don't neglect goalkeeper training in your practice sessions.
- Learning and perfecting goalkeeper techniques comes first.

Guidelines

- Play-Oriented
- Age-Appropriate
- Goal-Oriented
- Practical

- Goalkeeper training should be consistent with demands of play.
- Make sure that exertion levels correspond to match conditions.

From this, we can draw a few guidelines for exertion levels in goalkeeper training: Exercises should be relatively few in number, but they should run at top speed and alternate with long, active breaks.

Goalkeeper training should be flexibly organized.

Probably not too many coaches enjoy the privilege of having an assistant they can entrust with goalkeeper training. And especially at the lower levels, there's usually hardly any time left for goalkeeper training after the team's regular practice sessions once or twice a week. So coaches have to be creative, and we can help with some suggestions:

• If at all possible – in spite of work and other time commitments – try to plan occasional goalkeeper training sessions in addition to regular practices with the team; these are the best opportunity for focused goalkeeper training.

You can minimize the extra effort for everyone involved by scheduling goalkeeper training immediately before or after your regular sessions. Another advantage is that this makes it easier to include position-specific training for some of the fielders (e.g. forwards) as well.

• However, team training sessions also provide plenty of opportunities to combine some goalkeeper training concepts with fielder training. Many of the games and exercises in this book involve the goalkeeper, which means they involve goalkeeper training as well.

• It's ideal if you can make special group training for goalkeepers a league tradition. All goalkeepers should participate, whether they're youth players, adults or seniors. Then, if you can find a former goalkeeper who has some coaching expertise and will commit to leading the group, significant improvements are guaranteed.

And this is not just because the young goalkeepers can learn something from the example of their older colleagues. You can also expect to see a positive change in your goalkeepers' motivation and team spirit as the players give each other mutual encouragement and inspiration, as an almost automatic result of the group dynamic process.

Goalkeepers can usually practice on their own during some phases of the practice session (e.g. warm-up).

Illustration 4

How to Organize Goalkeeper Training

	Objectives/Contents	Organizational Tips
1 Individual Training	• Special exercises for the basic techniques and tactics of goalkeeping • Special exercises for basic goalkeeper condition	• Schedule individual training before or after team training. • Include certain fielders (forwards, wing players).
2 Group Goalkeeper Training	• Special training with an expert • Teaching younger goalkeepers by example • Creating "team spirit" among league goalkeepers	• Make group goalkeeper training a league tradition. • Find an expert goalkeeper coach for the league.
3 Goalkeeper/ Fielder Exercises	• Combining goalkeeper training with fielder training • Saving time by dispensing with special goalkeeper training sessions	• Some exercises are perfect for warm-up. • Adjust the exercises to fit fielders' and goalkeepers' ability levels.
4 Games Including Goalkeeper	• Match-character exercises (= high motivation) • Combined practice for fielders and goalkeepers	• Use special rules to put the focus on specific aspects of goalkeeping. • Use small-sided games to force goalkeeper plays.

Youth Goalkeeper Training

Developing a Long-Term Training Plan

Like fielders, goalkeepers also have to start at a young age and lay the groundwork for the complex technical, tactical, conditional and psychological challenges of the game. However, youth goalkeeper training must always take into account the "typical" developmental characteristics of each age level. The objectives, methods, content and exertion levels must match young goalkeepers' physical and mental capacities.

As with fielders, coaches can orient themselves according to a three-stage concept:
• basic training
• intermediate training
• advanced training.

Basic Training

At this level, practice focuses primarily on coordination. Without a solid basis in coordination with and without the ball, peak performance would be impossible later on. Comprehensive coordinative development is what enables players to optimize goalkeeper-specific movement sequences, instant assessments of the situation, skillful movements to the ball and sudden reactions.

Since basic coordinative skills are so important, you should avoid training players for specific positions too early. The youngest players should switch back and forth between goalkeeper and fielder positions regularly. Once players reach the age of 9 or 10, you can start assigning the goalkeeper role more regularly to those players whose inclinations and talents lie in that direction.

Intermediate Training

10- to 12-year-old boys and girls demonstrate an eagerness to learn, improved concentration and, above all, excellent coordination, so that quick and skillful movements are generally easy for them. This is the last and best opportunity to start position-specific goalkeeper training. Now the focus shifts to learning goalkeeper-

By ages 12 to 14, young goalkeepers should already have mastered basic techniques such as stopping shots on the ground.

specific techniques and using them in competition.

With 12- to 14-year-olds, we find improvements in power and speed. Players should start expanding the basic techniques they've learned into movement sequences requiring more dynamic play (and therefore more power). At this age, mobility training and full-body strengthening are essential.

Advanced Training

As players enter the second stage of puberty at ages 14 through 18, their learning and performance abilities undergo another significant improvement.

At this level, the basic objective of any systematic goalkeeper training program should be to stabilize and refine basic techniques and tactics of goalkeeping, adapting them to the increased demands of match play.

Illustration 5

Goalkeeper Training by Level

6- to 10-Year-Olds

Training Objectives

- Promoting coordination with and without the ball (the foundation of the goalkeeper's game) in an age-appropriate way
- Teaching a few carefully chosen basic techniques and essential technical-tactical skills

Notes on Practice and Match Play

- For the youngest players: Don't assign players to be goalkeepers too soon. Players should always switch roles, especially at ages 6 through 10.
- Players should switch back and forth between goalkeeper and fielder positions during practice too.
- Use ball training to make all players familiar with basic goalkeeping skills (catching, falling, punching, etc.).

10- to 14-Year-Olds

Training Objectives

- Systematically learning all basic goalkeeper techniques
- Using basic skills appropriately in a variety of situations
- Teaching basic tactics such as 1 v. 1 play, attack building and how to handle set plays
- Adapting techniques to increased speed and power (10- to 12-year-olds)

Notes on Practice and Match Play

- Starting no earlier than age 10, players can start to specialize in goalkeeping.
- At this age, the "golden age of learning," you should systematically teach every element of goalkeeping.
- Goalkeeper training should be challenging, focused, interesting and appropriate in terms of exertion levels.

14- to 18-Year-Olds

Training Objectives

- Continuing to perfect all elements of goalkeeping (more accurate and reliable movements)
- Greater focus on developing mental abilities (objective: personality development)
- New concepts: playing as a fielder, dominating the penalty zone
- Reinforcing motivation to play soccer, particularly to play goalkeeper

Notes on Practice and Match Play

- Include opponents in most exercises (practice with match character).
- Include goalkeepers in team training sessions more often, with the help of specialized exercises.
- Practice should be intense, but with appropriate rest periods. Don't overstrain your goalkeepers!
- Get your goalkeepers involved in every aspect of their training process.

Bibliography

Books on Soccer

BAUER, G./UEBERLE, H.: Fußball. Faktoren der Leistung. Spieler- und Mannschaftsführung. München 1984.

BAUER, G.: Lehrbuch Fußball – Erfolgreiches Training von Technik, Taktik und Kondition. München 1997.

BAUER, G.: Fußballtechnik heute. München 1998.

BISANZ, G./GERISCH, G.: Fußball. Training, Technik, Taktik. Reinbek bei Hamburg 1999.

BISANZ, G./VIETH, N.: Fußball von morgen, Teil 1. Münster 1999.

BISCHOPS, K./GERARDS, H.-W.: Handbuch für Mädchen- und Frauenfußball. Aachen 1996.

BRÜGGEMANN, D./ALBRECHT, D.: Modernes Fußballtraining. Schorndorf 1987.

FRANK, G.: Fußball-Konditionsgymnastik. Frankfurt/Berlin 1994.

HOEK, F.: Torwarttraining. München 1990.

KNEBEL, K. P./HERBECK, B./HAMSEN, G.: Fußball-Funktionsgymnastik. Reinbek bei Hamburg 1988.

KONZAG, J./DÖBLER, H./HERZOG, H.-D.: Fußball spielend trainieren. Berlin 1998.

MAYER, R.: Spieltraining Fußball. Reinbek bei Hamburg 1999.

MAYER, R.: Fußball trainieren. Reinbek bei Hamburg 1999.

WEINECK, J.: Optimales Fußballtraining, Teil 1. Konditionstraining. Erlangen 1999.

ZEEB, G.: Fußballtraining. Wiesbaden 1993.

Articles From the DFB Magazine "fußballtraining" (Philippka-Sportverlag, Postfach 15 01 05, 48061 Münster, Germany)

(Issue and volume numbers in parentheses)

BARUTTA, B.: Ideen und Investitionen für die Talentförderung (11+12/1998)

BAUER, G.: Taktik – was ist das eigentlich? (7/1999)

BAUER, G.: Spiele richtig analysieren – Siege erfolgreich vorbereiten (5/1998)

BAUER, G.: Die Trainingsplanung – ein wichtiger Schritt zum Erfolg (5+6/1995)

BIERMANN, S./THEUNE-MEYER, T.: So macht Athletiktraining Spaß! (11+12/1997)

BISANZ, G.: Wieso 4 Verteidiger gegen 1 Angreifer? (5+6/1999)

BISANZ, G.: Die Kondition immer mit Ball trainieren! (3/1997)

BISANZ, G.: Welche Einflußmöglichkeiten hat der Trainer? (2+3/1996)

BRÜGGEMANN, D.: Nachwuchsförderung: Antreten zum Drill? (11+12/1998)

BRÜGGEMANN, D.: Talent-Förderung oder Talent-Nutzung? (4/1995)

DANIEL, J.: „Ein guter Torwart ist die halbe Miete!" (7/1998)

DANIEL, J.: Angriffsfußball – Garant für Erfolg!? (10/1997)

DAUM, CH./KOCH, R.: Mit Angriffsfußball zum Erfolg! (3/1997)

ERKENBRECHER, U.: Die Manndeckung ist out! (11+12/1995)

GERISCH, G.: Coaching ist ein schwieriges Aufgabenfeld (2+3/1996)

GREIBER, P.: Wann muß ein Nachwuchstorhüter was lernen? (4/1999)

HITZFELD, O./HENKE, M.: Die Belastungsgrenze für die Spieler ist erreicht! (4/1997)

HOFMANN, T.: Eckstöße – aber mit Köpfchen! (7/1999)

KIEFERLE, R.: Vitaminpillen sind nicht alles! (11+12/1997)

LIESEN, H.: So bleiben die Spieler in Form! (11+12/1997)

PETER, R.: Schritt für Schritt zu zeitgemäßem Verteidigen (5+6/1999)

PETER, R.: Viererkette – Schritt für Schritt zum Ziel (11+12/1996)

PETER, R./VIETH, N.: So bilden wir Spitzenfußballer von morgen aus (10/1998)

RUTEMÖLLER, E.: Das Spiel in und aus engen Räumen (3/1997)

RUTEMÖLLER, E.: Keine Fouls im Strafraum! (9/1996)

THEUNE-MEYER, T.: Mit Teamwork zum Erfolg! (2+3/1998)

THEUNE-MEYER, T.: Geschickter, schneller, erfolgreicher…! (7+8/1997)

VIETH, N.: Keine Ausreden: Ein Torwarttraining kann jeder organisieren! (4/1999)

WEISE, D./SCHOTT, U.: Talente noch individueller fördern! (11+12/1999)

ZEMPEL, U.: Wie plane ich das Training im Jugendbereich? (4/1998)